A volume in the series

Anthropology of Contemporary Issues

EDITED BY ROGER SANJEK

Caribbean New York

BLACK IMMIGRANTS AND
THE POLITICS OF RACE

Philip Kasinitz

Cornell University Press

Ithaca and London

First published 1992 by Cornell University Press.

International Standard Book Number 0-8014-2651-0 (cloth)
International Standard Book Number 0-8014-9951-8 (paper)
Library of Congress Catalog Card Number 91-55539

Printed in the United States of America

*Librarians: Library of Congress cataloging information appears on the
last page of the book.*

⊗ The paper in this book meets the minimum requirements of the
American National Standard for Information Sciences–Permanence of
Paper for Printed Library Materials, ANSI Z39.48-1984.

For Frenchy,
the first immigrant
I ever knew.

Contents

Contents

Tables and Figures

[ix]

Figures

Preface

The research for this book began with a visit to the West Indian American Day Carnival in 1983. Over the next several years it took me to many corners of the city: to churches and after-hours joints, "pattie shops" and lawyers' offices, back-room political clubs and receptions at City Hall, and to a great many living rooms. In all these places I incurred a large debt of gratitude to those without whose help the book would not have been possible.

First and foremost I must thank the many Caribbean-American New Yorkers who generously and patiently gave me their time and hospitality. They will not all entirely agree with my portrayal of their community, and some will no doubt take issue with some of my conclusions. Nevertheless, they shared parts of lives with me with no preconditions, and for this I am deeply grateful. All I can offer by way of recompense is that I have tried to get the story right. Obligations of confidentiality and limitations of space prohibit my acknowledging by name everyone who has helped me. A special thanks must be extended, however, to certain individuals: Anthony Agard, Rex Archibald, David Brusch, Una Clarke, Locksley Dyce, Austin Ebanks, Donnie Forde, Maurice Gumbs, Herman Hall, Roy S. Hastick, Marco Mason, Colin Moore, Carl Roberts, Karl Rodney, the Reverend Heron Sam, Oswald Silvera, Ernest Skinner, Lamuel Stanislaus, Waldaba Stewart, Graham A. Stroude, and all the members of the Harriet Tubman Democratic Club.

The present work was shaped in many ways by Richard Sennett, Constance Sutton, and Dennis H. Wrong. They deserve a large part of whatever credit is due. In addition, earlier drafts were read by Juan Corradi, Kathleen Gerson, Stephen Gregory, Robert Jackall, Jonathan Rieder, Jim Sleeper, and Dessima Williams, all of whom provided useful comments and much encouragement. A crucial early phase of the research was supported by the New York University Center for Applied Social Scientific Research. Thanks are due to its director, Barbara Heyns, and to my office mate at CASSR, Kathleen Montgomery, who listened enthusiastically, if not exactly voluntarily, to the bits and pieces of this work as it progressed.

This book has also benefitted immensely from my interactions with other writers and scholars working on similar issues. Once again it is impossible to name them all, but I especially thank Linda Basch, Remco van Capelleveen, Shellee Colen, Judith Freidenberg, Laurie Gunst, Calvin Holder, Milton Vickerman, and Basil Wilson.

The final stages of my work were greatly facilitated by the assistance and patience of Roger Sanjek, the general editor of this series, and Peter Agree of Cornell University Press. In addition, substantial editing was provided at various points in the process by Janelle Yates, Anne Just, Joel Ray, and Donna Chenail. Shirley Bushika, Margaret Bryant, and Lori Toole gave me word processing assistance above and beyond the call of duty. Several of the photographs are the work of Ernest Brown. All have my gratitude.

Portions of Chapter 4 have previously appeared in *Ethnic Groups* (1988). They are included in this volume by the permission of Gordon and Breach, Science Publishers Inc.

Finally, a very special thanks is due to Lisa Jane Gibbs, who lived with this work, and with me, throughout the years of its long gestation. Being married to an ethnographer is, I suspect, a lot less fun than being one. Nonetheless, she has consistently been a source of both critical insight and unqualified support. My deepest gratitude and love to her.

Shortly after this book went to press, tragic events thrust many of the people and places it discusses into the headlines. On August 19, 1991, a car driven by a Hasidic Jew jumped a curb in Crown Heights, killing a seven-year-old Guyanese boy named Gavin Cato and critically injuring his cousin. Rumors, never substantiated, quickly spread throughout the neighborhood that a Hasidic ambulance service had ignored the children while rushing the uninjured driver from the scene. Several hours later a group of appoximately twenty black youths fatally stabbed a Hasidic student named Yankel Rosenbaum. Three nights of rioting followed in which groups of blacks and Hasidim clashed in the streets, Jewish families were attacked in their homes, and stores belonging to black, white, and Asian merchants were looted. Black youths marched to the world headquarters of the Lubavitcher Hasidic sect on Eastern Parkway, where some hurled rocks and bottles and shouted anti-Semitic slogans. Mayor David Dinkins, who repeatedly called for calm, was briefly trapped by rock-throwing black youths during a condolence call on the Cato family.

By week's end a massive police presence had quelled the violence. Yet the anger on both sides remained. At a loss to explain the outburst in the generally stable Caribbean community, some observers attributed the violence to young people "from the projects" spurred on by "outside agitators"—in other words, to an African-American "underclass." This analysis was half true at best. While most of the Caribbean community was horrified by the violence, many of the youths in the streets were immigrants and their grievances went far beyond the accident. "This is like trench town," a Jamaican teenager told a reporter, referring to the notorious slum in Kingston. "The wicked and the rich have had their day. Now we can stand up and be heard."[1] Many of Caribbean community's leaders, while denouncing the violence and condemning anti-Semitism, also gave voice to their own long-standing grievances against the Hasidim. The easy equivalence they drew between the accident and the murder revealed the depth of their sense of historical injustice. For their part, the Hasidic leadership saw the killing as only the latest chapter in their own narrative of victimization. Many were quick to describe the Crown Heights events as a "pogrom," and some even drew comparisons to Kristallnacht.

It is true that most of the self-appointed spokesmen for the angry youths in the streets-were from outside the neighborhood and only one of the most visible protest leaders, the attorney Colin Moore, was Caribbean. The African-American activists who dominated the

1. Quoted in David Kocieniewski, "Both Sides Are Angry." *New York Newsday*, August 24, 1991.

media coverage of the Crown Heights events proved more effective lightning rods for popular discontent than were most of the Caribbean leadership. Yet, as tempers cooled, many in the Caribbean community came to see these actors as exploiting a tragic situation. In addition one of the most visible of these activists, Sonny Carson, only hurt his own cause by clumsy attempts at ethnic politics—such as unfurling a Guyanese flag at Gavin Cato's funeral.

The Crown Heights riot occurred less than two weeks before Labor Day. Understandably, city officials viewed the prospect of hundreds of thousands of Carnival revelers on Eastern Parkway with considerable trepidation. Hasidic leaders called for the event to be canceled, and even some politicians friendly with the organizers quietly suggested that it might be moved to a less charged location. Yet the organizing committee insisted that Carnival should go forward on Eastern Parkway, as always. "Nothing is going to happen!" Carnival Association president Carlos Lezama insisted on the Thursday before Labor Day. "I am going to walk down the Parkway and if the head Rabbi wants to come with me, he is welcome! This is what the city needs now!"

The thought that Carnival could bring Crown Heights together, even for a day, struck me as charming but naive. Going ahead with the event was an enormous risk. Violence would gravely threaten its future and any overture to the Hasidim would certainly be attacked as a sellout by some in the black community ("a shame before God" is how Sonny Carson later described it). Yet Lezama, a retired machinist who has made the Carnival his life's work, understood the community better than I did. To my surprise, the next morning he put aside years of bad feelings and invited representatives of the Hasidic community to march in the parade. To my even greater surprise, they accepted. On Labor Day the crowd was a bit more subdued than usual, but it greeted the rabbis politely, and the day came off without incident. "Peace on the Parkway" was the year's slogan. To be sure, the deep wounds that drive New York's racial politics were not healed or even forgotten. Yet, for most of the people on the Parkway, two weeks of tension had been enough. For one day, at least, peace on the Parkway seemed a good idea.

The next week the Democratic party primary elections for the New York City Council were held. Redistricting had created two predominately Caribbean districts in East Flatbush. In one, activist

Colin Moore, along with six other Caribbean candidates, was soundly defeated by the white Jewish incumbent, Susan Alter. In the other Una Clarke, a Jamaican-born educator, narrowly defeated Carl Andrews, an African American, and Trinidadian Maurice Gumbs (see Chapter 7). Both Alter and Clarke easily won the general election in November.

PHILIP KASINITZ

Brooklyn, New York

Caribbean New York

Introduction

For most New Yorkers, Labor Day is a time for squeezing out the last few drops of summer. According to upper-middle-class lore, it is the close of one of those weekends when "nobody's in town." People with the means take off for the mountains or the sea. Others head for local beaches and backyard barbecues. A few working men and women still answer the call of solidarity and turn out to watch the aging union leaders and politicians lumber up Fifth Avenue. More often, however, they choose to spend the day in less formal surroundings. Coney Island is packed, and Queens is bathed in the sounds of the last block parties of the season.

On Brooklyn's Eastern Parkway, however, there is another Labor Day going on. Here too are the aromas of holiday food: roti and cod cakes, pulori and curry goat. And there is plenty of beer, along with stout and rum. But even the most casual observer would not mistake this for the usual Labor Day gathering. The crowd is huge; by midafternoon the street will be thick with people as far as the eye can see. The crowd is mostly black, although much of the music that resounds from the sound trucks along the Parkway would not be familiar to most black people in other U.S. cities. And when the weather is hot and the music loud the crowd seems charged with an intense energy. A sudden loud pop can send it scrambling, a clever sign can set it laughing, a change in music can start it dancing. The crowd is both sexy and serious, playful and volatile. It is hot, sweaty, and as an elaborately costumed reveler bursts into view, suddenly quite beautiful.

It is Carnival day in Brooklyn. The people who line the streets are, for the most part, West Indians. Many come from the surrounding neighborhood, while others have come from across the United States to be here. Some are recent immigrants, others have been here for decades, and still others are the grandchildren of immigrants. Among the 800,000 or so who fill the Parkway are young toughs and U.N. ambassadors, dreadlocked Rastas and churchgoing grandmothers. In recent years, many of the community's more respectable members have complained about the raucousness of Carnival. Still, they continue to come and to bring their U.S.-born children.

Scarcely noticed by the rest of the city, Carnival is in some ways the nation's largest block party. Yet there is also something serious going on. Next to the stilt walkers and the fantastic dragon, signs comment on U.S. and Caribbean politics. A band of masqueraders in elaborate African garb is accompanied by slogans about black pride and the liberation of Nelson Mandela. And the year the Duvaliers were overthrown, the old blue and red banner of pre-Papa Doc Haiti waved above some of the most uninhibited of the dancers. Local politicians, always the first to sense a shift in the political climate, started to come to Carnival in the early 1980s. As the decade went on, national political figures as well began to add Brooklyn to their Labor Day itineraries.

In Brooklyn and elsewhere, Carnival is a time when people play with the idea of identity: it is a moment when who one "is" can be questioned and redefined. So it is strangely fitting that this event has become the most visible public symbol of New York's West Indian community at the historical moment when that community's identity is being redefined. Like the West Indian community, Carnival is now too huge to ignore, and thus it serves to make visible a group of people who have long felt invisible.[1] A festival full of uncertainties and contradictions, Carnival presents an appropriately ambiguous public face for a people whose role in the city's political life is now in flux.

1. For a thoughtful discussion of the issue of "invisibility" of black immigrants, see Bryce-Laporte 1972.

Who are the people on the Parkway? For the most part they are people who trace their roots to what anthropologists term the "Afro-Creole" Caribbean: the non-Hispanic Caribbean basin societies in which the descendants of enslaved Africans have generally been demographically and culturally dominant.[2] A large majority are English-speaking, although in recent years the number of Haitians in the Carnival crowd has grown. They are overwhelmingly black people according to the way race is thought about in the United States (although not always according to the racial distinctions that operate in the Caribbean societies). Most are new immigrants, members of the massive wave of non-European people that flooded into the United States after 1965. In a time and place where ethnicity is considered an important element of identity, they are also undeniably "ethnics." Like so many other groups, they bring to New York distinct cultural and political traditions that may help or hinder their incorporation into North American society.

All of these factors and many others determine how individual West Indian New Yorkers would answer the question "Who am I?" No doubt, as with all modern people, that answer varies not only from individual to individual but also for the same individual in different contexts. This book addresses the issue of racial and ethnic identity in one of those contexts, that of public life. It seeks to understand the political situation of a group of people who do not easily fit into the categories by which ethnic and racial political relations are usually understood.

The issue here, though far narrower than the issue of how personal

2. There are exceptions, of course; the "red legs" of Barbados, the Germans of rural Jamaica, and the scattered Portuguese, Jewish, and Lebanese populations throughout the region. Also two historically "Afro-Creole" Caribbean societies, Trinidad and Guyana, have large Asian populations, in the latter now a slight numerical majority. For the most part, however, the European populations of the Commonwealth Caribbean, the Francophone Caribbean, and the Netherlands Antilles have been demographically insignificant. Moreover, the white populations in these places have tended to see themselves as a colonial elite and have had little interest in or influence on local culture.

The Hispanic Caribbean, by contrast, not only had a larger European population from its initial colonization, but that population quickly came to see itself as native to Cuba, Puerto Rico, or Santo Domingo. Interestingly the same word, "Creole" (Criollo), used in the Anglophone Caribbean to refer to Caribbean-born blacks in the Spanish Caribbean, refers to native (as opposed to Iberian) whites. White elites often led nineteenth-century independence struggles in the Hispanic Caribbean, whereas in the British colonies whites generally fought to hold off independence until the 1960s. This is not to minimize the African influence on Hispanic Caribbean culture; many African traditions were preserved in the Hispanic islands (particularly Cuba) in purer forms than in the Afro-Creole ones.

identity is constructed, is nonetheless fairly complex. There are more than half a million Afro-Caribbean immigrants living in New York City today—perhaps twice that figure if undocumented immigrants and U.S.-born minor children are included. These people are historically situated at the intersection of two different conceptions of group identity: "race" and "ethnicity." Both are slippery concepts. In recent years the terms have sometimes been used synonymously, and in practice they often overlap. Nevertheless, the two terms represent different ways of thinking about social groups, and in American society they have had markedly different political implications.

"Race" is, of course, a highly problematic concept; the word should probably always be surrounded by quotation marks. For a long time the term was used to imply inherent, biological differences between groups of human beings, signified by, but far more significant than, phenotype. By the 1960s a general (although by no means unanimous) consensus had emerged that this biological notion of race was scientifically useless and politically dangerous (Sanjek 1990). Yet in the face of twentieth-century history the importance of race as a *social construct* could hardly be denied. Regardless of its dubious roots in biology, race is real because, to paraphrase W. I. Thomas, people act as though it is real and thus it has thus become real in its consequences. Nevertheless, because race is a social construction rather than a biological reality, its meaning changes from time to time and place to place.[3]

"Ethnicity," a newer term that became popular in the 1970s, shifts our attention to how a group defines itself. While ethnicity implies that a group shares a real or mythological common past and cultural focus, the central defining characteristic of ethnic groups is the belief in their own existence as groups. As Katherine O'Sullivan See writes, "it is not a set of cultural characteristics *per se* that makes ethnicity; rather it is a *sense* of commonality and of shared history" (1986:3). Over the past two decades social scientists have often struggled with the question of why these seemingly irrational bonds of group iden-

3. Note for example that members of one of the groups most negatively impacted by the pseudobiological conception of race during the twentieth century, the European Jews, generally ceased to be considered a "race" at all after emigrating to the United States. For studies of how the notion of "black" differs in various multiracial societies, see Degler 1986; Banton 1983; Harris 1964. For examples of how racial definitions have changed over time within the United States, see Dominguez 1986; Williamson 1980; Blu 1980.

tity stubbornly persist in the face of the rationalizing and individu-
alizing effects of modernity. Their answers can generally be divided
into two rough categories. "Primordialist" approaches point to a fundamental psychological need to "experience a sense of affinity" with
those supposed to share a common origin (Shils 1968:4; see also van
den Berghe 1978; Isaacs 1975). By contrast, "mobilizationalist" or "in-
strumentalist" theories see ethnicity as arising from "the conscious
efforts of individuals and groups mobilizing ethnic symbols in order
to obtain access to social, political and material resources" (McKay
1982:399; see also Patterson 1975; Cohen 1974).

In practice the distinction between racial and ethnic groups tends
to blur. "Black American" is clearly an ascribed racial identity that
was violently imposed. The boundaries of this identity were defined
not on the basis of any cultural (that is, "ethnic") characteristics of the
group, but rather for the convenience of their oppressors. However,
once historical circumstances created black Americans, their shared
historical experience and cultural commonalities did produce a sense
of ethnicity. Thus, while "black" may be a purely racial term when
used to describe a person's phenotype, it is clearly also an ethnic one
when it refers to a self-conscious group of people, their history, or
their culture (as in "Black History Month"). When this group re-
defines itself as "African Americans," a further ethnic dimension is
added to its definition of self, albeit one that the group's African
ancestors, brought together against their wills on the basis of race,
might not have shared.

The concept of ethnicity restores a much-needed sense of the creative and subjective aspects of the process of group formation, but it
should not obscure "the central questions about power and inequality
that *race* forces upon us" (Sanjek 1990:111). It is significant that
while there are Polish, Irish, and Jewish Americans, there have not
been (until quite recently) Yoruba or Asante Americans. The historical conditions under which groups are incorporated into a society
shapes the amount of latitude these groups have in creating their
"ethnic" identity (see Banton 1983). In the United States the descendants of Europeans who are defined as "white" have generally had
the most such latitude; the descendants of Africans who are defined
as "black" have had the least, and other groups have fallen somewhere in between.

Thus the racial/ethnic distinction as used in the United States has

[5]

more or less overlapped with the distinction between voluntary immigrants of European descent and involuntary incorporated "racial minorities": blacks, Amerindians, Puerto Ricans, and some Mexican Americans.[4] Though both groups have been the victims of prejudice and sometimes of systematic discrimination, the latter have also endured the legally sanctioned denial of citizenship rights, government policies of segregation, and institutionalized racism (Ringer 1983).[5] In this regard the often quoted title of Irving Kristol's 1966 essay, "The Negro Today Is Like the Immigrant Yesterday," summarizes with notable clarity a fundamental (and common) misunderstanding of American race relations. The ways in which the experience of the descendants of enslaved Africans has been *unlike* that of the European immigrants is among the key problems of twentieth-century American history.

What of people who are both black *and* immigrants? For Caribbean immigrants to the United States, both racial and ethnic identities are clearly central in shaping their political life. Yet these two

4. This distinction was made more than half a century ago in one of the classics of American sociology, William Lloyd Warner's "Yankee City" studies. Nevertheless it was often overlooked as ethnicity took center stage in the 1970s, a fact pointed out by Sanjek (1984).

It should of course be noted that not all voluntary "immigrants" were voluntary "emigrants." Unless one has a rather broad notion of the role of agency in human life, it is hard to consider the Irish immigrant fleeing the potato famine or the Jewish refugee fleeing the Nazis as acting "voluntarily." Nevertheless, these emigrants usually had some control over their *immigration* experience in two important respects. First, they were often able to determine to an extent where they went, and as a result they tended to end up in those sectors of the U.S. society (i.e., the industrial north) which were expanding. Involuntary immigrants, by contrast, were often restricted to the most backward agricultural areas of the country (i.e., the south and, in the case of Mexican Americans, the southwest). Second, voluntary immigrants were free to maintain substantial control over their cultural lives after arriving, a fact that led to a rather different mindset in regard to the immigration process. As a result, after a few generations, descendants of European immigrant groups to the United States almost universally remember the process as voluntary and positive, even when this view clearly contradicts historical facts. Needless to say, blacks and other involuntarily incorporated groups have seen the process otherwise.

5. Of course, this juxtaposition of racial and ethnic modes of group definition vastly oversimplifies reality. While government bureaucracies increasingly use the concept "Hispanic" as if it were a racial category, the term clearly incorporates both voluntary and involuntary immigrants and their descendants. These groups have had a range of experiences regarding government policies such as segregation. "Asians," although for the most part voluntary immigrants, have at times been excluded from American social life and from the United States itself by clearly racial government policies. Even some European groups have occasionally been considered members of alien "races." Still, these important exceptions should not obscure the very real and systematic difference between the roles that racial categories and ethnic categories have played in American life.

ways of thinking about group identity have informed their relations with the broader society in different ways. The relationship between race and ethnicity and its impact on the choices the group has made, I will argue, have been generally shaped by historical circumstances.

West Indians have lived in New York in significant numbers since the turn of the century, and for most of that time race, not ethnicity, dominated their public activities. As with all immigrants, members of the group manifested various attitudes toward their new country. Some clung to the past. Others, bitterly rejecting the United States and its racism, pursued utopian futures, ranging from pan-Africanism in both religious and political variants to socialism in all its myriad forms. Others rooted themselves squarely in U.S. culture and political traditions, usually to find that assimilation meant, for them, assimilation into *black* America. Many maintained a strong devotion to West Indian culture, what we might term "ethnic" culture, in their private lives. Yet, particularly for the large wave of migrants who came before the Depression, identification with native-born African Americans was the key defining fact of their *public* activities. Indeed, they and their descendants have been disproportionately well represented among the political and economic leaders of New York's black community.

During the 1980s, however, ethnicity played an increasingly public role in the lives of Afro-Caribbean New Yorkers. West Indians have brought this ethnic identity into the public sphere.[6] This emergence does not necessarily imply a sharp division or conflict of interests with the rest of the black community (at times this has been the case, at times it has not), but it does mean that the black community has become more ethnically diverse—or to be more accurate, it has become more conscious of its ethnic diversity.

A central question of this book, therefore, is why does an immigrant group play down its separate identity and merge itself within a larger category at one point in its American experience, only to choose to emphasize its cultural distinctiveness at another, much later point?

There are a number of interrelated reasons. The most obvious is

6. This discussion of identity may give the impression that I am concerned with the social psychology of ethnicity. Let me state at the outset that this is not the case. Most people have a variety of equally valid social identities. The question that interests me is what use people make of them.

the massive growth in the size of the community. West Indian migration to the United States started in earnest in the first decade of this century and grew steadily until the Depression. From the end of the Depression until the mid 1960s, migration from the Anglophone Caribbean slowed to a trickle. Then, quite unexpectedly, the immigration reforms of 1965 changed the trickle to a flood. During the late 1960s and 1970s more West Indians migrated to the United States than in the preceding seven decades, and about half of these people settled in New York City.

Yet numbers alone do not explain the new ethnic awareness of New York's West Indians. During the 1920s Caribbean immigrants made up almost as large a proportion of the black population in New York City as they do today, and their total numbers were certainly not so small as to fall below the necessary critical mass for ethnic mobilization. They also maintained at least the rudimentary beginnings of what Martin Kilson (1984) has called an "ethnic infrastructure": a network of formal and informal ethnic associations. Yet most of these groups and organizations remained outside U.S. politics.

Individuals who were involved in both U.S. and Caribbean politics sought to keep these roles distinct. The Jamaican-born Harlem Renaissance figure W. A. Domingo, for instance, was a vocal advocate of black rights when working in the American political context and a leading advocate of Jamaican independence in the Caribbean context. But he was never an advocate of the interests of Jamaicans in the United States, because here it was racial identity that was politically relevant. Caribbean New Yorkers of the 1920s and 1930s might have been immigrants in a city of immigrants, but it was race that structured their life chances. Being black determined where they lived and could not live, where they could and could not go to school, what type of job they could get and the way they were treated by Americans of all colors.

Thus, despite maintaining strong ties to their nations of origin, West Indians of the first immigrant wave generally played down their ethnic separateness as far as North American affairs were concerned. In fact, contrary to the idea that group strength grows with numbers, members of this group and their descendants came to increasing political prominence in New York's black community during those decades when the Caribbean portion of New York's black population was in decline.

[8]

As with numbers, differences that predated the North American experiences of the two major immigrant cohorts can only partially explain the dissimilarities. To be sure, they came from very different Caribbeans: most of the pre-1965 immigrants left small, largely agricultural colonies, still economically and culturally oriented toward Great Britain. Most of the post-1965 migrants left independent or soon-to-be independent micro-states increasingly within the political, cultural, and economic sphere of the United States. Yet despite these historical disparities, the two cohorts do not exhibit markedly different characteristics—none comparable to the regional and linguistic differences that separated different waves of Jewish immigrants, for example. Virtually all territories and all social classes in the Anglophone Caribbean are represented in both immigrant waves. In fact, family connections between the two cohorts are common.

Thus, in order to complete the explanation, we must look beyond the immigrants themselves to their American context. As Abner Cohen notes, "Ethnicity is a variable" that is "interdependent with many other variables" (1974:xx). The emergence of a West Indian ethnic identity in New York is directly related to several other developments in the North American political culture.

In the first place, I will argue that changes in the role of race in American culture since the late 1960s have made West Indian political distinctiveness possible. This is not to say that race has ceased to be tremendously important in self-definitions and in shaping the life chances of all black Americans. That even the most separatist West Indian leaders in New York today are in almost complete accord with the rest of the black leadership on issues such as police brutality, discrimination, and South Africa shows how central race remains in their political thinking. Nevertheless, for all its importance, race is not the monolithic force it was when the first cohort of West Indian migrants came to political consciousness. Further, the ways in which race is defined and conceptualized, and the relative importance of African imagery (which Caribbean immigrants can share) versus traditional African-American imagery, are increasingly subject to renegotiation.

Yet political identities do not spring forth automatically simply because the conditions for their emergence exist. Nor does the changing role of race, in and of itself, make ethnicity more salient. Such

[9]

ideas must be introduced into public discourse by specific people with specific interests. And during the 1980s some such people chose to make public claims on behalf of what they termed the "Caribbean community."

One reason they did so had to do with changes within New York's African-American political structure. During the 1970s, black political power in New York was roughly divided between, on the one hand, various groups of Democratic "regulars" who had come up through the party system and, on the other, activists who had their political roots in the struggles for school decentralization and community control of the late 1960s. Many of the older party regulars were persons of West Indian ancestry. This fact should not be overemphasized; with the exception of Congresswoman Shirley Chisholm, members of this group had never made a public issue of their heritage. Nevertheless, had these politicians stayed in power, their connections to the Caribbean might well have smoothed over relations with the newer immigrants then becoming politically active. The replacement of the "regulars" by insurgents who were overwhelmingly African Americans (in many cases emigrants from the South) created a decided drop in the number of West Indian officeholders at the very moment the West Indian community was growing most rapidly.

At the same time, white politicians generally encouraged expressions of West Indian ethnic assertiveness. Prominent whites including Mayor Edward Koch and Brooklyn borough president Howard Golden publicly courted Caribbean leaders and would-be leaders during the 1980s. Local white politicians made considerably more use of Caribbean symbolism than did black politicians, including West Indian politicians. In fact, I will argue that the state's willingness at a certain historical juncture to respond to "ethnic" demands, and perhaps even create ethnic constituencies, accounts for a significant part of the growth of such demands and constituencies.

As the 1980s came to a close, race reasserted itself as a dominant factor in black immigrant politics. Once again, circumstances external to the community, in this case the city's worsening racial climate, played a central role in this change in emphasis. As of this writing the intertwining of race and ethnicity within the community remains highly dynamic. Nevertheless, leaders willing to play the ethnic card

[10]

in New York politics now exist and will probably continue to influence events for some time to come.

It should also be noted that ethnic politics cuts both ways within the West Indian community. While a focus on ethnicity differentiates West Indians from African Americans as well as from white Americans, it clearly unites people from various national origins. On the Parkway we see immigrants from throughout the Anglophone Caribbean, including those from nations with no Carnival tradition. In bringing together the dozens of similar but nonetheless distinct and often insular strains of Afro-Creole culture within the context of contemporary New York, West Indian New Yorkers are creating something quite new. Far from being a sentimental last gasp of an identity no longer relevant in people's daily lives (the "symbolic ethnicity" that Herbert Gans (1979) has identified with the resurgence of white American ethnicity of the early 1970s), West Indian ethnic activity is a new and I will argue at least partially conscious strategy of adaptation. Born in New York of Caribbean parents, this sense of pan–West Indian identity is fast becoming a cultural and political force, both in New York and in the Caribbean as well.

This book approaches the problem of public identity from two different angles and is divided into two parts. Part I deals with what I refer to as "ethnicity from the ground up." This section is an attempt at a fairly conventional immigrant community study, with the aim of exploring the social origins of the racial and ethnic stances taken by West Indians at various historical junctures. Chapter 1 briefly sketches the Caribbean background of West Indian immigration and some of the differences in racial categorization in the United States faced by various immigrant cohorts. Chapter 2 describes the different ways West Indians have organized their community life in New York during various historical periods. Chapter 3 deals with the economic roles West Indian immigrants have played in New York, and Chapter 4 with community groups and voluntary organizations.

The second half of the book directly addresses the formation of ethnicity as a public identity. As such it focuses on the authors of that identity, community activists. This "ethnicity from the top down" is certainly rooted in and bounded by the realities described in the first half of the book. Nevertheless, the articulation of this identity constitutes a highly contested terrain in which actors exercise considerable independence in creating competing formulations. Thus this part of the book addresses the side of race and ethnicity that is less often discussed: the mechanics of "making" ethnicity. It deals with the public stances political actors take and the interaction between these actors and their audiences.

In Chapter 5, on the Labor Day Carnival, we will see the point at which "ethnicity from the ground up" and "ethnicity from the top down" come together, literally, on the streets. Various leaders and groups struggle over the control of this, the most public expression of West Indian–American identity. Yet despite their best efforts, Carnival refuses to speak with one voice: the mass participatory nature of the event both attracts and frustrates those who seek to make of it a political statement. Chapter 6 examines the various modes of leadership that have emerged in the community. Finally, Chapter 7 focuses on the history of West Indian participation in New York City electoral politics and the multifaceted relationships between the community, the polity, and the men and women who seek to mediate between them.

I have made use of a variety of research techniques: the examination of historical records and official documents, ethnography, and participant observation. I collected the lion's share of the original data, however, from in-depth interviews with New York-based political activists between 1984 and 1987. Since that time I have frequently been asked how a white, Jewish researcher was able to gain access to the people and events described here. I wish that I could attribute this success to years of ethnographic diligence, or to my skills as an interviewer. In fact the answer is simpler. Most of the people I spoke to were activists, accustomed to dealing with outsiders, and more to the point they believed that they were involved in something important, something they felt merited scholarly attention. In at least a few cases they seemed surprised and perhaps mildly irritated that it had taken me, as a representative of the social scientific community, so long to get there.[7]

I made contact with these individuals, in part, on the basis of "clustering," which is a fancy way of saying that some informants led

7. Interviewing activists accustomed to journalistic conventions does present other problems. In some cases interview subjects launched reflexively into something of a standard line on various topics. Probing and patience often revealed other, quite different information.

me to others. It is important to state at the outset that this technique leads to two serious limitations and that the book should be read with these in mind.

First, although I believe I was able to make contact with a wide spectrum of activists in the community, the view on events presented here is generally an activist's view. I made no attempt to use survey techniques in order to derive the views of a mythical "average" West Indian New Yorker. The people I interviewed were informants, not respondents, and I spoke to them precisely because they were not typical. Their positions have given them greater access to information and a greater role in the formation of group opinion than the typical community member has. I have attempted to balance this activist-centered point of view with indicators of aggregate behavior: demographics, voting patterns, attendance at cultural events. Nevertheless, it was the leadership group and their understanding of the world that I was primarily interested in. It would be wrong to conclude that the degree of self-consciousness such individuals bring to their activities is typical of the community as a whole.

A more serious limitation is that the view presented here is probably a male view. Most of the people interviewed were men (as was the interviewer), and most of the women interviewed worked with largely male organizations. This situation in part may reflect who leads political organizations in the community and in part may be the result of a male bias as to what counts as "political." It may also reflect the weakness in using informants to locate other informants: male informants sent me to people they thought of as interesting and important, and these were generally (although not always) other men. This limitation is significant in light of the facts that the post-1965 migration of West Indians to the United States (in sharp contrast to most international migrations) is predominantly female and that both West Indian and African American women have long histories of political participation. Predominantly female organizations and networks do play an important role in this community (see Basch 1987) and they are somewhat underrepresented in the book. Whether a more "female" perspective on the issues dealt with here would be substantially different might make an interesting question for further research.

One cannot, a friend reminds me, study everything—particularly not in what William Styron calls "a land as strange as Brooklyn."

[13]

What follows then is a limited, but I hope nonetheless informative slice of social reality.

A Note on Terminology

Throughout this book the term "West Indian" refers to people of African descent from the English-speaking Caribbean, including the mainland nations of Guyana and Belize, as well as their descendants from the English-speaking black diaspora communities in officially Spanish- and Dutch-speaking countries. It should be noted that this is not the preferred self-description among members of this group in New York City, who most often call themselves "Caribbean." The widespread use of the broader term reflects the fact that ethnic boundaries are currently in flux. However, despite the pan-Caribbean sentiments expressed by both Hispanic and Anglophone Caribbean intellectuals, the two groups form quite separate communities in New York, as the rest of this work will make clear. Thus I use the somewhat unfortunate term "West Indian" to differentiate the Anglophone Caribbean community from New Yorkers of the Hispanic Caribbean origins.

The boundary between West Indians and other Caribbean immigrants is more nebulous. Although this book does not concentrate on New York's large Haitian community and Haitians are not included in the notion of "West Indian" as used here, it became apparent during the course of my work that in some areas of public life the boundaries between English-speaking West Indians and Haitians are now blurring.[8] Thus at some points in the text I refer to "non-Hispanic Caribbean" people, which includes Haitians.

Caribbean immigrants of East Indian descent are not dealt with specifically here, although they are, by necessity, included in those immigration statistics reported by nation of origin. They are not in-

8. In New York this distinction is often thought of as a matter of race. English-speaking West Indians and Haitians are both considered "black," whereas immigrants from the Spanish-speaking Caribbean are generally categorized as "Hispanic." Yet this fact only points to the looseness of race as a conceptual category: many Puerto Ricans and Cubans and most Dominicans are of African ancestry, and, language aside, the culture of the "Hispanic" Caribbean is at least as West African as it is Iberian.

cluded in those statistics reported for "foreign-born blacks."[9] East Indians and other Asians make up about half the population of Guyana and nearly half the population of Trinidad and are present in smaller numbers in Jamaica as well. They are for the most part the descendants of indentured workers recruited to replace slaves after emancipation. Although they have historically been underrepresented among Caribbean migrants to New York, in recent years East Indian emigration has risen sharply, particularly from Guyana. While this group constitutes a distinct ethnic minority in the Caribbean, many of its members have come to share much of the Afro-Creole culture of these societies, a fact some become aware of only when they leave.

The position of these immigrants regarding the racial categories of the United States clearly differs from that of other West Indians. In some cases Caribbean-Asian immigrants may merge with New York's other Asian populations. In other contexts they may continue to be defined by their cultural connections to the Caribbean. How this will eventually work out is far from clear.

The term "African American" is used in the book to refer to North Americans of African descent, as opposed to "West Indians." The term "black," unless otherwise noted, is used to refer to *all* non-Hispanic New Yorkers of African descent, of both Caribbean and North American origin.

Not all the persons written about will be completely happy with these categorizations, and in a book about people who define themselves in a variety of different ways, such terminology is inevitably inadequate to convey a complex reality. Where informants are quoted using racial terminology, the words presented are their own; I made no attempt to standardize their usage with mine.

9. Listing immigrants by country of origin also underestimates the size of the West Indian community by missing English-speaking West Indians from enclave communities in predominantly Hispanic nations and those holding British passports. On the other hand the "foreign-born blacks" statistics derived from the U.S. census includes non–West Indian immigrants from Africa. Both statistics miss the children of Caribbean immigrants born in the United States. For more on the problem of defining West Indians statistically, see Chapter 1.

PART I

Ethnicity from the Ground Up

[1]

The Three West Indian Immigrations

The character of West Indian communities abroad reflects not only the conditions of reception but also the extent to which overseas emigrants remain part of West Indian society. . . . Such allegiance is not necessarily incompatible with a desire to be recognized as American, British, French or Dutch—one can send remittances to Paramaribo without ceasing to participate in Amsterdam life, support Martiniquais separatism without losing pride in being French, or run for political office in New York without forgetting to be Barbadian. But the degree and quality of separation are affected by the nature and strength of these home ties as well as by responses to circumstances.
—DAVID LOWENTHAL, "West Indian Immigrants Overseas"

Since the beginning of the century people have been leaving the West Indies and coming to New York City. Their numbers have ebbed and flowed at various times. The societies from which they came have experienced enormous changes, as has the America they have come to. Yet all West Indian migrants to the United States (and to Canada, Great Britain, and other nations for that matter) share a common migratory tradition.

Few societies on earth have been as shaped by the movement of their people as those of the Caribbean. Subject to the chronic overpopulation, scarce resources, seclusion, and limited opportunities of small island nations, West Indians have utilized migration as a survival strategy whenever they were free to do so. In much of the Anglophone Caribbean, migration has become a normal and expected part of the adult life cycle, a virtual rite of passage (Hennessy 1984; Richardson 1983; Marshall 1980; Thomas-Hope 1978).

Well before such voluntary migration was possible, the movement of people was creating and defining Caribbean societies. Their Amerindian populations wiped out soon after discovery, the islands of the Caribbean were "born modern." Populated primarily by Africans who grew an Asian product to be sold in Europe, the early West Indian colonies were from their inception part of a world economic system. Though it would be an exaggeration to say that these nations have no pre-Columbian past (the roots in West Africa are deep and often evident), West Indian cultures primarily reflect the historically recent merging of a dozen African strains, along with those from Europe, Asia, and the Middle East.

The labor-intensive sugar plantation economy required large numbers of slaves, and the low fertility rates of most West Indian islands meant that the major source of slaves throughout most of the pre-emancipation period was importation (Klein 1986; Mintz 1974). As David Lowenthal notes, in the West Indies "it seemed easier to work Negroes hard and replace them with newly bought slaves than to look after them and encourage them to reproduce. The Negro was a replaceable machine" (1967:308).

Thus first-generation Africans constituted an important segment of the slave population until emancipation, in contrast to the overwhelming predominance of New World–born slaves in the American South by the nineteenth century (Genovese 1979). Even after emancipation, the Caribbean black population continued to be "re-Africanized" by the importation of indentured workers from West Africa (Knight 1978).

At the same time, slave owners made little allowance for natural population growth and imported slaves beyond the capacity of many of the islands to support them. As a result, the most successful of the sugar plantation islands were considered overpopulated before the close of the seventeenth century (Richardson 1983; Lowenthal 1967). This led to the sale of slaves to other islands and colonies—and occasionally to starvation—until a periodic upturn in the sugar industry increased the labor demand and brought a new group of imported Africans.

After emancipation in 1838 this pattern of alternately importing and exporting labor intensified. Large numbers of East Indian, Chinese, Portuguese, and African contract laborers were imported to replace the slaves during the mid-nineteenth century. At the same time, those blacks who had a choice generally sought alternatives to the plantations (Thomas-Hope 1978). As Karl Marx noted in 1857, many former slaves rejected wage labor altogether, seeking instead to become "self-sustaining peasants working for their own consumption" (1974 [1857]:325–26). Most of the time, however, this option was not available. In the ecologically devastated Leewards, densely populated Barbados, and some of the larger islands as well, the only way out of the slavery-like conditions of the local plantations was migration. As early as the 1840s the former slaves from St. Kitts were boarding small boats for the perilous journey to labor-starved Trinidad (Richardson 1983). By the 1850s Jamaicans were being recruited for labor in Panama and Costa Rica in such numbers that the island's governor would compare the emigration to "the Irish Exodus" (Thomas-Hope 1978:67).

Agricultural labor circulated throughout the Caribbean during the nineteenth century. Movement from the older colonies to the expanding economies of Trinidad and Guyana continued alongside the importation of Indian indentured workers until the price of sugar fell dramatically in the late 1880s (Rodney 1981; Marshall 1980). This was followed by the movement of agricultural workers to Cuba after slavery ended there in 1886 (Thomas-Hope 1978). Canal construction in Panama drew approximately 100,000 West Indian workers, primarily from Jamaica and Barbados, between 1881 and 1914 (Petras 1987). During the same period a smaller flow of migrants left the islands for Costa Rica, British Honduras, and the eastern coast of Nicaragua. The existence of predominantly black, English-speaking cities in Central America (Limon in Costa Rica, Bluefields in Nicaragua, and Belize City in the new nation of the same name) is the heritage of this migration (Priestley 1989; Bourgois 1989; Gordon 1989). The oil industry in Venezuela and Aruba, the sugar plantations in the Dominican Republic and Cuba, and labor shortages in the U.S. Virgin Islands and Bermuda continued to draw Caribbean migrants throughout the twentieth century (Conway 1989).

Though small now by comparison with the migration to metropolitan societies, intra-Caribbean migration continues. Today several Caribbean nations simultaneously export numerous skilled and unskilled workers while they import labor for seasonal agricultural work

[21]

and low-wage jobs in the tourist industry (Marshall 1985; Miller 1985). On small islands this pattern has been a particular cause for concern. A University of the West Indies mission to St. Vincent in 1969 noted: "In a situation of institutionalized migration people come to see migration as the only means of achieving anything. The young grow up to think that this is the only way to make anything of themselves" (1969:106).

Unfortunately, the high unemployment and limited opportunities of most West Indian nations mean that migration *is* often the only way for young people to "make anything" of themselves. This, plus the drive for experience and opportunity that cannot be had in small insular societies, has produced a uniquely outward-looking culture and a steady stream of migrants (Maingot 1985; Anderson 1985).

This migrant tradition has affected West Indian political ideology. The common experience of work in foreign lands has been a cornerstone of most efforts to establish a pan-West Indian identity. As Bonham Richardson notes in regard to the labor migration from the Anglophone Caribbean to the Dominican Republic in the 1930s:

> The workers' friendships extended from their home islands as black men from all over the Antilles became acquainted with one another. . . . Home islands provided stories, anecdotes and informal comparisons of similarities and differences that existed among the small insular colonies of the British Caribbean. Men from St. Kitts and Nevis learned secondhand, for example, of the prevalence of drought in Antigua or of the Stevedore wage levels in St. Vincent. . . . An incipient pan-Caribbean identity was thus formed around the camp fires on the cane plantations in Santo Domingo. (1983:139).

In the twentieth century this identity has at times taken the form of pan-Africanism. Marcus Garvey was a Jamaican whose widespread following reflected his extensive travels to Central America, Europe, and the United States. Many other leading anti-colonialist and pan-Africanist figures such as George Padmore, C. L. R. James, Frantz Fanon, and Stokely Carmichael spent most of their careers far from the lands of their birth. Alexander Bustamante and Norman Manley, the rival cousins who led Jamaica to independence, both went abroad for periods in their youth, and Eric Williams, Trinidad's first prime minister, taught for a time at Howard University. Eric Gairy, who dominated Grenadian politics for two decades, got his start in public life as a union leader in the Aruba oil industry. The father of Maurice Bishop (who overthrew Gairy) worked at the same refinery, as did Herbert Blaize, who succeeded Bishop after the 1983 American invasion (Maingot 1985; Thomas-Hope 1985; Taylor 1976).

West Indians who seek opportunities abroad have traditionally maintained close ties with their home communities. Indeed, given the importance of remittances in the Caribbean economy, many appear to have strengthened these ties. While West Indians did establish permanent settlements within Hispanic nations, most intra-Caribbean migrants moved back and forth between home and labor, and a sojourn abroad was usually seen as a way to better one's position *at home*.

The current pattern of migration to the metropoles represents a break with earlier migrant patterns, although in Britain, Canada, and the United States, West Indian migrants have continued to maintain strong ties to their home communities. Relatively few have come to these nations as short-term migrants.[1] Many plan to return home eventually (at least to retire), and visiting is common, but immigration policies in all of these nations favor those planning long stays.[2] For contemporary migrants return may also be less necessary than before, as the increased cultural contact and ease of travel between the West Indies and Caribbean diaspora communities in the metropolises has made them part of one social sphere. Thus an incipient transnationalism may be developing, in which the division of home and host society is increasingly less relevant (see Glick-Schiller et al. 1987; Sutton 1987).

The Three Cohorts

West Indian migration to the United States has come in three distinct waves. A large group came in the first three decades of this

---

1. Approximately 10,000 Anglophone Caribbean workers travel to southern Florida each year to cut sugar cane under the U.S. government's "H-2" temporary agricultural labor program (see Wilkinson 1989). A few thousand more, mostly Jamaicans, come to New England for a few weeks each fall to pick apples. Although an unknown number of "H-2" workers simply walk off at the end of their contract periods and join the growing Caribbean communities of New York, Miami, and Hartford, Connecticut, they do not constitute a significant portion of the new immigrants in these communities.

2. Whether such policies will continue since the Immigration Reform and Control Act of 1986, with its bias in favor of temporary workers, remains to be seen.

century. A much smaller and somewhat more middle-class group came between the waning of the Depression and the changes in U.S. immigration policy of the mid 1960s. The largest wave began in 1966 and continues to the present with no sign of abating. Each group reflected the unique situation that propelled it toward the United States, and each was incorporated into U.S. society under distinct historical circumstances.

The first migration began about 1900 and peaked during the early 1920s. Black immigration, almost all of it West Indian, rose from 412 immigrants admitted in 1899, to 832 in 1902, to 2,174 in 1903, to 5,633 in 1907. It then stabilized at rates of between 5,000 and 8,000 per year until, on the eve of immigration restrictions, it swelled to 12,243 in 1924. Restrictions sharply cut the numbers admitted after 1924, but significant migration continued from the colonial Caribbean (with many West Indians entering the United States through the underutilized British quota) until the Depression. It then fell off sharply, dropping from 1,804 in 1930 to 187 in 1932. From 1932 to 1937, the number of West Indians returning home exceeded the number entering the United States (Reid 1939).

By 1930 there were 177,981 foreign-born blacks and children of foreign-born blacks in the United States, constituting 1.5 percent of the total black population.[3] The vast majority of these were West Indians. Of the 98,620 black immigrants in 1930 (see Table 1), 72,138 came directly from the non-Hispanic Caribbean; most of the rest

---

3. There is some difficulty over what statistic to use when defining "West Indians." If one counts all those born in the Anglophone Caribbean nations and territories, one misses those born in Britain or France of Caribbean parents as well as a large number of English-speaking black immigrants from Central and South America. Most researchers use the number of "foreign-born blacks" as a proxy for West Indians (including Haitians). While not perfect, this measure was reasonably reliable through the 1980 census, as the number of black immigrants from non-Caribbean backgrounds was quite small and regionally concentrated. It should be noted however, that the increase in African migration to the United States during the 1980s means that this proxy measure cannot be used with the 1990 census.

This problem becomes even more difficult when one tries to measure the number of Americans of Caribbean descent. In 1980 the old category of "foreign stock" (persons whose parents or grandparents were born abroad) was eliminated from the census. It was replaced by a subjective question on "ancestry." This tended to increase the membership of European "ethnic" groups because many people not of "foreign stock" did report an ancestry designation. And it tended to decrease the numbers in categories from the Americas. For example, many of the U.S.-born children of West Indian immigrants gave their birth place as the United States, their race as black, and their ancestry as African, British, or mixed. Similarly, Haitians often listed their ancestry as African, Argentines as Spanish or Italian, and so forth.

Table 1. The foreign-born black population of the United States

Year	Number	Percentage of total black pop.
1890	19,979	0.3
1900	20,336	0.2
1910	40,339	0.4
1920	73,803	0.7
1930	98,620	0.8
1940	83,941	0.7
1950	113,842	0.8
1960	125,322	0.7
1970	253,458	1.1
1980	815,720	3.1
1980—urban areas only	783,881	3.5
1980—north-east U.S. only	491,922	10.1

Source: U.S. Census of Population, 1890–1980.

came from Central and South America and were of West Indian origin. More than half of all black immigrants had settled in New York City.[4]

Some of this immigrant group originated in the "brown" middle classes of the islands (Richardson 1983), but a large majority appear to have come from the working class. Ira Reid indicates that of those reporting a pre-migration occupation, 31.4 percent had been industrial workers and 40.4 percent had been servants or laborers (1939:244). Despite their modest island beginnings, by the 1930s these immigrants constituted a disproportionately high percentage of those in the professional, economic, and political leadership of New York's black community.

The second wave of West Indian immigrants, those arriving between the late 1930s and 1965, was the smallest. Though the frequent use of British passports makes it difficult to report their numbers precisely, net migration from the Commonwealth Caribbean

---

4. The largest group of clearly non–West Indian "foreign-born blacks" enumerated by the 1930 census were the approximately 6,000 Cape Verdeans. As the Cape Verdean community was located primarily in southeastern New England, it is safe to assume that well over 90 percent of New York's foreign-born blacks were West Indians. It should be noted, however, that the binary racial distinction (black/white) employed by the Census Bureau was never adequate to describe the reality of groups like the Cape Verdeans, among whom "racial" (that is, phenotypical) characteristics vary widely even within families.

probably never exceeded 3,000 per year until the close of this period and was generally far below that. Immigration virtually came to a halt at the height of the Depression, climbed slightly after World War II, but was cut back again in 1952 when the McCarran-Walter Act restricted the use of the "home country" quotas by colonial subjects. During this period the main body of Caribbean out-migration was directed toward Great Britain, then experiencing postwar labor shortages. The small number of West Indians who did enter the United States during this period continued to settle, for the most part, in New York. This middle cohort was largely made up of people joining family who had migrated during the first wave, and of young professionals who entered the country on student visas and stayed after completing their degrees. Many of the elder statesmen of today's West Indian community were part of this group (Buffenmeyer 1970).

After independence in 1962, tiny quotas of one hundred immigrants per year were provided for Jamaica and Trinidad within the McCarran-Walter framework, and it was assumed that similar small quotas would be assigned to other West Indian nations that became independent subsequently (Reimers 1985). But two developments during the next three years altered the history of the West Indies and of New York City by redirecting the main body of West Indian out-migration back toward the United States.

The first was the severe restriction of Commonwealth immigration to Britain in 1962. West Indian migration to the "home country" had been unrestricted during the 1950s, and in 1962 it peaked at more than 50,000 (Davison 1963). The almost complete shutdown of this important population safety valve might have had dire consequences for Caribbean nations on the eve of independence, had it not been for a second development.

In 1965 the Hart-Cellar Immigration Reform Act changed the entire focus of American immigration policy, opening the way for a dramatic surge in immigration. The bill eliminated the national quota system first established in 1924 and reaffirmed under McCarran-Walter. In its place Congress established uniform limits of 20,000 persons per country for the eastern hemisphere, within an overall hemispheric limit of 170,000. A limit of 120,000 immigrants was set for the western hemisphere, with no quotas per country (the maximum of 20,000 immigrants per country was extended to the western hemisphere in 1976). This reform proved a boon for the new micro-states of the Caribbean, effectively making more and more West Indians eligible to immigrate as more Caribbean territories became independent nations after 1962. In the ten years after the Hart-Cellar reforms went into effect, West Indian immigration exceeded that of the previous seventy years, and the numbers continued to grow after that. By the early 1980s approximately 50,000 legal immigrants from the Anglophone Caribbean and another 6,000 to 8,000 from Haiti were entering the United States annually. Approximately half of these people settled in New York City.

Coming a mere thirteen years after the McCarran-Walter Act, the Hart-Cellar reforms represented a remarkable shift in policy. That they were passed with little controversy reflects the broad rethinking of the roles of race and ethnicity in American life taking place during the period. Nathan Glazer, whose own work was a major part of this shift in thinking, recently noted that in the wake of "the radical change in American attitudes towards race that accompanied the rise of the civil rights movement . . . [the] attempt to freeze the composition of the American people by favoring (immigrants from) Northwestern Europe was increasingly seen as basically immoral and wrong. (1985:6)

Yet while the reforms of 1965 signaled an increased acceptance of American ethnic divisions, the immigration policy debate that begot them revealed U.S. insularity. No one, particularly not the bill's supporters, envisioned that Hart-Cellar would produce a dramatic change in the ethnic composition of new arrivals. On the eve of the bill's passage, Attorney General Robert Kennedy testified that the number of new immigrants was not expected to increase greatly, and other experts, while acknowledging that immigration from Jamaica and Trinidad would exceed the limit of one hundred, predicted that it would stabilize at approximately 5,000 to 7,000 per year for the Caribbean as a whole (Reimers 1985:77). Not one witness or legislator disagreed with this estimate. By the early 1980s, however, immigration from Jamaica alone would total approximately 20,000 persons annually.

This third and largest cohort of immigrants (see Table 2) has come from virtually every sector of Caribbean society. It has included well-educated members of the urban elite seeking to protect their wealth in volatile economies, children of the middle class searching for

Table 2. West Indian immigration by country or region of birth, 1960–1984

Country/region of birth	1960–1965	1966–1970	1971–1975	1976–1980	1981–1984	Total
Antigua	NA	NA	1,969	4,131	7,124	13,224
Barbados	2,377	7,312	7,878	13,070	7,781	38,418
Dominica	NA	NA	1,182	3,399	2,278	6,859
Grenada	NA	NA	2,388	5,377	3,210	12,085
Guyana	1,434	5,760	14,320	33,211	34,194	88,919
Jamaica	9,675	62,676	61,445	80,550	81,637	295,983
Montserrat	NA	NA	932	1,007	583	2,522
St. Kitts-Nevis	NA	NA	1,960	4,474	6,327	12,761
St. Lucia	NA	NA	1,305	3,642	2,465	7,412
St. Vincent	NA	NA	1,613	3,122	2,984	7,715
Trinidad-Tobago	2,598	22,367	33,278	28,498	14,187	100,928
Other[a]	—	—	8,489	14,125	11,186	
Other[b]	11,343	16,806	—	—	—	61,944
Total Anglophone West Indies	27,424	114,921	136,759	194,606	134,638	640,104
Haiti	10,820	27,648	27,130	41,786	33,725	141,109

Source: U.S. Department of Justice, *Statistical Year Books of the Immigration and Naturalization Service*, 1969, 1980, 1983, 1984.
[a]Includes Anguilla, Bahamas, Belize, The British Virgin Islands, Cayman Islands, The Netherlands Antilles, Turks and Caicos.
[b]Includes the places listed in note *a*, plus Antigua, Dominica, Grenada, Montserrat, St. Kitts-Nevis, St. Lucia, and St. Vincent.

broader opportunities, and large numbers of poor people looking for a standard of living above mere subsistence. Though political developments in the region account for certain peaks in migration, the flow of migrants has grown steadily in the most stable nations as well as the more volatile ones. The reasons for this exodus, as for most Caribbean migration of the last 150 years, are primarily economic.

Development has been slow in coming to the Caribbean, and where it has come it has seldom generated much local employment. In spite of—or, as some have argued, because of—the infusion of American capital since the mid-1960s, large segments of the West Indian population remain unemployed or underemployed (Marshall 1985).[5] Unemployment rates of 15 to 25 percent are the norm in the region, and in Jamaica they have at times gone considerably higher.

5. Ricketts (1987), for example, demonstrates a strong positive correlation between U.S. investment in Caribbean nations and migration from those nations to the United States, a pattern Sassen-Koob (1981) had previously described as "exporting capital and importing labor" (see also Watson 1985).

The situation is worse for the young. Since 1972 the unemployment rate for Jamaicans under age 24 has seldom been below 40 percent (in 1980 it topped 50 percent), a grim situation that has persisted despite changes in government and economic policies (Anderson 1985).

The situation is comparable in many of the smaller nations of the region. Though in a few cases such as Bermuda and the Bahamas the per capita Gross Domestic Product (GDP) approaches first world levels, most of the Anglophone Caribbean lags far behind. Falling oil prices have adversely affected Trinidad, the region's major success story, and the Jamaican per capita GDP in 1980 was only $1,339 (compared to $11,536 in the United States). In Dominica, St. Vincent, and Grenada, the 1980 per capita GDP was less than $600 (Pastor 1985). As in other parts of the third world, a combination of economic and ecological factors have made agriculture increasingly problematic (Richardson 1983; Miller 1985). The result is rapid urbanization, a large informal sector, and a growing number of people outside the labor force altogether.

Perhaps even more important than persistent poverty and unemployment in explaining Caribbean migration is the nature of the development that has occurred in these nations. Ricketts (1987) argues that capital-intensive development strategies driven by foreign investment have tended to disrupt local labor patterns. Once people are displaced from jobs, high unemployment and limited options in these small countries make emigration often the only viable option, even for members of the middle class. Thus large numbers of legal and illegal immigrants come not only from the region's poorer nations but from those that according to aggregate levels of development are doing relatively well.

U.S. penetration of the Caribbean is not limited to economics (see Watson 1985). Satellite dishes bring American television directly to Jamaica and the spread of VCRs has brought it to the rest of the islands. The tourist industry, which brings the first world to the Caribbean in person, is spreading into the remotest corners of the region. Thus American popular culture pervades the nations of the West Indies, which are also increasingly within the American sphere politically and militarily. Is it any wonder then, given a culture in which migration is already the norm, that the young and the ambitious often see the United States as their only option?

[29]

The number of those who choose this path is larger than the official statistics indicate. The growth of the West Indian community in the United States after 1965 facilitated a significant increase in the number of illegal immigrants, who can rely on friends to provide places to live and help them get jobs. They can live and work in these communities with little risk of detection. Nor do illegals form in any sense an "underground" group; it is not unusual to find U.S. citizens, legal resident aliens, persons holding valid student or tourist visas, and illegal immigrants within the same families.

Table 3. Non-Hispanic Caribbean immigrants admitted to the United States by country or region of birth, 1984

Country or region of birth	Total	New arrivals	Adjusted
Anglophone Caribbean			
Anguilla	61	53	8
Antigua	953	746	207
Bahamas	499	262	237
Barbados	1,577	1,295	282
Belize	1,492	1,256	236
Bermuda	154	104	50
British V.I.	93	77	16
Cayman Is.	26	14	12
Dominica	442	390	52
Grenada	980	823	157
Guyana	8,412	7,794	618
Jamaica	19,822	17,159	2,663
Montserrat	80	64	16
Panama[a]	2,276	1,776	500
St. Kitts-Nevis	1,648	1,273	375
St. Lucia	484	344	140
St. Vincent	695	565	130
Trinidad-Tobago	2,900	2,293	602
Turks and Caicos	20	6	14
Total Anglophone Caribbean	42,614	36,294	6315
Haiti	9,839	8,032	1,807
Guadeloupe	31	27	4
Martinique	30	22	8
Netherlands Antilles	179	84	95
Total other Afro-Creole sending societies	10,079	8,165	1,914
Total non-Hispanic Caribbean	52,693	44,459	8,229

Source: INS Year Book, 1984.

[a]Although the Panamanian census indicates that only 14 percent of Panama's population is officially considered to be "West Indian" (persons of African descent whose first language is English), an analysis by the New York City Department of City Planning indicates that the large majority of Panamanian immigrants to the United States come from this group.

Of course many illegal immigrants eventually adjust their status and become legal immigrants. Most years about 15 percent of those immigrants "admitted" from the non-Hispanic Caribbean are not new immigrants at all, but rather persons whose status was adjusted to immigrant from some other form of visa (see Table 3 for 1984 data). Others return to their homelands in order to get a visa issued by the U.S. consulate when in fact they have lived in the United States for years.

In addition to facilitating illegal immigration, the existence of a West Indian community in New York greatly encourages further legal immigration, primarily because American immigration law encourages family reunion. Preference to the relatives of those already here was written into the Hart-Cellar bill, in part to placate nativist opposition. It was argued that if the relatives of those now living in the United States are given first preference in immigration, then new immigrant populations will tend to reflect the present U.S. ethnic composition without the overt bias of the old quota system (Reimers 1985; Briggs 1985). For a while this was, in fact, the case. Many of the post-1965 immigrants were sponsored by earlier immigrants. But as the number of immigrants in the United States started to swell, the number of people in the Caribbean that they were eligible to sponsor increased geometrically. Thus for legal as well as economic and cultural reasons we can expect high levels of West Indian immigration to continue.

Immigration policy also tends to encourage naturalization, as the relatives of U.S. citizens have preference over the relatives of permanent residents. The first cohort of West Indian immigrants were notoriously reluctant to become U.S. citizens, for reasons that will be explored. Among the current cohort there is also great reluctance to give up ties to the Caribbean, but contrary to popular belief this has not been a hindrance to naturalization. As Table 4 indicates, naturalization rates for black immigrants are now higher than for Hispanics and, once adjusted for length of time in the country, higher than for whites as well. The desire to sponsor others is probably the main force behind these rates, but undoubtedly there are political reasons, too. Naturalized citizens can, and generally do, vote.

This issue of citizenship demonstrates one of the clear historical differences among the three cohorts. Though all three groups were reluctant to give up ties to home, for the third wave such sacrifice

[31]

Table 4. Naturalization rates for immigrants by race, 1980

	% naturalized citizens	Standardized for date of arrival
Blacks	43	51
Whites	66	49
Hispanics	30	34
Other races	33	49

Source: U.S. Census of Population and Housing: 1980. Public Use Micro Data Sample. In Walter Allen and Reynolds Farley, *The Color Line and the Quality of Life: The Problem of the Twentieth Century* (Sage, 1987).

was not necessary to have the advantages of U.S. citizenship. With the single exception of Trinidad, the new nations of the Anglophone Caribbean permit full citizenship rights to their subjects abroad whether or not they have become U.S. citizens (in some cases such rights are extended to their U.S.-born children and grandchildren as well). Under pressure from their people abroad (and needing to keep the emigration channel open), these nations have passed some of the world's most liberal citizenship laws. Thus most West Indian New Yorkers may become fully involved in political life in New York without losing any of their rights in the Caribbean—largely because independence allowed the Caribbean states to set their own citizenship policies.

This transnationalism extends beyond the issue of legal citizenship. It is reflected in cultural attitudes as well. Caribbean newspapers frequently report stories about emigrants who are doing well in the United States, including those in the military. So casual is the "hometown-boy-makes-good" style of these stories that one might forget that serving in the armed forces of another nation is, in most countries, grounds for loss of citizenship, or worse. The idea that loyalty to one nation contradicts loyalty to another is fast disappearing among contemporary West Indian immigrants.

Encountering Race in the United States

All West Indian immigrants have faced a double process in being incorporated into American life, coming simultaneously into "America" and into "Black America." They entered a society far more prosperous than the ones they left, but in so doing they also joined the ranks of America's most consistently oppressed minority group. This dilemma—economic upward mobility at the price of downward mobility in status—has confronted all three cohorts of immigrants, but its effects have been different for each.

Historically the United States has exhibited a highly unusual system of racial categorization that contrasts sharply with the way race is conceptualized in the rest of the Americas (Degler 1986; Harris 1964). All persons of *any* known or discernible African ancestry, regardless of somatic characteristics, are considered "black" and have been subject to all of the social and legal disadvantages that this implies. Hence Americans may describe someone as a "light-skinned black person" without giving much thought to the Alice-in-Wonderland quality of the phrase.[6]

Thus the first wave of West Indian immigrants entered a society in which they were considered "black," regardless of appearance.[7] More important, it was a society in which being black was, in the jargon of sociologists, a "master status." That is, race played an overwhelming role in shaping the life chances of African Americans; all other statuses paled by comparison. The outcome for most was segregation, discrimination, and poverty. In 1930, perhaps 5 percent of American blacks could be described as middle-class, and the majority of these were professionals working in segregated institutions or service providers to all-black clienteles (Patterson 1987).

Of course, most contemporary West Indian immigrants are still considered black. But this fact does not necessarily mean what it used to. One need not completely accept William Wilson's assertion that the significance of race has "declined" in U.S. society to recognize that the situation is now a good deal more complex. By the late 1970s approximately 40 percent of black U.S. households could be counted as middle- or lower-middle-class, and often the wage earners in these households worked in integrated settings (Wilson

---

6. While it has roots in slavery, this binary notion of race was not formalized until after Reconstruction, when segregation necessitated that legal and social definitions of race be firmly fixed. Its imposition was, not surprisingly, sharply resisted by the descendants of the antebellum "free persons of color" (see Johnson and Roark 1984; Williamson 1980). A number of racially ambiguous groups, including both immigrants and isolated mixed race groups dating from the eighteenth century, have at times avoided being categorized as "black" by invoking a variety of cultural and legal strategies (see, for examples, Machado 1981; Blu 1980; D. Cohen 1974). The overwhelming majority of such people, however, were incorporated into the black community by the early twentieth century.

7. For a vivid account of the impact this designation had on light-skinned migrants from the "colored" middle class, see Michelle Cliff's novel *No Telephone to Heaven* (1987).

1978). By contrast, the black poor, who according to some now constitute an "underclass," are increasingly isolated from both the industrial economy and the institutions of mainstream society (Wilson
1987). This group, which is defined by both race *and* class, is, as
Orlando Patterson has recently commented, "more segregated than
blacks have been at any time in American history" (1987:232).

Thus contemporary black immigrants enter a society in which the
role of race is in flux. While overt racism continues to affect the daily
life of African Americans, many of the older, blatant forms of segregation have been replaced by "forms of discrimination that are
more indirect, more subtle"; these forms are often based on an interaction of racial and class factors producing "critical effects that cannot
be explained simply by combining the main effects of the two" (Pettigrew 1981:245). For middle- and working-class African Americans,
opportunities have expanded during a period when the black poor
face an unprecedented level of social isolation.

Of course, saying that race constitutes less of a structural barrier to
economic opportunity than it once did is not at all the same thing as
saying that prejudice and discrimination have declined. In fact, they
may have increased. As several of Wilson's critics have pointed out,
the disappearance of institutional structures of segregation means
that middle-class blacks are more likely to be competing directly
with whites and thus to encounter prejudice more frequently in both
its overt and subtle forms (Clark 1980; Willie 1978). Further, recent
incidents of mob violence against blacks in white neighborhoods
demonstrate clearly that blacks continue to be treated as a singular,
racially defined category.

Nevertheless, Wilson and others who have examined the growing
bifurcation of the black community have pointed to an undeniable
shift in the nature of American race relations. While race remains a
central influence on the position of West Indian immigrants in the
American social structure, its effect on the post-1965 immigrants is
multifaceted and contingent on a variety of other factors in a way it
was not for their predecessors.

The West Indian Response

The first cohort of West Indian immigrants arrived and settled in
the United States during the height of racial segregation. Given this
fact, they were faced with two options.

They could remain "birds of passage," and consider themselves only temporary sojourners in North American society. No matter how economically established in the United States such immigrants were, the dream of return remained vital and they organized their lives around this expectation. Any indignities they suffered while sojourning in this strange land were but part of the tribulations they endured in expectation of a specific end, and were bearable because they were temporary. The self-image of those who chose this option was tied to their former status in their homeland, or to their anticipated improved status upon return (Piore 1979). Manifestations of this strategy included a propensity to retain close personal and financial ties to the homeland, a reluctance to take out U.S. citizenship, and participation in organizations of fellow countrymen devoted to maintaining past statuses or to giving the migrant a continuing voice in home country affairs.

The other option was for the migrants to immerse themselves within the North American black community, and to work for the betterment of that community. Such immigrants could make use of their immigrant advantages—education, access to rotating credit associations, the drive to success of a proven risk-taker—to achieve positions of prominence within the larger black community. This did not mean that ethnicity was nonexistent or forgotten. It generally did mean, however, that ethnic ties, which threatened racial unity and might lead others to question their position within the African American community, remained private.

As we shall see, neither of these strategies of accommodation lends itself to "ethnic" politics of the type practiced by white immigrant groups. The "sojourner" stays out of American politics. While he retains his cultural distinctiveness, he does so on a nation-of-origin basis. Thus West Indian migrants have formed many organizations concerned with the parochial affairs of the various islands and territories, reflecting thereby the consciousness of exiles, not of "ethnics." The "settler" strategy, though it affirms involvement in U.S. affairs, seeks to play down ethnic distinctions. Public activity is based on race and other identities become distinctly secondary.

The post-1965 immigrants now coming into their own in New York are handling the issues of race and ethnicity quite differently from their predecessors. In some ways their activities resemble those of white immigrant ethnic groups. They have founded their own "ethnic" neighborhoods and thus given an ethnic flavor to local institutions. They have used culture to make political statements and they have turned their attentions to local politics. At the same time, the relative ease of travel between the Caribbean and the United States, combined with the flexible citizenship policies of the new Caribbean nations, has blurred the sharp choices that confronted earlier immigrants. It is now easier than ever to retain a foot in both societies; commitment to one implies no lessening of commitment to the other.

Of course West Indians differ from white "ethnics" in many other important respects. Though an ethnic cultural identity is more available to contemporary black immigrants than it was to earlier cohorts, cultural activity still takes place within the context of pervasive racial stratification. Thus, while white immigrants stand to gain status by becoming "Americans"—by assimilating into a higher status group— black immigrants may actually lose social status if they lose their cultural distinctiveness.

At the same time, both because they share a strong sense of black identity and because they are confronted by white racism in their everyday lives, most West Indians I have spoken to appear deeply ambivalent about being the more favored blacks in the eyes of some whites. Even those who maintain a strong sense of cultural distinctiveness express suspicion of what they describe as "divide and conquer" strategies. Yet though they may resent white attempts to differentiate them from native blacks, they also frequently note that such attempts may have practical value. A politically active banker puts it thus:

> Informant: Since I have been here, I have always recognized that this is a racist country and I have made every effort not to lose my accent.
>
> PK: Your accent is an asset?
>
> Informant: Yes.
>
> PK: In dealing with blacks or whites?
>
> Informant: With whites! But then later, when the time is appropriate, you can confront these people with their racism.

Thus the new black immigrants are confronted by the changing and at times contradictory meanings of race and ethnicity in the contemporary United States. They often express both a deep sense of kinship with other African Americans and a heartfelt urge to retain and perhaps institutionalize their ethnic distinctiveness. As the people of Marcus Garvey, contemporary Caribbean Americans defer to no one in the expression of black pride. Yet in a society in which ethnic identity has become increasingly salient, they have begun to express that pride in terms distinctly their own.

[2]

From a Presence to a Community: New York's West Indian Neighborhoods

Fulton Street today is the aroma of our kitchen long ago when the bread was finally in the oven. And it's the sound of reggae and calypso and ska and the newest rage, soca, erupting from a hundred speakers outside the record stores. It's Rastas with their hennaed dreadlocks and the impassioned political debates of the rum shops back home brought out onto the street corners. It's Jamaican meat patties brought out and eaten on the run and fast food pulori, a Trinidadian East Indian pancake doused in pepper sauce that is guaranteed to clear your sinuses the moment that you bite into it. Fulton Street is Haitian Creole heard amid any number of highly inventive, musically accented versions of English. And its faces, an endless procession of faces that are black for the most part—for these are mother Africa's children—but with noticeable admixtures of India, Europe, and China, a reflection of the history of the region from which they have come in this most recent phase of the diaspora.

—PAULE MARSHALL, "The Rising Islanders of Bed-Stuy"

The growing number of West Indian immigrants in New York City in the wake of the 1965 Hart-Cellar immigration reforms has been reflected in a related development: the growth of distinctly West Indian neighborhoods in Brooklyn and Queens. This fact is not surprising. During the past several decades we have become used to thinking of New York and other older American cities as mosaics of "ethnic" neighborhoods, and it is generally expected that ethnic com-

[38]

munities will be concentrated in geographical areas. It is the significance of population concentration that concerns us here.

Not all ethnic groups establish distinct geographic enclaves; in particular, earlier cohorts of West Indians did not do so. Further, the formation of neighborhoods is not merely a matter of demographic concentration; it also may serve as the basis of a self-conscious community. Geographic concentration means that institutions in an area may start to serve predominantly one group; thus they become, perhaps quite unintentionally, "ethnic" institutions. As Martin Marger notes, "The emergent ethnic community consists of members who are increasingly conscious of their ethnic identification vis-a-vis other ethnic communities and who interact regularly on the basis of their shared ethnicity. In addition, it displays in some degree an institutional structure catering to a particular clientele" (1986:2).

At some point an ethnic population will reach a critical mass that promotes the founding of enterprises and institutions that serve this constituency. These enterprises and institutions in turn contribute to the ethnic identity of those who use them. They form the locus where certain aspects of a group's culture may be selected and reified so as to become the symbols of an ethnic identity within the host nation, and where sentiment, symbol, and geography may become intertwined (Firey 1947). Thus, to draw on Marshall's description, on Fulton Street the mundane act of eating "Jamaican" meat patties assumes a symbolic significance it never had in Jamaica. It may take on a further significance for the second-generation West Indian-American, for whom in some sense the pattie shop *is* Jamaica.

In a city where people are used to thinking of ethnicity and geography as connected, the founding of neighborhoods may also help to create boundaries that others recognize. As Gerald Suttles has demonstrated, ethnicity forms a vital part of the symbolic conceptual shorthand that urbanites routinely use to mentally divide up territory (1968). Such symbolism has probably increased in importance in recent years as more traditional forms of neighborhood interaction have declined. The boundaries drawn by local institutions, the marketing practices of the real estate industry, and the use of ethnic symbolism are all factors contributing to the way urbanites think of the geography of the city. Thus churches, clubs, meeting halls, and bakeries that cater to a population in one area serve to make the ethnic group real in the minds of both members and outsiders.

In addition, the establishment of distinct neighborhoods contributes in a direct way to the politicization of ethnicity. American urban politics is largely based on geographic notions of community. Since the 1960s, with the movement for "community control," this has been increasingly the case. Even the left has tended in recent years to emphasize neighborhood (and thus ethnic) ties over those of the workplace: as early as 1972, Dennis Wrong noted that the phrases "'member of the community' and 'community control' had acquired the aura that once attached to 'worker' and 'worker's control'" (1972:43).

Of course the notion of community implicit in this rhetoric is based as much on myth as on reality. Modern urban "communities" often rise as much out of political conflict and bureaucratic manipulation as from a sense of communal solidarity, a fact attested to by the hyphenated name of the site of the most famous community control struggle of the 1960s: Ocean Hill-Brownsville (Suttles 1972:81). In electoral politics the malleable and occasionally spurious nature of the urban "community" becomes clear. The customs and culture of the Forty-third State Assembly district do not differ drastically from those across the street in the Forty-second, yet a political candidate crossing that line will be challenged on the grounds that he or she is a carpetbagger. Further, geographically based political boundaries are subject to all manner of manipulation of which gerrymandering is only the most obvious.

The fact remains, however, that in the United States race and ethnicity often determine where people live and, as Ira Katznelson notes, "the system of territorial districts puts a premium on identities that are found where people live" (1981:71; see also Rae 1967). Thus, to the extent that ethnicity shapes a group's location, it often shapes its political activity as well. The "ethnic competition over the territorial supply of municipal services" has long been "the stuff of urban politics" in most American cities (Bender 1983:18).

Because this connection between geography, ethnicity, and politics is widely understood, it can also be self-fulfilling. Once an enclave is formed, those who would be leaders of that ethnic community are likely to settle in that enclave, seeing it as a potential power base. This further solidifies the neighborhood's ethnic identity. By the early 1980s several Caribbean political activists had moved into Brooklyn's West Indian neighborhoods, and one unsuccessful congressional candidate, himself long affiliated with activities in other parts of the city, sought office in Brooklyn specifically to capitalize on his Caribbean background.

The formation of ethnic neighborhoods by West Indian New Yorkers in the 1970s and 1980s presents a sharp contrast to the behavior of earlier cohorts of West Indian immigrants. For the earlier immigrants, race, not ethnicity, was the most crucial factor shaping both where they lived and their political identity, despite undoubtedly deep attachments to their Caribbean heritage.

Racial Segregation and Ethnic Integration, 1900–1965

The first wave of Afro-Caribbean migrants to New York City was part of a much larger migration of black people into the cities of the northern United States. As in other northern cities, the black population of New York swelled dramatically in the first three decades of the century, growing two and a half times faster than the total population (see Table 5). What was unique about New York was the diversity of the black migrants. It was the only city in the United States where a significant proportion of the black population was of Carib-

Table 5. New York City's black population, 1900–1960

Year	Black population	% N.Y.C. total	% increase black population	Foreign black population	% black foreign-born
1900	60,666	1.8	—	NA	—[a]
1910	91,709	1.9	51	11,757	12.8
1920	152,467	2.7	66	36,613	24.0
1930	327,706	4.7	115	54,754	16.7
1940	458,444	6.1	40	48,418	10.6
1950	747,608	9.5	63	(est. 53,570)	(7.2)[b]
1960	1,087,931	14.0	45	(est. 67,655)	(6.2)[c]

Source: U.S. Census of Population.

[a]In 1920, only 1,960 of New York's foreign-born black population reported arriving in the United States prior to 1901.

[b]In 1950, foreign-born blacks were not enumerated by locality. As it is generally assumed that the vast majority of New York State immigrant blacks lived in the city (Rosenwaike 1972), the estimate here is based on 90 percent of the total for New York State.

[c]In 1960, the census reported nativity data for all "non-whites" together, not reporting data for individual races by state or locality. The estimate here, derived by Rosenwaike (1972:168) is based on the assumption that nearly all foreign-born "non-whites" not born in Asian countries were, in fact, blacks.

Table 6. Nativity of New York City's black population, 1930

Place of birth	Number	Percent
Southeast[a]	142,165	43.4
South central[b]	10,815	3.3
New York State	79,264	24.2
Other U.S.	40,708	12.4
Foreign	54,754	16.7
Total	327,706	100

Source: Gilbert Osofsky, *Harlem: The Making of a Ghetto* (Harper and Row, 1963), p. 129.
[a]In order of percentage, Virginia, South Carolina, North Carolina, Georgia, Florida, Maryland, and the District of Columbia.
[b]In order of percentage, Alabama, Louisiana, Tennessee, Texas, Kentucky, Mississippi.

bean origin. By 1930, 16.7 percent of New York's black population was foreign-born. The black population of Manhattan was 17.7 percent foreign (Reid 1939:248), and Osofsky estimates that by the mid-1920s the black population of Harlem—the fastest growing black area—was 25 percent immigrant (1963:131). Table 6 reveals the high proportion of recent arrivals from both the South and the Caribbean among black New Yorkers at that time. Less than 25 percent of the city's black population had been born in New York State.

During the first three decades of the century, southerners and West Indians alike found themselves confronted with a tightly segregated housing market. Few areas were open to blacks; after 1920 the black population of New York was largely concentrated in central Harlem and the Bedford-Stuyvesant section of Brooklyn. During the twenties the white population of Manhattan dropped by 18 percent as the children of Jewish and Italian immigrants left Harlem and the Lower East Side for the outer boroughs, and during the same period the black population increased by 106 percent. In Harlem almost 120,000 whites were replaced by over 87,000 blacks and 45,000 Puerto Ricans. The main reason for these concentrations was discrimination. In 1931 a presidential commission examining housing conditions in New York wrote that "the factor of race and certain definite racial attitudes favorable to segregation, interpose difficulties to . . . breaking physical restrictions in residence areas" (quoted in Osofsky 1963:129). The result was overcrowding and a rapid escalation of rents in Harlem, which by 1930 were one third higher than those for comparable apartments in white working-class areas of the city. As Osofsky puts it, "The economic and residential mobility permitted whites in the city was [during the twenties] and would continue to be largely denied to Negroes. Most Negroes were 'jammed together' in Harlem—even those who could afford to live elsewhere—with little possibility of escape" (ibid.:131).

The combination of increasing racial segregation and rapid black population growth meant that West Indian migrants, who were treated as blacks, had few options as to where they could live. Invariably they settled among African Americans in areas where West Indians were in the minority. Given the stiff competition for space in the zone of black settlement, the formation of a distinct Caribbean enclave within the black community would have been difficult, even if West Indian immigrants had desired it. W. A. Domingo, while acknowledging social differences between African Americans and West Indians in Harlem, noted that "congestion in Harlem has forced both groups to be less discriminating in accepting lodgers, thus making for reconciling contacts" (1925:650).

One should not assume, however, that the concentration of new migrants within established black communities was entirely an imposition of the restricted housing market. The influence of Garvey and his pan-Africanist vision was never stronger than at the height of the first wave of West Indian migration, and for many immigrants Harlem was the "black metropolis"[1] where the various strains of the race would be reunited. Ira Reid describes it as the "new world mecca of the negro peoples" (1939:86). The growing mass media and personal communications spread Harlem's reputation throughout the Caribbean and the South, and this exerted a powerful pull on young migrants. Many leading intellectual figures from the Caribbean made their homes in Harlem during this period, including authors Claude McKay and Eric Walrond, journalist Cyril Briggs, socialist organizers Frank Crosswaith, Hulbert Harrison, and Richard Moore, Caribbean nationalist leaders such as Domingo and Ethelred Brown, and of course Marcus Garvey. For such men, nothing could have been further from their intentions than self-seclusion in West Indian en-

---

1. The phrases "black metropolis" and "negro metropolis" were commonly used by the black press in describing the black communities of New York and Chicago. The Jamaican author and poet Claude McKay published *Harlem: Negro Metropolis* in 1940 and St. Clair Duke and Horace Clayton used similar wording for the title of their famous study of Chicago, *Black Metropolis*, in 1945.

claves; it was precisely Harlem's diversity and excitement that had attracted them. As Jervis Anderson has written:

> Harlem has never been more high-spirited and engaging than it was during the 1920's. Blacks from all over America and the Caribbean were pouring in . . . word having reached them about the "city" in the heart of Manhattan that blacks were making their own. It was chiefly earlier migrants to Harlem that were spreading the word. . . . [T]heir letters, read in churches, lodges and gatherings, set off the new wave of migration that reached a flood tide during 1923. (1981:137)

New York's other rapidly growing black ghetto of the time, Bedford-Stuyvesant in Brooklyn, had little of Harlem's cachet, but its somewhat superior housing stock was also attracting large numbers of black immigrants by the mid-1930s. A smaller black Brooklyn enclave also formed on the edges of predominately Jewish Brownsville.

So whether by choice or not, the first cohort of West Indian immigrants lived in neighborhoods that were segregated by race and integrated by ethnicity and class. Harlem and Bedford-Stuyvesant were primarily home to the masses of the black poor, but also housed the black working class and much of the then tiny black middle class as well. This middle class, McKay writes in 1940, was "not large enough to establish an exclusive residential district," despite "strenuous and pathetic" efforts to do so. "Wherever they move, the common people follow and threaten to submerge them" (1940:23). At best they formed small and fragile islands of relative prosperity within the ghettos, such as Harlem's "Striver's Row."

Even when new areas opened to the black middle classes in the postwar era, these quickly became almost exclusively black and home to residents of wider income disparities than neighboring white communities, and they included blacks of different national or ethnic backgrounds. While there were areas within these black communities where large numbers of West Indians had settled, nowhere were they concentrated in such numbers as to create "West Indian" neighborhoods prior to the large-scale immigration in the late 1960s.

This is not to imply the residents of these neighborhoods were unaware of their ethnic differences, or that the immigrants were easily integrated into the larger black communities. Ethnic division was only one aspect of the intraracial discord which became more pronounced as New York's black enclaves grew during the twenties. As

Anderson notes, "Northern-born blacks looked down on the speech and manners of those recently arrived from the rural South; an upper class, consisting mainly of light-skinned professionals, fought to be recognized as Harlem's most representative social grouping; West Indians and black Americans often glared at each other xenophobically across borders of accent and style" (1981:137).

However much the leadership of both groups may have preached racial unity, resentment and competition often characterized the relations between West Indians and African Americans. Blacks were hardly unaffected by the general rise in anti-immigrant sentiment during the 1920s and, as the *Herald Tribune* noted in 1930, many shared "the white American's scorn for foreigners of any kind."[2] West Indians, the direct competitors for jobs and space with American blacks, bore the brunt of this scorn. In their account of pre-World War II Harlem, Roi Ottley and William Weatherby note that "the islander's tropical clothes were ridiculed. Frequently his white suit and cane brought him a shower of stones from Harlem street urchins" (1967:193). West Indians were known by the epithets "King Mon," "black Jews,"[3] and, most often, "monkey chasers." A popular song of the day demonstrates much of the prevailing attitude:

> Got my grip and trunk all packed,
> Steamship I'm gwine take her,
> So long to old New York Town,
> I'se gwine to Jamaica.
>
> When I get to the other side,
> I'll hang around the waters,
> I'll make a living sure as you born,
> A-divin' after quarters. . . .

2. Quoted in Anderson 1981:299. It should be remembered that the black nativism of this period arose in the context of an overall rise in nativism in America. Black leaders, often strong opponents of immigration restrictions in earlier times, became more conservative on the immigration question during the twenties, although they never exhibited the xenophobia of many native white politicians of the era. If anything, blacks appear to have been consistently less anti-immigrant than whites of the same income level—a remarkable fact given that blacks had the most to lose from competition with immigrants (Hellwig 1981).

3. The phrase "black Jews" was occasionally applied in a less derogatory manner, as in Adam Clayton Powell's description of West Indian entrepreneurial energy in *Marching Blacks* (1945). Shirley Chisholm claims that during the 1920s and 1930s the phrase was used by other West Indians to describe Barbadians.

> Done give up de bestest job,
> A' runnin' elevator,
> I told my boss "Mon" I'd be back
> Sometime soon or later.
>
> When I git back to this great land,
> You better watch me Harvey,
> 'Cause I'm gonna be a great big "Mon"
> Like my frien' Marcus Garvey.

> ("West Indies Blues," by Dowell, Williams and Williams,
> Clarence Williams Music Publishing Company,
> New York, 1924)

A bit of street doggerel of the same era that makes the point even more strongly:

> When I get to the other side
> I'll buy myself a mango
> Grab myself a monkey gall
> And do the monkey tango. . . .
>
> When a monkey-chaser dies
> Don't need no undertaker;
> Just throw him in the Harlem River,
> He'll float back to Jamaica.
> (quoted in Ottley 1943:46)

While Ottley reports that such taunting was sometimes sung good-naturedly, Reid (1939) leaves the reader with precisely the opposite impression. There can be little doubt as to the attitude of Harlem journalist Robert L. Vann, who in a speech during the height of the depression proclaimed: "If you West Indians don't like how we do things in this country you should go back where you came from. . . . We are good and tired of you. There should be a law deporting the whole lot of you. Failing that, you should be run out of Harlem" (Anderson 1981:303).

The West Indian immigrant was ridiculed for his supposedly aggressive behavior and crafty business practices as well as for his accent and dress. He was attacked in the New York black press for both his reluctance to become a naturalized citizen and for seeking to dominate New York black politics when he did. It was often said that when a West Indian "got ten cents above a beggar" he would open a business (Ottley and Weatherby 1967), Adam Clayton Powell, Jr., noted that the economic success of West Indians had made them the object of "envious scorn" in Harlem (1945:81).

But the immigrants' aggressiveness was also admired. Langston Hughes described them as "warm, rambunctious, sassy . . . little pockets of tropical dreams on their tongues." These qualities were not always appreciated by whites. In 1925 the *Saturday Evening Post* reported that West Indians were "notably lacking in the Southern Negro's diplomacy" and made "lots of noise about their rights" (Anderson 1981:299–300). The Pullman company, a major prewar employer of black men, avoided hiring West Indians as a matter of policy, according to Gilbert Osofsky, "because of their refusal to accept insults from passengers" (1963). This observation is echoed by Domingo: "The outstanding contribution of West Indians to American Negro life is the insistent assertion of their manhood in an environment that demands too much servility and unprotesting acquiescence from men of African blood" (1925:650).

The mixture of emotions West Indians inspired in some black Americans can be seen in Ottley's description:

> Legend has it that the West Indian came to Harlem to "teach, open a church or start trouble." He has done all of these things. But he has made a fundamental contribution to public education out of his zeal to improve the lot of black men. He joined the stepladder brigade, or the street corner meeting, and in the best traditions of the American town meeting has grappled with the questions facing the race. The development of left wing organizations among Negroes is largely attributed to him, to the extent that the typical Negro Radical was described as "an overeducated West Indian without a job." (1943:47)

For their part, West Indians appear to have been less than enamored of African Americans. Many seem to have resisted incorporation into black America, maintaining and perhaps exaggerating their separateness. McKay, for example, chastises his countrymen for being "incredibly addicted to the waving of the Union Jack in the face of their American cousins" (1940:135). This sentimental attachment to things British helped Caribbean blacks maintain the "sojourner" role and perhaps provided a psychological defense against the indignities of American racism. West Indians emphasized this British connection by holding coronation balls and church services on the king's birthday and, of course, playing cricket—a game they would make very much their own. All of this was a source of great amusement for *The New Yorker* magazine, which ran several articles on the doings of uptown's black Britons.[4]

This attachment to the colonial power may seem surprising in light of subsequent events. Such sentiments were certainly not shared by all, but for many West Indians, faith in Britain and British fair play remained strong. Thus, while the founding of the Jamaica Progressive League (JPL) in September of 1936 mobilized much of the intellectual leadership of New York's West Indian Community around the issue of independence, the League's early meetings drew only a few hundred supporters,[5] whereas a ball in Harlem celebrating the coronation of George VI in May of 1937 drew more than 5,000.[6] Pro-British attitudes would diminish after the labor riots of 1937 and 1938 and be further eroded during the independence struggles of the 1940s and 1950s, but widespread and profound disillusionment with Britain would set in only after migration to the "home country" gave a large number of West Indians firsthand experience with racism in England.

The British connection may have had practical benefits as well. Most sources on West Indian life in prewar New York note the supposedly common cry of the West Indian confronted by racial discrimination: "I am a British subject, I will report this to my consulate!" While there is no real evidence that the consular authorities were much concerned with the difficulties faced by their black subjects in New York, the threat may have had its own value, as did the confidence that it reflects.

Whether for practical or psychological reasons, the first cohort of West Indian immigrants were hesitant to lose the British connection and were slower than European immigrants to become naturalized U.S. citizens. This was itself a cause of resentment among African Americans as it reduced the numbers of potential black voters. Yet in

4. "Coronation Ball," *The New Yorker*, 27 May 1937; "Houdini's Picnic," *The New Yorker*, 6 May 1939; "Well Caught Mr. Holder," *The New Yorker*, 25 Sept. 1954. For other descriptions of these events see Reid 1939:124–29).

5. "Jamaica: Twenty-first Anniversary of Independence Celebration, Souvenir Journal," 1983, The Jamaica Progressive League, Inc.; Secretary's Report of the Jamaica Progressive League, 26 May 1939 (handwritten, JPL archives).

6. *New York Amsterdam News*, 22 May 1937.

light of American racism this reluctance is understandable. As Reid observed:

> For the Negro immigrant from the French or British West Indies, particularly, the label of democracy is found to be fictional. Accustomed to class lines that he has learned to respect even though he may hate them, he can find little solace in a system that brands him as inferior before he is even known. Acceptance of inferior status that is urged upon him abruptly is not easily done even if the economic conditions are materially improved. (1939:163)

In many spheres of life, the first cohort of West Indian immigrants in New York retained a strong sense of identity. They founded mutual assistance organizations that kept alive the connection to the territories of origin and thus generally excluded African Americans. West Indians often differed from African Americans in religion as well, the former being largely Anglicans, Episcopalians, and Roman Catholics while the latter were mostly Baptists, Methodists, and members of various evangelical and pentecostal sects. The churches tended to perpetuate ethnic differences and traditional practices among the immigrants (Dunbar 1935), and religious differences may have also helped perpetuate class differences between the two groups, as the churches that West Indians and African Americans did share were those associated with elite status in the American South (Spurling 1962).

Migrants of this period often sought out each other's company socially, even with countrymen of different classes whom they would not have met socially at home. Marriage to African-Americans was uncommon, particularly among the well-educated (Johnson 1938), although rates of intermarriage appear to have increased with time. As the first cohort of West Indian immigrants were predominantly male, intermarriage tended to be between West Indian men and African-American women (Reid 1939).

For all their separation and occasional rivalry, West Indians and African Americans shared geographic communities and therefore common interests at the local political level. A study of the middle-class black community of St. Albans, Queens, conducted during the late 1950s, notes that although "West Indian families, by and large, tend to form a separate community in St. Albans . . . this does not mean a separate community in the physical sense—that is within one part of the neighborhood. American Negroes and West Indians are living next door to each other in many instances" (Spurling 1962:49).

Faced with this physical proximity, the impossibility of remaining sojourners indefinitely and, increasingly, a second generation who were at least partially assimilated into their African-American surroundings, the first cohort of West Indian migrants eventually joined the mainstream of New York's black community. For much of the intellectual leadership this was always a desirable goal, consistent with Garveyite philosophy. For others it was a practical response to the fact that race, not national origin, was the factor that most directly shaped their lives. As early as 1926, Wilfredo Domingo could write: "By virtue of the presence of thousands of West Indians in the United States, a bond is being forged between them and American Negroes. Gradually they are realizing that their problems are in the main similar and that their ultimate successful solution will depend on the intelligent cooperation of the two branches of Anglo-Saxonized Negroes" (1926:342).

William Bridges, a West Indian-born radical of the 1920s, made this point in even more impassioned terms: "There is no West Indian slave, no American slave; you are all slaves, base, ignoble slaves. . . . West Indian Negroes are oppressed. American Negroes are equally oppressed. West Indians, you are black, Americans, you are equally black. It is on your color upon which white men pass judgement, not your merits, nor the geographical line between you" (quoted in Reid 1939:123).

Thus a feeling of commonality, based partially on an awareness of a common history and heritage, but also on an awareness of common problems faced in racist America, helped forge a shared black identity. Osofsky may have put it too strongly when he wrote in 1962 that "Young Harlemites today, even third-generation descendants of Negro immigrants, are often unaware of these old divisions. The unique type of intra-racial hostility so prominent in the twenties has never reappeared" (1962:135). He is correct, however, in asserting that the issue of ethnic division subsided in New York's black communities with the Depression. Even as economic competition was bringing nativist feelings to a head, the decline in immigration was lessening these tensions, and the realization that race was the central problem created an awareness of common goals and common enemies for both groups.

While West Indians maintained many of their own social networks and organizations, they also became part of the broader black community, not only as members but often as political and economic leaders. This dual sense of identity marks the first cohort of West Indian migrants, who saw no contradiction between being the businessmen, spokesmen, and political leaders of black New York and simultaneously maintaining an ethnic identity that made them distinct if not separate from their African-American neighbors.

West Indians in the United States continued to be concerned with the affairs of the islands, but they were perhaps the largest immigrant group in New York that, prior to the 1970s, did not have some form of community press. This was hardly due to a lack of financial resources, for West Indians owned several of the leading newspapers serving the black American community. Rather it was a result of their unwillingness to employ ethnic modes of self-identification in that particular sphere. As Edwin Lewinson notes: "Most West Indians, despite the antagonism of portions of the black community, quickly perceived themselves as part of that community rather than as a separate entity. . . . The West Indians never had a newspaper of their own. Although the *Amsterdam News*, the leading black weekly in New York, and the *Boston Chronicle* are owned by West Indians, this fact could not be discovered by reading them" (1974:170).

It is often pointed out that West Indians and their descendants have been disproportionately overrepresented in the political and economic leadership of New York's black community. Some, notably Thomas Sowell, have used these observations as part of an argument against the centrality of racial prejudice in explaining the continued disadvantaged status of American blacks.[7] Yet if West Indians have often been among the leaders of the black community it is only because they are regarded as—and have generally regarded themselves as—part of that community. However successful a few members of the first cohort may have been, their success was sharply constricted

---

7. Sowell argues in effect that if West Indians, being black and theoretically equally subject to discrimination as American blacks, can be "so successful," then racism alone cannot provide an explanation of the relative failure of the latter.

by racial boundaries in an example of what Norbert Wiley (1967) has called the "ethnic mobility trap." As Lewinson writes:

> In New York West Indians not only formed a percentage of the black professionals far out of proportion to their numbers, but also became labor leaders and businessmen. Yet the role of the West Indians has largely been limited to that of leadership within the black caste. They have become doctors, lawyers, labor leaders, politicians and business- men within the black ghetto. . . . They have played leadership roles within the black community, but in general have not held jobs which have not also been held by native born members of the race. (1974:171)

Sowell, by contrast, imputes West Indian political success to suc- cessful manipulation of ethnicity:

> Paradoxically the very success and prominence of West Indian individ- uals has contributed to their invisibility as a group. West Indians, as such, are too small a group to have any political power, so West Indian individuals in public office hold their positions as "representatives" of the black population as a whole. To stress their specifically West In- dian background would undermine their positions. . . . Moreover, the many West Indians in the civil rights movement must attribute black poverty and unemployment almost solely to white racism, although the West Indian experience itself seriously undermines the proposi- tion that color is a fatal handicap in the American economy. (1981:220)

Yet it was color that confined West Indians to positions within the black community in the first place. Given the racial divisions of the society in which they found themselves, was any other strategy possi- ble? The first cohort of West Indian immigrants lived in black com- munities. Race limited their economic opportunities and structured most of their dealings with whites. Leadership roles within the black communities were the only ones available to them. They shared the black communities' interests because they were, whether they liked it or not, members of it. In many aspects of their private lives the first cohort of West Indian migrants retained a strong sense of ethnic pride, which was often passed on to their children. But for a very long time ethnic distinctions were feared as a threat to black unity. Thus they were considered inappropriate for the public spheres of journalism or politics.

If the question of multiple social identities was complicated for the first cohort of West Indian migrants, it was far more so for their American-born children. Like other second-generation immigrants they were faced with conflicts between the urge to assimilate and feelings of loss. Furthermore, "assimilating" meant assimilating into *black* America, which, for many, created a dual sense of identity. One informant, a political activist today, notes: "It was different when I was a kid (in the late 1950s). We got the total Caribbean thing at home, you know, the music, the food, the talk, what have you. But out on the street we got black American music, food, slang. We wanted to fit into that. But my kid, now, he gets the Caribbean at home, and out in the street too. The record store, what you hear on the street: all Caribbean."

For others, the two identities eventually merged. Paule Marshall makes this point in an essay describing a trip to the Apollo Theater that an African-American neighbor, "Miss Jackson," took her on when Marshall was not yet a teenager:

> She had taken it upon herself to put me in closer touch with the Afro-American culture that was also my birthright. She was as much a teacher as my mother, the Bajan "mout'-king" and kitchen poet, who flooded my childhood with the customs and rites and brilliant dialect of her native Barbados. My mother claimed me in the name of Afro-West Indian culture, Miss Jackson in the name of the Apollo and all it represented. . . . [I]n fact the two strands, the two cultures had merged to become one in me. (1985b:60)

The commitment of the second generation to unity with the broader black community can be seen in terms of race, especially the role of race as the central determinant of their life chances. When this group faced discrimination, exclusion, and prejudice it was due to race, ethnic origin notwithstanding. When they were successful it was almost always as professionals and tradesmen serving the black community. Those who would go furthest would do so as the leaders of that community. Their primary interests were in pushing back the limits on opportunities imposed on the entire black community, limits that chafed them more than their parents, for they had no Caribbean to return to, no dubious British connection to take some measure of comfort in. Endowed with much of their parents' striving confidence, but with a native's sense of entitlement, second- and third-generation West Indian Americans led many of the early fights for black political representation in New York.

Speaking to the members of this generation today, one is struck by how at ease they seem with the sense of dual identity. Many take a fierce pride in their Caribbean backgrounds, yet they have muted their assertions of ethnic difference to serve as power brokers for their largely African-American constituencies.

Ethnic Geography, 1965–1989

For the post-1965 immigrants the geography of ethnicity has changed dramatically. By the 1980s New York had distinctly West Indian neighborhoods, neighborhoods that supported a lively self-proclaimed West Indian press, that gave a Caribbean flavor to their educational, social, and religious institutions, and that could potentially provide the power bases for a more ethnic politics.

The 1980 U.S. census reported 300,000 New Yorkers born in the non-Hispanic Caribbean, 80 percent of whom had arrived since the reforms of 1965 (see Table 7). Using the somewhat higher figures for "foreign-born blacks," Table 8 confirms the recent growth of the community.

Table 7. Non-Hispanic Caribbeans in New York City by period of immigration

		Period of immigration to the United States		
Birthplace	Total	Pre-1965	1965–1974	1975–1980
Jamaica	93,100	16,820	52,620	23,660
Haiti	50,160	6,380	29,940	13,840
Trinidad-Tobago	39,160	4,860	23,660	10,640
Guyana	31,960	2,540	13,700	15,720
Panama[a]	20,840	8,720	7,580	4,540
Barbados	19,680	5,160	9,040	5,480
Grenada	5,660	720	2,960	1,980
St. Vincent	2,700	480	1,340	880
Antigua-Barbuda	2,380	560	1,220	600
Dominica	1,660	460	660	540
Bahamas	1,540	780	340	420
Aruba	1,140	480	500	160
St. Kitts-Nevis	1,000	520	380	100
St. Lucia	960	300	520	140
Curacao	500	120	300	80
All others	27,160	9,680	12,160	5,320
Total	299,600	56,580	156,920	84,100

Source: 1980 U.S. Census Microdata Sample, prepared by NYC Department of City Planning.
[a]Panamanians in New York tend to be of British West Indian, not Hispanic, ancestry.

Table 8. Foreign-born blacks in the United States and New York City, 1970–1980

Year	U.S.	% U.S. black pop.	NYC	% NYC black pop.
1970	253,458	1.1	NA	NA
1980	815,720	3.1	345,360	19.3

Source: U.S. Census.

As Table 9 shows, the number of legal immigrants from the non-Hispanic Caribbean (four fifths of them from the Anglophone Caribbean) remained steady at slightly over 25,000 per year until at least 1986. Thus it can be conservatively estimated that the number of legal non-Hispanic Caribbean immigrants in New York was close to half a million by the late 1980s.

These figures tell only part of the story. In addition to the substantial undocumented population, the census statistics do not include the U.S.-born children of Caribbean immigrants. While it might be argued that the adult children of earlier immigrant cohorts do not really form part of the Caribbean community today, the minor children of recent immigrants certainly do. Since the new immigrants tend to be young adults, the number of such children is probably considerable. (In the part of central Brooklyn where the West Indian concentration is the highest, Community Districts 9 and 17, the 1980 census found the median age to be 28.3 and 27.9 respectively, whereas the median age for the city was 32.7.[8])

Besides outnumbering previous cohorts, the post-1965 immigrants have settled in different areas. The core of the community shifted during the 1970s from Harlem and Bedford-Stuyvesant to the Crown Heights, East Flatbush, and Flatbush sections of central Brooklyn. As Table 10 indicates, in 1980 over half of New York's (and almost one fourth of the nation's) West Indian population lived in Brooklyn. Large West Indian settlements have also grown up in southeastern Queens and the northeast Bronx. Despite the community's long historical ties to Harlem, the 1980 census found less than 8 percent of New York's West Indians living in Manhattan.

It should also be noted that the various English-speaking Caribbean immigrants tend to live together. Where one finds large num-

8. *Community District Statistics*, New York City Department of City Planning, 1984.

Table 9. Caribbean immigrants to New York City, 1982–1986

Birthplace	1982	1983	1984	1985	1986
Anglophone Caribbean					
Anguilla	11	8	8	5	5
Antigua-Barbuda	443	365	337	383	337
Bahamas	80	60	61	73	81
Barbados	1,256	1,021	984	1,033	965
Belize	522	478	498	455	375
Bermuda	29	28	25	21	12
B.W.I.	9	9	6	49	73
Cayman Islands	12	9	5	6	7
Dominica	161	124	131	120	120
Grenada	758	778	739	688	765
Guyana	6,932	5,953	5,913	6,151	7,285
Jamaica	9,117	8,278	8,982	8,507	8,772
Montserrat	42	43	21	27	67
St. Kitts-Nevis	85	106	257	170	119
St. Lucia	169	176	155	182	172
St. Vincent	482	460	503	500	413
Trinidad-Tobago	1,776	1,461	1,455	1,357	1,350
Turks and Caicos	6	2	8	5	5
Total Anglophone Caribbean	21,890	19,359	20,088	18,802	20,923
Other non-Hispanic Caribbean					
French Guinea	1	2	1	0	0
Guadeloupe	11	8	12	9	5
Haiti	4,773	4,126	5,159	6,151	7,385
Martinique	10	5	7	10	8
Netherlands Antilles	86	54	63	32	45
Suriname	27	24	20	28	28
Other	1	3	0	0	0
Total other non-Hispanic Caribbean	4,909	4,222	5,262	6,230	7,471
Total	26,799	23,581	25,350	25,032	28,394

Source: New York City Department of City Planning.

bers of Jamaicans, one also finds Trinidadians, Guyanese, and Barbadians as well as citizens of Haiti and the United Kingdom (almost certainly West Indians holding U.K. passports), but only rarely immigrants from the Hispanic Caribbean. Conway and Bigby, using data from the U.S. Immigration and Naturalization Service, have constructed indexes of residential segregation among recent immigrants which show not only that English-speaking Caribbean immigrants are substantially segregated from Spanish-speaking groups, but also that the nationality groups of English-speaking West Indians are far more integrated internally than the Hispanic groups. Even

Table 10. Persons born in the non-Hispanic Caribbean in New York City and by borough, 1980

NYC	Bronx	Brooklyn	Manhattan	Queens	Staten Island
299,600	45,320	164,300	22,140	66,280	1,560
(100%)	(15.1%)	(54.8%)	(7.4%)	(22.1%)	(.5%)

Source: 1980 U.S. Census, Microdata File.

the two groups that Conway and Bigby found were the least likely to live near each other in New York (Barbadians and Guyanese) displayed a level of segregation from each other that is less than half of that between Cubans and Dominicans, and far less than that between English- and Spanish-speaking Caribbean immigrants in general.[9] Haitians were also far more likely to live near English-speaking West Indians than near Hispanic Caribbean immigrants (Conway and Bigby 1987).

This new spatial organization has occurred for two reasons: the greatly increased immigration of West Indians after 1965 and, during the 1960s and particularly the 1970s, the increased availability of places in the city where it was possible for blacks to live. This is not to say that the city was desegregated; blacks are still excluded from buying or renting throughout much of New York (Tauber 1983; Massey and Denton 1988). But the nonwhite zones of settlement have now grown to the point that many distinct neighborhoods are possible within them.

Branching out from their original enclave in Crown Heights, the new immigrants moved steadily into East Flatbush and Flatbush during the late 1960s and 1970s. At the same time a smaller concentration of West Indians developed in formerly Italian neighborhoods in the northeast Bronx. By the mid-1980s, many of the more prosperous had moved to the Springfield Gardens, Cambria Heights, and Laurelton sections of Queens. Their reasons for avoiding traditionally black areas such as Harlem may have been an aversion to stigmatized ghettos and the declining physical conditions in such areas, but a central reason seems to have been architecture. By the mid-1970s,

9. The moderate segregation of these two groups is probably explained by differences in time of arrival rather than by the existence of separate communities. Barbadians were well represented among the earliest wave of West Indian immigrants, whereas the Guyanese exodus reached its height only recently.

[57]

Central Brooklyn and southeastern Queens offered a large stock of relatively inexpensive small one- and two-family houses to black home buyers.

Located near long-established black enclaves, all these neighborhoods experienced substantial "white flight" during the late 1960s and 1970s as younger whites left for the suburbs and more distant parts of the outer boroughs. Yet, perhaps because of the high rates of owner occupancy, these areas did not suffer the kind of rapid deterioration that followed the white exodus from the South Bronx, Brownsville, and other areas.

West Indians were by no means the only nonwhites to take advantage of this new opportunity, but they were among the leaders. This influx was made possible by shifts in the overall pattern of racial segregation, but it was also greatly facilitated by distinctly Caribbean cultural traditions and familial ties. One Guyanese immigrant whose family owns four houses on the same Flatbush block describes the pattern in this way: "It's like our own little village here. . . . It's an old Caribbean tradition of families living close together. What happens is one person will come here, and with hard work and some help, he'll eventually be able to afford a house. Other members of the family follow and you begin to have something like a neighborhood" (Blauner 1986:72).

If "Caribbean tradition" explains much of the impetus towards home buying, it turned out that this tradition was highly functional in the U.S. context. For lower- and middle-income people in the United States, housing is generally by far the largest single expenditure, and home ownership the major form of savings as well as the only significant tax break. During periods of high inflation, home owners are particularly at an advantage, since mortgages are paid in ever cheaper dollars while the equity value of the property continues to accrue (Hanretta 1979; Kain and Quigly 1972). Varying rates of home ownership are frequently identified as one reason for the continuing economic disparity between whites and minority groups, even when income levels are similar. Purchase of a home is particularly important across generations, for the equity in a parent's home is often the only source of capital that lower- and middle-income people have to help them become homeowners (Krivo 1986; Parcel 1982). By buying small houses, West Indian homeowners were starting a pattern of capital accumulation for themselves and their children.

[58]

This pattern was facilitated by the establishment of several real estate agencies that dealt with predominantly West Indian clientele and by a "sell-to-your-own-kind" ethos that became effective once there were enough of one's own kind to guarantee home sellers a fair price. Rental apartments are often discovered by word of mouth within the community (simply answering newspaper ads or visiting unknown brokers remains a chancy business for blacks), and this too serves to develop ethnic enclaves. While the vast majority of West Indians continued to live in areas where "you can walk throughout and not see a white face except passing in a car" (Foner 1983:27), their neighbors were increasingly likely not only to be fellow blacks but also fellow West Indians.

The New West Indian Neighborhoods

The desperately ambitious mother figure in Paule Marshall's 1959 novel *Brown Girl, Brownstones* describes the West Indian American dream, circa 1950: to leave crowded Bedford-Stuyvesant for the stately streets of Crown Heights: "Every West Indian out here taking a lesson from the Jew landlord and converting these old houses into rooming houses—making the closet self into rooms some them!—and pulling down plenty-plenty money by the week. And now the place is overrun with roomers the Bajans getting out. Every jackman buying a swell house in ditchy Crown Heights" (312).

New York's oldest and most diverse Caribbean neighborhood, Crown Heights is a wide rectangle of row houses and apartment buildings in the heart of Brooklyn. It extends from Atlantic Avenue on the north to the huge wall of hospitals along Clarkson Avenue on the south, and is bounded by Prospect Park to the west and Brownsville on the east. The area has been home to blacks since the 1830s,[10] but in the early 1950s large numbers of Caribbean and African-American blacks moved into what was then a predominantly Jewish neighborhood.

While both native and immigrant blacks initially lived in the northern part of the area (directly south of Bedford-Stuyvesant), after

10. Weeksville, a settlement of free blacks, was one of several semirural communities that were merged into Crown Heights as the area took its current shape in the 1870s.

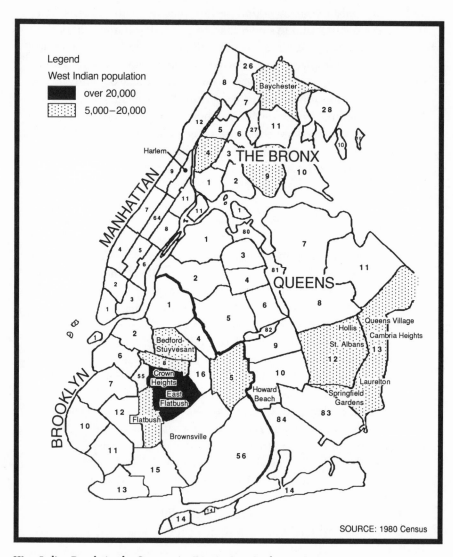

West Indian Population by Community District New York City: 1980

1965 Caribbean blacks became increasingly concentrated south of Eastern Parkway, a six-lane boulevard that serves as a natural boundary. Architecturally this area presents stark contrasts. Along the Parkway and the other main thoroughfares are large, almost palatial apartment buildings, some well-maintained and others in serious disrepair. On the main shopping streets are small buildings with housing above stores. Some of the side streets contain handsome limestone row houses and brownstones, and a few have single-family homes with small yards (14 percent of neighborhood households own their own homes). Others streets, by contrast, feature decrepit tenements and squat four-story brick apartment buildings. At still other points the street grid is broken by multistory housing projects.

This neighborhood, which roughly corresponds to Brooklyn Community District 9, was overwhelmingly black and largely Caribbean by the late 1970s.[11] The 1980 census reports that 81.6 percent of its 97,000 people was black, 9.6 percent Hispanic, and about 9 percent non-Hispanic whites. Since 1980 the white population has been increasing. The Lubavitcher sect of Hasidic Jews has its world headquarters in Crown Heights, and many of its members continued to move into the area after other whites had left. In 1987 *New York Newsday* estimated that about 15,000 Hasidim and 80,000 mostly Caribbean blacks were competing aggressively and sometimes violently for space. "The bottom line is a territorial problem," a Guyanese minister comments. "It's a question of vying for limited turf" (quoted in Bernstein 1987). Both groups are noteworthy for their large families and modest incomes: in 1980 almost a quarter of the area's residents reported incomes below the poverty level.[12] (The black median household income for the area was slightly higher than the white.)

Crown Heights remains the home of many of New York's largest

---

11. The part of what is traditionally considered Crown Heights north of Eastern Parkway is now Community District 8. The division of the area between two community boards in the 1970s reflected the increased division between the Caribbean and Hasidic Jewish area south of the Parkway and the largely African-American community to the north. Unless otherwise noted, all statistics for Crown Heights are from the U.S. Census as reported for Brooklyn Community District 9, compiled by the New York City Department of City Planning.

12. While this is higher than the citywide rate of 20 percent, it is still considerably lower than the 40 percent in nearby Bedford-Stuyvesant or the nearly 45 percent in adjacent Brownsville.

Foreign-Born Blacks Living in Brooklyn

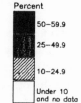

Data by census tract.
Scale: 1 inch=9900 ft.
Source: 1980 Census STF–4

New York Department of City Planning

1970

Percent

50–59.9

25–49.9

10–24.9

Under 10
and no data

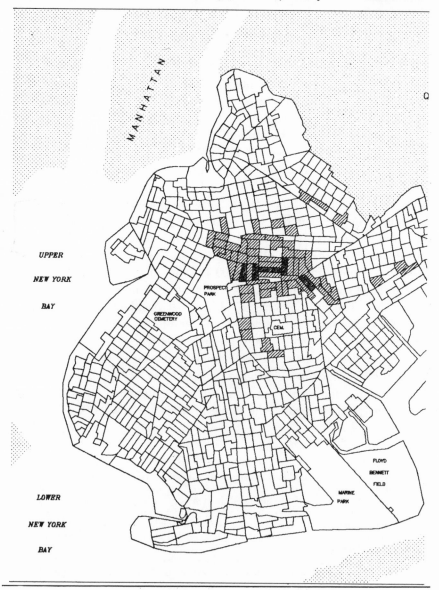

Source: Elizabeth Bogen, *New Immigrants in New York City* (New York: 1987). Reprinted with permission of Praeger Press.

1980

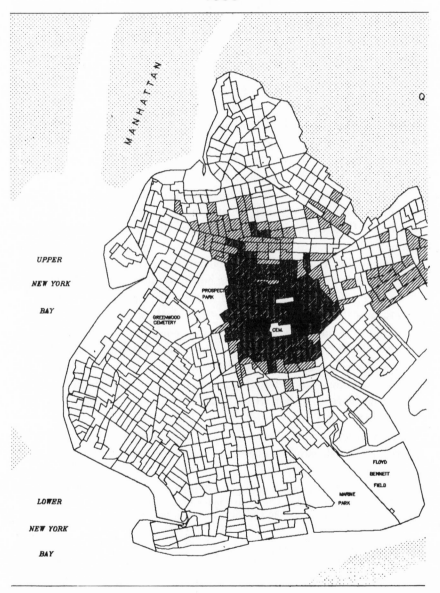

UPPER

NEW YORK

BAY

LOWER

NEW YORK

BAY

Caribbean churches[13] and businesses and many of the West Indian community's most prominent members. It is notably well served by public institutions including the Brooklyn Museum, the Brooklyn Children's Museum, and the Brooklyn Botanical Gardens. Since the 1970s, however, it has also been afflicted by increased crowding and crime. As the community has grown, its more prosperous members have moved south into East Flatbush[14] during the 1960s, Flatbush[15] during the 1970s (see Figure 2), and further south into largely Jewish Midwood and Flatlands as the 1990s approached.

Today East Flatbush is probably New York's most West Indian neighborhood. Home to only a handful of blacks in 1950 (baseball's Jackie Robinson was among the first), by 1980 80.2 percent of its 154,473 residents was black and 46.3 percent was foreign-born. While most of these people were far from wealthy (19.6 percent reported incomes below the poverty level), they were generally somewhat better off than those in Crown Heights: the median household income in the area was only a hair below the city-wide median, and 45 percent higher than that of neighboring Brownsville.[16]

Boasting few of Crown Heights cultural amenities, East Flatbush was shaped by its topography and history. It remained rural into the 1890s, and its flat, open landscape was ideal for the commercial development of relatively low-density lower-middle-class housing. The neighborhood was created in three successive housing booms. In the 1890s, as street car and subway lines connected it to the rest of the city, speculators started to break up its farms into small building plots that were soon dotted with Queen Anne-style cottages. In the late 1930s Fred Trump, the father of Donald, built row after row of attached brick homes. These "Trump bungalows" were quickly sold to young Jewish families eager to escape the tenements of Browns-

13. The location of churches is often an unreliable indicator of a population's residential location. Several of the largest Caribbean congregations have acquired or inherited church buildings in predominantly white Park Slope, an area containing many more grand nineteenth-century churches than its current secular population requires.

14. Unless otherwise noted, statistics for East Flatbush are those derived from the 1980 U.S. Census for Community Planning District 17.

15. Unless otherwise noted, statistics for Flatbush are those derived from the 1980 U.S. Census for Community Planning District 14.

16. The median household income in New York City in 1980 was $13,854. The median for southern Crown Heights was $11,702, for East Flatbush $13,552, and for Brownsville $7,530.

ville and the Lower East Side. Thirty years later, many of these would pass on to West Indian families for not dissimilar reasons. Finally, around 1950, the area's remaining open land was taken up by high-rise developments. The result was an area of little architectural distinction but nonetheless ideal for the growing Caribbean community.

Today about one third of East Flatbush's 53,628 housing units are small one- and two-family homes, and 27.6 percent is owner-occupied (compared with 23.4 percent citywide). Although the local real estate market slumped after the initial black influx, it recovered in the 1980s as Caribbean immigration swelled the demand for housing. Despite rising crime and drug-related violence, in 1988 one developer built seventy-two condominium units in East Flatbush, the first substantial new construction in the area in three decades. The units were specifically marketed toward Caribbean households with incomes in the $35,000 to $45,000 range. Hailing the development, *The New York Times* noted how "both rental and for-sale housing have made a comeback" in East Flatbush, "aided by a growing demand from an industrious West Indian immigrant population" (Oser 1988).

In the 1970s this demand spread across Bedford Avenue into Flatbush proper. Perhaps the most quintessentially "Brooklyn" of Brooklyn neighborhoods, Flatbush was 32 percent black in 1980, and the black population has steadily increased since. Since the late 1960s the eastern portion of the neighborhood, which includes central Brooklyn's main shopping area along Flatbush Avenue as well as the historic center of the old village of Flatbush, has been largely black, and since the mid 1970s largely Caribbean. Much of the southern and western part of the neighborhood resisted black immigration until the mid-1980s, when the area saw an influx of Asians and young white professionals as well.

Despite this diversity, increased Caribbean migration and the Caribbean domination of the commercial strip have signaled to many that Flatbush has become a Caribbean neighborhood. This identification was reinforced in 1990 when a weekly radio drama entitled "Flatbush USA" went on the air over WRTN-FM. Directed at a Caribbean audience and sponsored by a Caribbean food company, "Flatbush USA" is both highly contemporary and a throwback to another era. Set in a Flatbush apartment building populated by immigrants from throughout the Caribbean, the show explores the drama, humor, and pathos in the immigrant experience.

Taken together, southern Crown Heights, East Flatbush, and the eastern part of Flatbush proper now make up a contiguous Caribbean core neighborhood that runs across three community districts and is home to over 300,000 people. A smaller neighborhood evolved about the same time in the Baychester section of the northeast Bronx. As Figure 1 shows, many West Indians also continued to live in predominantly African-American Bedford-Stuyvesant, and in smaller Caribbean enclaves that sprang up in black and Hispanic East New York and parts of the Bronx during the 1970s.

The rising crime rates in these areas during the late 1980s makes them hard to catergorize. Is the Crown Heights-East Flatbush-Flatbush area a lively working-class enclave of striving "industrious" immigrants, as the *Times* real-estate section reassures potential investors (Oser 1988), or is it one of the city's worst centers of the crack business and of deadly competitive retailing practices, as that paper's crime reporters would have us believe? In fact it is both. In Caribbean neighborhoods the drug trade has not been relegated to out-of-the-way corners and alleys. It often takes place alongside thriving vegetable stores and restaurants, and in discos and social clubs, most of whose patrons are simply working people having a good time. This openness probably accounts for the large number of innocent bystanders who fell victim to violence in this area during the late 1980s.

During the late 1970s the ecology of West Indian ethnicity in New York entered a new phase. Once again relatively prosperous members of the community led the search for greener pastures. Some moved, block by block, into predominantly white middle-class areas on the fringes of the West Indian neighborhoods. A few brave souls bought homes in the epicenter of Brooklyn's racial backlash, Canarsie, in some cases only to see their property torched before they could move in (Roberts 1990). For the most part, however, middle-class Caribbean home buyers moved into the semisuburban communities of southeastern Queens.

The St. Albans neighborhood in southern Queens was one of New York's first middle-class black enclaves. From the 1950s it was home to a mixture of African-American and Caribbean blacks. At the same time a poorer African-American neighborhood grew up to the west in

South Jamaica. Then in the late 1970s and throughout the 1980s a growing number of West Indians moved into the sprawling neighborhoods of Community District 13, notably Queens Village, Laurelton, and Cambria Heights.

Although there are pockets of poverty in these areas, for the most part they are thoroughly middle-class. The average price paid for a home in Laurelton in 1989 was $160,000 (Bohlen 1989).[17] What is truly striking about southeastern Queens, however, is the overwhelming predominance of modern single-family homes along its tree-lined streets. In 1980 the owner-occupancy rate of District 13 was 69.8 percent, the highest in the city outside of Staten Island.

It thus came as a shock in 1987 when southeastern Queens found itself in the midst of a drug war involving both Caribbean and African-American gangs. While the level of violence never approached that of East New York or the South Bronx, the number of murders in the area jumped from fifteen to thirty-six in one year. A series of gangland-style slayings were used to intimidate those who might testify against the dealers, and in one case a policeman was gunned down while guarding the home of a Guyanese Indian witness. This provoked a crackdown, and by the end of the decade crime appeared to be on the decline. The strife was sufficient, however, to make many who had sacrificed to achieve the dream of home ownership wonder if it had all been worthwhile.

At first glance southeastern Queens appears less obviously an "ethnic" neighborhood than does central Brooklyn. It is home to fewer recent immigrants and the lines between African-American and Caribbean enclaves are less firmly drawn. Drug dealing aside, most of its commercial strips show less of the pulsating verve that characterizes East Flatbush. Yet just as ethnicity continued to play a role in the housing choices of white ethnics long after they left urban "ethnic villages" for suburbs further out on Long Island, we cannot assume that ethnicity is becoming less important in southeastern Queens simply because it is becoming less obvious. Whether race or ethnicity will be the central factor shaping the development of these communities—that is whether they will come to be "Caribbean" or "black middle-class" neighborhoods—remains to be seen.

17. The 1980 median income for Queens Community District 12, which includes Jamaica, was $14,912. In Community District 13, then 41 percent black, it was $22,022.

Local Merchants: New Flavors on the Street

Housing alone does not a neighborhood make, and the new Caribbean presence in New York is more than simply a matter of location. In recent years central Brooklyn, the symbolic as well as demographic heart of the community, has seen the growth of businesses, churches, private schools, and health care institutions with a decidedly Caribbean flavor. This is a striking contrast to earlier periods. These areas are not only more Caribbean than the black ghettos of earlier periods, they are more publicly so. Though geographical concentration was mainly the result of common housing preferences and familial and social ties, it had cultural results. As Claude Fischer (1976) notes, the critical mass of people in a given place sharing certain characteristics will promote awareness and perhaps even an exaggeration of those characteristics.

One of the most distinctive features of urban neighborhoods (particularly in contrast to "suburbia") is the various use of space. Neighborhoods such as those most West Indians occupy in central Brooklyn and the northern Bronx (and southeastern Queens also, although to a lesser extent) comprise a mixture of residential housing and small commercial strips, often with lower-cost housing above ground-floor commercial enterprises. Even on purely residential streets one is seldom farther than "up the block and around the corner" from a commercial area of some kind. The commercial enterprises—"mom and pop" stores, local services, and particularly restaurants and bars—are meeting grounds that are public without being anonymous. They help to create a sense of public life largely missing in the more "single minded" spaces of the suburbs (Walzer 1986).

These commercial enterprises have a great deal to do with the vitality of a neighborhood in the mind of the residents, and the proprietors of such establishments are very important in setting the terms by which a neighborhood is defined. The types of stores in an area, the goods and services being sold, the signs and symbols that the owners use to proclaim their identity on a public street, all help to shape the collective definition of an area for residents and outsiders alike. Urbanites become adept at "reading" the commercial street for indicators of ethnic, class, cultural, and occupational identity.

[68]

Today on long stretches of Brooklyn's Utica, Nostrand, and Church Avenues many businesses display some Caribbean referent: a flag, a country's name, a few words in dialect, or perhaps just a painted palm tree. This is true even of merchants who are not themselves West Indians. Korean-owned vegetable stands often display signs proclaiming that they specialize in West Indian products (though complaints about Korean businesses have been a source of bitter contention in the community and led to a controversial boycott on Church Avenue in 1990). In 1986 *The New York Times* reported with some amusement that the Jewish owner of a chain of ornate carwashes celebrated the grand opening of a branch in Crown Heights decorated in an island motif ("Carib Clean") with a steel drum band.

Regardless of who the owners actually are, the concentration of businesses that appeal to an ethnic group helps to connect that group with that particular location. Such a concentration of businesses will help define a given area as a core neighborhood even when the group is fairly widely dispersed. During the mid-1980s, when many West Indians were moving to Queens, the Bronx, and even Westchester and Nassau counties, many commercial strips in central Brooklyn took on an increasingly Caribbean atmosphere.

Some businesses are "ethnic" by nature. Record stores, restaurants, and bakeries all draw their customers by virtue of the "authentic" ethnic product they sell. If an area is strongly identified with such businesses, it may retain its ethnic connections even long after its residential demographics have changed.[18] Other businesses are concentrated in ethnic neighborhoods for more mundane reasons: shipping businesses and travel agencies that operate between the Caribbean and the United States, for example, are concentrated in central Brooklyn because that is where the customers are. Yet they too serve to make the area a distinctly West Indian center of commerce, albeit inadvertently.

In businesses where there is nothing particularly ethnic about the

18. In a few cases, for example Mulberry Street in New York's "Little Italy" or Hanover Street in Boston's "North End," the commercial strip may become more ethnic as the population becomes less so. Here the sale of a reified version of the ethnic experience, primarily to tourists and second- and third-generation ethnics, has become the primary industry of the area. While this is certainly not yet true of Brooklyn's West Indian areas, many Brooklyn restaurants and bakeries already rely on customers from outlying areas for a large portion of their business.

enterprise, the visible ethnic connection is made either as an expression of the owner's pride or as an attempt to attract customers. In some cases, such as real estate agencies, an island-oriented name or a palm tree on a sign may serve as an assurance that one's business is welcome. In the case of personal services the symbol may assure the customers that their accent will not be ridiculed, and that they will deal with people they feel at home with. In other cases such a symbol may simply be a way of attracting the customers' attention, as in the case of the steel drum band at the car wash. Also certain commercial enterprises may take on secondary social functions; bakeries and small groceries are often places to hang out, meet friends, and exchange gossip, as well as to buy goods.

All of these businesses, by becoming centers of ethnic activity, help to associate the locality with the ethnic group. Proclaiming the connection publicly in signs and symbols, they make the connection plain for all to see. The fact that West Indian identity is so displayed speaks not only of pride, but also of a security not characteristic of earlier migrants. A bank manager originally from Trinidad notes that in East Flatbush "I feel like I'm home. I won't move from Brooklyn because I am home. You get the music, you get the food. You get everything" (*New York Times* 1987). This security in ethnic expression contributes to the creation of geographic neighborhoods that are not only demographic concentrations but actual Caribbean communities.

Community Press

The creation of neighborhoods also facilitates the creation of a community press, which in turn may become a major factor in creating consensus on neighborhood identity and boundaries (see Janowitz 1952). Historically, ethnic newspapers in the United States have tended to go through two distinct phases. They start out with a cosmopolitan orientation, but as more of the immigrant population learns English and starts to utilize the better-financed English language media, the ethnic press, if it is to survive, becomes more specialized, taking on a specific political, regional, or neighborhood orientation. Often it becomes less a source of information than of points of view.

For West Indian New Yorkers the cosmopolitan phase was made unnecessary by the English-speaking immigrants' ability to use both the mainstream and African-American media.[19] Thus the creation of a viable ethnic press during the 1970s probably bespeaks less a need to communicate than a desire to express ethnic identity. Also the growing numbers in the community promised opportunities for would-be publishers. As a result, several publishing ventures were initiated in recent years, at least two of which have been fairly successful.

Everybody's magazine, a glossy monthly founded by a young Grenadian immigrant named Herman Hall, has been published continuously since 1977. Its circulation of 75,000, though spread throughout the United States and the Caribbean, is concentrated in New York, with most of its subscribers in central Brooklyn. In addition to mail subscriptions the magazine is sold in neighborhood newsstands, bakeries, and pattie shops.

According to its editors, the readership of *Everybody's* reflects the demographics of the American West Indian community, Jamaicans being the largest subgroup, Trinidadians and Guyanese being the next largest, and a small percentage belonging to each of the small islands. "We always get somebody asking why we don't cover more news from Anguilla," Hall reports. "It's hard to get news about Anguilla." While much coverage is given to music, entertainment, and social events, the magazine attempts to balance this with political coverage of the Caribbean and New York, social criticism, essays, and occasionally short fiction. While originally focused on "news from home," in recent years it has become more concerned with coverage of the West Indian community in the United States. In 1985, for example, it published a long interview with New York's Mayor Koch, with his picture on the cover.

While *Everybody's* strives to the more than a neighborhood publication, it nevertheless provides coverage of neighborhood activities, and neighborhood businesses are prominent among its advertisers. In turn the geographical concentration of West Indians makes it pos-

---

19. For earlier immigrants the availability of at least one Caribbean paper, the *Jamaica Weekly Gleaner* (which has long published a North American edition), probably satisfied the need for news from home. But this had changed by the mid-1970s. For one thing, the independence of a growing number of Caribbean nations had increased the immigrants' appetites for wider Caribbean news, thus making the increasingly parochial *Gleaner* inadequate.

sible to market the relatively expensive publication to its select audience. Thus *Everybody's* has developed a local focus, and the presence of the publication itself helps to generate local news, since political actors can utilize it as a forum for reaching a West Indian constituency.

This is even truer of the *New York Carib News*, a weekly tabloid with a circulation of 64,000. Founded in 1981 by Karl Rodney, a former president of the Jamaica Progressive League, the paper had covering the Caribbean as its original purpose, and much of its space is still devoted to that. The paper's coverage of Caribbean affairs was largely responsible for its initial success, and during the 1983 Grenada invasion its sales more than doubled. Once established, the *Carib News* became the logical focus for discussion of West Indian participation in New York politics as well. It provides coverage for various political groups and its lively editorial pages have given community activists a forum in which to debate ideology and strategy. Editorially the paper has tended to endorse most, but not all, West Indian candidates for public office (in 1986 it endorsed the African-American incumbent congressman Major Owens over Virgin Island-born Roy Innis), and it has supported increased West Indian political participation.

These publications, along with about half a dozen less successful efforts, help to shape the terms in which people think about the community. They allow politicians and city officials to address a specifically Caribbean audience, and allow commercial enterprises to advertise to a selected Caribbean clientele. Their "Help Wanted" sections give employers access to a selected pool of West Indian workers and their editorial pages allow a West Indian point of view to solidify. Finally, the fact that these media define themselves as "Caribbean" rather than either "black" or specifically national helps to frame the New York West Indian identity.

Le Critique, an English language magazine founded in 1986, tried to push these processes even further. *Le Critique* was published by Haitian immigrant Joe Florestan and edited by Raymond Joseph, the publisher of New York's leading Haitian newspaper, *Le Haiti Observateur* (and later chargé d'affaires of Haiti's embassy to the United States). It was aimed at both Anglophone West Indians and assimilated, English-speaking Haitians. Several prominent English-speaking West Indians served on its editorial board, and the magazine's premier issue included articles on West Indians in business, a discussion of West Indians in New York politics, a story on a Virgin Island-born musician, and local restaurant reviews, as well as accounts of recent events in Haiti. Though *Le Critique* failed within a year, Florestan and Joseph went on to establish a glossy bilingual monthly, *Haiti Observateur Magazine*, affiliated with the French-language weekly.

This magazine represents a major shift in emphasis for the Haitian intelligentsia. Until recently the Haitian community has been primarily concerned with events in Haiti, and its two New York newspapers, with a combined circulation of 105,000, have tended to see themselves more as an opposition press in exile rather than an ethnic press in the United States. Indeed, during the Duvalier years papers published in New York and Montreal (and often smuggled into Haiti) were an important voice of opposition to the regime. Furthermore, Haitian intellectuals have been embroiled in a long and complex debate over the propriety of writing in French versus Haitian Creole (the *Observateur*, published in French, includes a few pages in Creole in each issue), and few had previously given much consideration to writing in English.

That Haitians have undertaken these ventures reflects the growth of pan-Caribbean sentiment, extending to English- and French-speaking but not necessarily to Spanish-speaking Caribbean immigrants. In Brooklyn and Queens, Haitians and English-speaking West Indians are discovering their commonalities and sharing institutions. That they share geographic neighborhoods means that they come to share a certain measure of social life as well, despite the language barrier.

Educational Institutions

The concentration of West Indians in certain neighborhoods has also facilitated the founding of private educational institutions as well as the gradual "Caribbeanization" of previously existing private and public schools. This is an important development as such institutions are vital in transferring a sense of ethnic identity to American-born children.

In the United States in general and New York in particular, it is commonly thought that public schools are the first step towards assimilation into the dominant culture; immigrant families keep ethnic traditions alive at home, but their children will learn American ways in school. At the present time, however, many immigrants have lost faith in the public schools. Among West Indians the belief is widespread that New York's public schools are inferior to those of their homelands. Thus many have abandoned the public schools for private institutions built along models derived from their nations of origin. Whether the motive is the wish for better educational quality or for stronger ethnic identity, the result is that school becomes an institution in which the ethnic culture is maintained rather than a vehicle for assimilation.

The tie between ethnicity and educational institutions starts early. In Brooklyn today several preschools and day care centers serve almost exclusively Caribbean populations. These schools advertise firm discipline and traditional values and portray themselves in sharp contrast to the more liberal public institutions. The advertisements of one of the largest of the nursery schools makes the connection between discipline and ethnicity explicit. "Children are trained just like at home in the West Indies," it reads, and the staff is "strictly West Indian."

This quest for a "back-home" style education may be seen in the many private and religious academies that have either been founded by West Indians or have become predominantly West Indian as neighborhood demographics have changed. Nowhere has this quest been better realized than in St. Mark's Academy, located in the heart of Crown Heights. Founded in 1977 with forty students, this primary school (kindergarten through eighth grade) had served over eight hundred youngsters by 1985. Almost all its students are of West Indian background and all its staff were trained in the Caribbean. The school features an "ethnic awareness" program, and its headmaster, a self-described Garveyite, emphasizes that black pride is an important part of the curriculum. Yet the colonial influence is also not hard to spot at St. Mark's, from the British-style school uniforms to the strict sense of discipline.

St. Mark's was founded by a prominent Guyanese minister who was disillusioned by his own experiences with the public schools, particularly his perception that integrated schools had lower expectations of black children. He recalls:

The need came from the parents. Also from what I saw happen to my own children in the public schools. They had an accent and the other children laughed at them for that. They couldn't find their place. Second of all, I recall I once came to a parent-teacher conference and the teacher said to this white parent ahead of me, "Johnny got a 90 in math and he must do better if he is going to get in to thus and so high school." Then it was my turn, and I knew my son had gotten a 70, and she said, "Your son is doing extremely well. Tell him to keep up the good work." Well, from that moment my mind was made up.

Wanting to raise children in a black environment that would place high educational demands on them, the founders of St. Mark's did not, however, make common cause with black Americans, and although nothing prohibits African-American students from attending St. Mark's, few do. Yet the demand for schools like St. Mark's did not arise solely from cultural norms about what constitutes a "good" education. It also reflects the desires of parents to shield their children from racism. Perceiving that integrated schools, private and public, could be racist and hostile, but that the predominantly black neighborhood public schools were inferior, parents preferred St. Mark's. Thus the school quickly became the first choice of many of the community's elite; its parents include doctors, college professors, and at least one political activist—who has run for the community's public school board but kept his children in the private institution.

This distrust of public education reflects an attitude on that is widespread among West Indian New Yorkers today. Having grown up in societies where blacks constitute the vast majority of the population, many West Indians have avoided feelings of inferiority to whites. They consider this experience a psychological advantage, and hope to pass it on to their children. They often feel that they can best contribute to the broader black community by maintaining their own distinct institutions. A large hand-lettered sign in the St. Mark's assembly hall—"NO ONE CAN MAKE YOU FEEL INFERIOR WITHOUT YOUR CONSENT"—bears witness to this search for equality through autonomy; and it sums up the atmosphere of the place almost as well as the one next to it: "NO TALKING IN ASSEMBLY."

Earlier cohorts of West Indian immigrants, who had neither the numbers nor the geographic concentration necessary to establish their own schools, sometimes sent their children back to the Caribbean for their education. One of these children was Shirley Chis-

[75]

holm, who writes: "Years later I would know what an important gift my parents had given me by seeing to it that I had my early education in the strict, traditional, British-styled schools of Barbados. If I speak and write easily now, that early education is the main reason" (1970:8).[20] This pattern of child circulation continues to this day and helps migrants maintain strong kinship ties with their home communities. Many migrants seem to prefer the primary education facilities of the Caribbean, bringing children to New York afterwards to get an American high school diploma and taking advantage of the greater opportunities for a college education available in the United States. However, as this pattern is becoming less practical for long-term New York residents, the existence of Caribbean schools in New York gives them a West Indian educational alternative that is not only local but also expresses an idealized "West Indianness" that is perhaps closer to the migrants' concept of a "Caribbean education" than what actually occurs at most schools in the West Indies.

The goal of St. Mark's and the other private and religious academies in Caribbean neighborhoods is quite different, then, from the assimilating function typically attributed to the public schools. As the St. Mark's headmaster states: "Our objective is to encourage our students to permeate the society, to appropriate, not to assimilate." Of course, St. Mark's does serve an integrationist function *within* the West Indian community, as students from throughout the English-speaking Caribbean come together here.

Private academies such as St. Mark's may help to link Caribbean ways of doing things with middle-class status: the more prosperous members of the community will send their children to the school that is culturally West Indian and so these children develop Caribbean modes of behavior. Children of less prosperous immigrants who utilize predominantly African-American institutions are less likely to grow up in a West Indian educational environment. Thus, contrary to the usual assumptions made about white immigrant groups, in the West Indian community the more advantaged members are slower to be incorporated into American educational institutions and are more directly involved in the creation of West Indian modes of identity.

20. Other prominent U.S.-born West Indians who were sent to the Caribbean for education include singer-activist Harry Belafonte and New York State assemblyman and 1985 mayoral candidate Herman "Denny" Farrell.

Of course, as the community has grown, many public schools have felt the West Indian ethnic influence. But here the record of the West Indian students is mixed. At least one predominantly Caribbean East Flatbush elementary school is considered among the city's finest and has been widely hailed for its achievements. Test scores indicate, however, that most of the public schools in West Indian neighborhoods are in the lower-middle range of the city system. Parents and teachers point to adjustment problems among students. Many children find themselves suddenly pulled out of extended family networks and living in a new country with relatives and stepparents they barely know. In addition, adjustment to big city life, often in tough neighborhoods, can be difficult (Soto 1987; Reid 1983). The mean streets extend into the high schools: in Brooklyn and southeastern Queens violence between Jamaican and Haitian students as well as between Caribbeans and African-Americans is not uncommon.

Teachers report a variety of experiences placing Caribbean students. Youngsters from rural Haiti or parts of urban Jamaica are often well behind their American peers, whereas those from smaller islands or more middle-class schools in Jamaica or Trinidad are generally well ahead. In Crown Heights' Wingate High, probably the most Caribbean high school in the city, teachers and administrators point to problems unknown in the school's predominantly Jewish past: students with full-time jobs or child-rearing responsibilities, educational careers interrupted by frequent relocation and greater levels of violence.[21] Still, Wingate reports higher attendance rates and lower drop-out rates than schools in adjacent neighborhoods, which is all the more noteworthy in light of the fact that many of the community's best students are "creamed off" into Brooklyn's selective high schools. Though only about half of Wingate students graduate, 90 percent of those who do enter college (Bernstein 1987).

The community has actively addressed its educational problems. During the 1980s an association of Caribbean educators and parents

21. Of course, as the effective memory of these teachers goes back only a few decades, the "Jewish" past they think in terms of is the 1950s and early 1960s, the time when the East Flatbush Jewish community was at its most prosperous. A comparison with the educational problems of first-generation Jewish communities, for example, with the Lower East Side of the 1890s or Brownsville of the 1920s would no doubt reveal some of the same problems faced by Caribbean immigrants today.

created programs to ease the adjustment of immigrant students in the public high schools in Crown Heights and East Flatbush, and political clubs and the *Carib News* have tried to encourage high performance with awards for academic excellence and small scholarships. All of these efforts serve to reinforce the connection between the Caribbean community and the schools.

Other youth activities in Brooklyn and Queens have become "Caribbeanized," and in many cases consular officials and Caribbean leaders have become involved in local activities. In 1985, for example, the graduation keynote speaker at Brooklyn's Winthrop Junior High School, where 70 percent of the student body is estimated to be Caribbean, was Jamaican consul general Lorell Bruce. In 1986 a forum on youth employment in central Brooklyn, cosponsored by the "Summer Jobs '86" program and the Caribbean American Chamber of Commerce, featured not only the borough president and the area's two African-American congressmen, but also Barbados prime minister Bernard St. John.

In recent years West Indian activity at the city's colleges and universities has increased. In 1985 the City University of New York Association of Caribbean Studies (CUNYACS), a group made up of graduate students and faculty members, launched a new quarterly journal of Caribbean and Caribbean-American affairs, *Cimmarron*. That same year Medgar Evers College, a two-year division of City University located in Crown Heights, opened a Caribbean studies institute (after much political wrangling over control of the institute's state-funded budget). In addition to a number of highly reputable social scientists, many of the community's aspiring political leaders were named to the board of directors. Other city campuses have also undertaken Caribbean activities. During the early 1980s conferences on Caribbean affairs took place at Hunter College and Long Island University, bringing together West Indian and non-West Indian academics as well as Caribbean artists, writers, and student groups. Caribbean student associations were founded at New York University and Long Island University, both private institutions, as well as on most of the City University campuses.

This intellectual activity is clearly associated with an increased interest in Caribbean culture. West Indian literature is currently in vogue; the works of C. L. R. James, George Lamming, Earl Lovelace, Rosa Guy, Derek Walcott, Michael Thellwell, and V. S. Naipaul have all attracted much attention. Caribbean dramas found their way onto New York's stages with some frequency during the 1980s, to say nothing of the continuing popularity of Caribbean music.

These educational and cultural activities, while they draw on Caribbean traditions, reflect an emerging ethnic identity that is the result of the critical mass of Caribbean people now coming together under the particular historical circumstances of contemporary New York City.

Caribbean Organized Crime

"Crime," Daniel Bell once observed, is "an American way of life." In New York some members of every major immigrant wave have availed themselves of this "queer ladder of social mobility," and West Indians have been no exception (Bell 1962:127). Until the mid-1980s Caribbean criminal groups tended to operate within their own community, and thus seldom came to the attention of the rest of the city. This changed dramatically around 1985, as the use of crack cocaine surged and predominantly West Indian gangs were among those that moved into this expanding industry. Since that time the "posses," as the gangs are known, have challenged the West Indians, "model minority" image with a combination of entrepreneurial drive, brazenly innovative business strategies, and frightening violence.

The posses have their roots in the slums of Kingston, Jamaica. The word "posse" probably reflects the popularity of American westerns among the "sufferers," as the slum-dwellers are known. In Jamaican popular culture, ghetto desperadoes have sometimes been portrayed as urban Robin Hoods, an image that came into full flower in the 1960s as the exploits of the "Johnny-Too-Bads" were celebrated in local legend and reggae music.[22] By the 1970s, however, it was clear that the Kingston gangs, far from being rebels, had become unacknowledged pillars of the establishment. In the feudal politics of post-independence Jamaica, both major political parties, the Jamaica Labor Party (JLP) and the People's National Party (PNP), used gang enforcers to control slum constituencies. In the words of journalist

---

22. This image was immortalized in Perry Henzell's film "The Harder They Come" and Michael Thellwell's novel of the same name.

Laurie Gunst, they relied "on their gang loyalists to hand pick the tenants for scarce housing, funnel jobs and money to supporters, stuff ballot boxes at election time, and kill sufferers in enemy territory" (1990:90). The gangs also took control of gambling and the ganja trade—the export of marijuana.

By the late 1970s the increased power of the gangs was causing alarm among the Jamaican elite. As drug profits and the accompanying importation of guns soared, many feared that "the tail had begun to wag the dog" (ibid.:91).[23] Gang violence during the 1980 election claimed over eight hundred lives and brought the country to the brink of civil war. Fearful that the politicians might well lose control altogether, the victorious JLP let loose a violent post-election crackdown on many of its own gun-men as well as those of the opposition. Soon, Gunst writes, many "young posse men had got the message. They began to head north" (1989:568).

Posses from Kingston had begun small-scale operations in the West Indian communities of New York and Miami as early as the late 1960s. Initially the groups moved into what they knew: extortion, gambling, and ganja. Many reportedly maintained close ties to their neighborhood bases back home, sending money and guns to Kingston and bringing trusted recruits from their home turf to the United States. Both the size and pace of these operations increased dramatically with the arrival of young gunmen during the early 1980s. While marijuana and eventually cocaine were increasingly the focus of gang activity, old political vendettas were not forgotten. During 1984 and 1985 a series of shootouts between the pro-JLP "Shower posse" and the pro-PNP "Spanglers" culminated in a machine-gun battle at a Jamaican Independence Day picnic in New Jersey which left two dead and dozens, mostly innocent bystanders, injured (*New York Carib News* 1985a). This incident aside, struggles over politics and turf almost always pitted posse members against each other, and as

23. For the elite, perhaps even more dangerous than the gunmen's ferocity in doing the politicians' bidding was their ability to stop doing it. In 1978, gang wars were halted by a short-lived "peace treaty" negotiated by pro-JLP and pro-PNP gang leaders without the politicians' approval. The truce was celebrated at a reggae concert at which Bob Marley coaxed PNP prime minister Michael Manley and opposition leader Edward Seaga into an uncomfortable onstage handshake as the gunmen looked on. But it quickly broke down, and the principal gunmen who negotiated it soon met violent ends: one was shot to death nine months later by Jamaican police, and the other assassinated in Brooklyn in 1980 (see White, 1983:299–302; Waters 1985:231–35).

their other criminal activities were largely restricted to the West Indian community, they aroused little alarm in the city at large.

The widespread distribution of crack, the cheap, smokable form of cocaine introduced around 1985, changed all that. While the Jamaican groups were not the first to market crack on a large scale (that dubious achievement is usually credited to gangs in New York's Dominican community), they played a significant role in its spread throughout the nation. "They're very good businessmen," says an agent of the Federal Bureau of Alcohol, Tobacco and Firearms. "They follow the law of supply and demand. When they see that a vial of crack selling for five dollars in New York will get fifteen in Kansas City, they'll move in" (Massing 1989:58). By 1986 posses based in New York and Miami had set up crack operations in Washington, D.C., Philadelphia, and Denver, as well as in such unlikely towns as Newburgh, New York, and Charles Town, West Virginia. In general the Jamaicans used a combination of lower prices and violent intimidation to muscle out the competition. In most cases their customers are African Americans.

The total number of people actually involved in these operations has been a subject of considerable controversy. In some venues federal officials report the existence of about twenty posses with several thousand members (Volsky 1987). At other times the same agencies have reported that at least forty identifiable posses with ten to twenty thousand members control 35 to 40 percent of the U.S. crack trade.[24] The larger estimates, however, contradict other descriptions by the same agencies which suggest that while the largest posses may have several hundred members, many number as few as twenty-five (Massing 1989). The fractious nature of the posses—splinter groups and breakaway factions are common—makes it difficult to measure the phenomenon precisely. Yet many who are familiar with them depict the posses as loose confederations of small groups with large numbers of part-time workers—a picture at odds with the federal government's portrayal of an organized conspiracy of full-time criminals numbering in the tens of thousands.

In March of 1989 the press reported that the Manhattan District

---

24. In a 28 March 1988 feature article, *Newsweek* magazine also reported the existence of thirty to forty posses, but estimated their total membership at about five thousand. In my estimation this figure is far more realistic.

Attorney's office had in its possession a list of thirty thousand Jamaican posse suspects. This immediately brought forth howls of protest from the Caribbean community. After initially denying the existence of the list, the office eventually admitted that it had at one time possessed a list of thirty thousand names assembled by the Federal Bureau of Alcohol, Tobacco and Firearms, which included the names of Jamaicans arrested for *any* offense, nationwide. The District Attorney's office also noted that it had collected the names of about two thousand suspected posse members operating in the United States (*New York Carib News* 1989a). That figure was subsequently revised down to 1,500 identified posse members, "mostly Jamaicans," but including immigrants from other Caribbean nations, Africans, and African Americans as well. Spokespersons for the office were quick to point out that these groups constituted only "a tiny fraction" of the Jamaican community (*New York Carib News* 1989b).

The existence of the larger list understandably infuriated Jamaican organizations in New York and was protested by the American Civil Liberties Union. It also drew the ire of Jamaican prime minister Manley, who, while noting the "duty to smash" the "brutal phenomenon" of the posses, expressed grave concern about the stigmatization of Jamaicans in New York, the "overwhelming majority" of whom, he asserted, are "hard working people" (*New York Carib News* 1989c). This notion of hard-working Jamaicans being suspected as posse members was the central theme of a number of *Carib News* editorials, which pointed out that white ethnic groups would never tolerate the existence of such a list, and which concluded: "Obviously, Jamaicans who make up one of the City's fastest growing and most law-abiding communities are not rated highly by the D.A., an elected official in an election year. If they were considered people with voting clout, the politically sensitive D.A. would not have started the list" (Best 1989:16).

The idea of the posse list clearly evoked fears of police harassment for many in the Caribbean community; indeed, the *Carib News* was soon publishing letters from West Indians claiming police harassment from as far away as Kansas City. But the Caribbean reaction bespoke even deeper insecurities. On the one hand Caribbean groups attacked the stigmatization of Jamaicans as "racist," but on the other, many seemed anxious to distance themselves from any association with drugs and drug-related violence, crimes that the media has often associated with African Americans. What was seldom pointed out was the resemblance the posses bear to criminal groups among first-generation white immigrants earlier in the century.

The posses were also a cause for alarm within the community because of the effects they have had on those around them. The groups do exist, and even if their numbers are smaller than the more overblown federal estimates, they have taken a heavy toll on New York's Caribbean neighborhoods. The fast money and tough-guy prestige of the drug trade has had an undeniable appeal to some of the community's youth, confirming many an immigrant parent's worst nightmare. By the late 1980s gun battles between heavily armed posse members, many very young, started to occur in previously stable working-class areas.

By the close of the decade violence and their own relatively small numbers appear to have taken a significant toll on the posses. The expansion of the crack business occurred so quickly that the posses found it impossible to staff operations with trusted running mates from Kingston. Soon it became necessary to recruit Jamaicans from other areas, immigrants from other Caribbean nations, Africans, and African Americans. These recruits were more likely to steal from their employers and, when caught, far more likely to inform on them. Many posses came to rely on gruesome violence to keep their associates in line, which in turn increased their unpopularity in the community and drew the attention of law enforcement.

The trial of crack kingpin Delroy "Uzi" Edwards in 1989 illustrated the rise and fall of such a posse. While his gang, "the Renkers" (patois that roughly translates as "stinking"), was not the largest of the Jamaican drug operations, they were probably fairly typical.

The Renkers were spawned in south-central Kingston, in a small JLP enclave within a larger PNP constituency. The neighborhood was among the fiercest battlegrounds in the gang wars of the late 1970s. By 1980 Edwards, then twenty-one, was employed as a ten-dollar-a-week pro-JLP gunman. He was implicated in several killings in the pre-election violence that year and during the post-election crackdown he fled to Brooklyn, where he was soon selling ganja in five-dollar bags out of the back of his father's grocery store on Rogers Avenue. After his father was murdered in 1982 Edwards took over the grocery and ganja business and eventually served time for gun possession. After his release in 1985 he reassembled his old Kingston posse, supplemented with new recruits from New York, and moved into the growing crack trade (Gunst 1990). The Renkers soon controlled a number of crack locations in Crown Heights and Bedford-Stuyvesant and in 1986 they expanded their operation to Washington, D.C., Maryland, and Philadelphia. According to prosecutors, by 1987 the Renkers had about fifty members and took in between $40,000 and $100,000 a day (Buder 1989b).

The gang had little time to enjoy their ill-gotten gains, however. The Renkers were almost constantly at war with local African-American gangs, and Edwards soon rekindled an old Kingston feud with a rival pro-PNP posse. Firebombings and drive-by shootings at drug locations became commonplace. At one point Edwards sent an associate to a Bedford-Stuyvesant street corner frequented by members of the rival group with orders to "shoot anyone who looks Jamaican." A reggae musician who happened to be walking by was paralyzed for life (Buder 1989a). Edwards was also pathologically suspicious of his employees, many of whom were local teenagers. Several were brutally beaten to death or shot when suspected of skimming profits from the gang. By the time Edwards was arrested on murder, assault, kidnapping, and racketeering charges in March 1988, fourteen other member of the Renkers were in custody and even his closest associates and relatives were ready to testify against him. In December 1989 he was sentenced to seven consecutive life terms (Buder 1989c).

What effect will this tiny but conspicuous minority of West Indians have on the future of the community as a whole? Some suggest that the posses are a passing phase, a response to the dislocations of the immigrant experience and the allure of the quick dollar. Others maintain that the highly volatile and violent nature of the crack trade itself will change; these observers predict that, as with white ethnic crime groups earlier in the century, a few large and stable criminal organizations will eventually come to dominate the crack business, perhaps even funneling profits into legitimate enterprises (Massing 1989). On the other hand, the sheer lack of numbers may prevent the posses from ever achieving Mafia-like stability. Compared to their potential rivals, African-American street gangs and Latin American immigrant groups, the "natural" base from which the posses draw their membership is tiny, and recruiting from outside of that base can be highly destabilizing, as the case of the Renkers shows.

The increasing unpopularity of the posses within the West Indian community may also threaten the groups' long-term survival. In Kingston even the most murderous of the posses have generally made some efforts to take care of their neighborhoods and maintain support of the sufferers. In New York, as retailers of crack, they have largely abandoned this role, and any residual support certain groups may have enjoyed among the transplanted Jamaican poor seems to be eroding rapidly. Unlike gambling or ganja, crack has no roots in Caribbean traditions, and whereas the labor-intensive ganja trade supports a large number of people in both the United States and Jamaica, the profits of the crack business are narrowly distributed. In the case of Edwards, most of the money went for flash: he owned two Mercedes-Benzes, a quarter of a million dollars worth of gold jewelry, and a house on Long Island paid for in cash, but he ended up on trial with a court-appointed lawyer. Finally, there is the sickening violence which has caused anger and shame in a community that prides itself on hard work and self-sufficiency. "None o' them try fi' help their brother and sister," a Jamaican nurse who came to watch the Renkers' trial noted with disgust. "Them just buy these damned expensive cars. Them was scavengers" (Gunst 1989:569).

Low-cost Social Sustenance

The emergence of distinct geographic communities has other results that, if more pedestrian than those discussed above, may be equally important in the long run. As Logan and Molotch have noted, urban neighborhoods create informal networks that provide life-sustaining products and services (1987:104). These networks may have a substantial economic as well as social impact on the lives of neighborhood residents (see, for example, Wellman 1979). It will be argued in the following chapter that West Indian economic activity in New York, concentrated as it is in the service sector, is directly tied to the larger changes in the city's economy since the late 1960s. The existence of an ethnic community supports the largely service sector labor force by reducing the costs of labor force reproduction. In other words, "ethnic" labor is cheaper for a society to maintain for a variety of reasons that have little to do with wage differentials.

We have already seen that some West Indians have voluntarily assumed much of the cost of educating their children (while at the same time paying taxes to maintain the public school system). Others send children to the Caribbean, where third world taxpayers subsidize the production of first world workers. The West Indian communities in New York also provide low-cost child care. On the streets of East Flatbush and Crown Heights one frequently sees signs in windows advertising babysitting or child care. These home-based informal day care facilities allow thousands of West Indian women to work in the wage economy without utilizing the already overcrowded state-funded facilities. While this type of arrangement is not exclusive to immigrant communities, the networks and mutual trust built along ethnic lines greatly facilitate them.

As unlicensed child care facilities are illegal, it is difficult to obtain accurate information on exactly how many children they serve, but they appear to be widespread. When a tragic fire killed two children at one such facility in 1986, the operating details (and the dangers) of what seems to have been a typical facility were revealed. In this case an immigrant from Guyana cared for ten children, aged eleven months to five years, in the basement of her home in the East New York section of Brooklyn. All of the children were from Caribbean families in the neighborhood who paid $40 per week for the service. While the *Carib News* portrayed the event as a community tragedy, it avoided blaming the day care operator: "The parents were pleased with the service they received. It was very economical . . . and located only a block from their homes. They also felt safe, knowing of [the operator's] love for the kids. Many felt the service rendered by the City had become dangerous, with child molestation, drugs being sold near the neighborhood Day Care, the cost, bureaucratic red tape and waiting period" (1986:16).

In response to city officials who blamed the illegal use of space for the children's deaths, the *Carib News* condemned what it saw as an accusatory finger pointing at the provider of an essential service:

> [The] type of home day care that is at the center of this tragedy is in some ways a response to the need for self help and self sufficiency. . . . Here is an individual providing a desperately needed service . . . [which] the families involved favored over the . . . large scale day care option with its many unknowns and bureaucratic obstacles. (1986:16)

Besides providing their own day care, West Indians demonstrate self-sufficiency with a host of other informal (and often illegal) home-based cottage industries within the immigrant community. These produce food items, clothing, and other goods and services at costs

far lower than those of the formal sector. While such informal economic activities (often barter) do not generate taxes, they contribute
to the economy by allowing workers to subsist on lower wages. As
sociologist Remco van Capelleveen notes, "many of these goods and
services are provided through social networks such as family, friendship and ethnic-national organizations" (1987:268).

These networks also help immigrants find housing and jobs.
Megan McLaughlin's survey of 101 West Indian immigrants in
Brooklyn found that 87 percent had moved in with friends or relatives upon arriving in the United States and 68 percent had located
their first job through the help of a friend or relative (1981:123–27).
Such help is not only useful for the immigrant, it also gives employers access to workers whose reliability is somewhat assured by
the fact that a friend or relative has put his or her own reputation on
the line for them.

The immigrant community also provides many of its own financial
services through rotating credit associations and other organizations
based on common ethnic identity (Bonnett 1981). Known as "boxes,"
"partnerships," or—most commonly—"susus," these savings clubs
have long been widespread in the Caribbean and are becoming so in
New York. The typical susu consists of ten to fifteen members who
each "throw a hand," that is, contribute a set amount into a communal fund weekly or biweekly. Each time the "hands" are thrown one
member of the club receives the entire fund. The order of payment
may be random, or it may be timed to individual members' needs. In
either case trust is the key to the club's functioning, since a member
who "draws a hand" early in the rotation order takes out far more
than he or she has contributed and must be relied upon to stay in the
club long enough to repay the group.

The amount raised for one payment typically ranges from several
hundred to a few thousand dollars. Bonnett reports that susus have
occasionally been used to finance small business ventures and down
payments on houses (1981), but more mundane uses are more common.[25] "It's for poor people who need a refrigerator, or they are hav-

---

25. Bonnett reports that interest-free loans from rotating credit associations are occasionally used to "top off" major purchases, that is, to complete a down payment on a house
when a member is $1,000 short. However, Bonnett also notes that one of the principal
advantages of the rotating credit system is to provide loans when the amount of funds
needed is too small to be obtained from a formal financial institution. In recent years the
widespread diffusion of credit cards has made even this function less important.

ing a wedding," explains a Guyanese minister who notes that many such groups function among his congregation. Why do people choose to save by this method, which pays no interest? For some recent arrivals with little knowledge of the American banking system the susu may be seen as more reliable. Certainly many undocumented aliens and others working "off the books" may prefer the fact that the susu operates in cash and generally keeps no written records. However, many highly sophisticated long-time New Yorkers with completely legal sources of income continue to use the savings clubs for social and motivational reasons. "When I get my paycheck the first money I take out is my hand," explains a Brooklyn construction company supervisor, who has saved one hundred dollars a week for nearly twenty years. "I don't think I'd be disciplined enough to do that on my own" (*New York Times* 1988). In addition, the other functions of such groups—camaraderie, fellowship, and information sharing—may well be as important as the actual savings.

These informal economic activities require the commitment to mutual support that comes with a shared identity. Without that bond, such sharing networks would be infinitely harder to operate. Though rotating credit associations do not always operate strictly along ethnic lines, they tend to be more successful when they do (Bonnett 1981). Churches, mutual benevolent societies, and other neighborhood institutions are also vital in establishing the networks through which knowledge, informal services, and other types of help can flow. To be sure, earlier West Indian immigrants maintained such networks, but the larger numbers in New York today have expanded their reach and scope.

These ethnic networks constitute a financial resource that may help the immigrant to function in the wider economy. Noneconomic relationships such as kinship, friendship, and ethnicity are at certain times more economically useful than more formal and rational ones. Thus the immigrant brings to New York the advantages of relative backwardness vis-à-vis the "modern" economy. The maintenance of the ethnic enclave helps them maintain some of these advantages, and assimilation may erode them. "I live in the suburbs and I still use them," says the construction supervisor of her susus, "but I don't see my children going into it. My kids do CD's"

The maintenance of a West Indian ethnic enclave is now not only possible; from the point of view of the immigrants it may be economically beneficial. It is thus not surprising that with the passage of time some of New York's black immigrants and their descendants have become more, not less, self-consciously Caribbean in their culture, settlement patterns, and, as I shall argue in the following chapter, in their work life as well.

[3]

From Ghetto Elite to Service Sector: The Changing Roles of West Indians in New York's Economy

America is all right if you have money.
—C. L. R. JAMES, *Mariners, Renegades, and Castaways*

Just as changes in the racial geography of New York City affected the social and political life of the two large cohorts of West Indian immigrants in different ways, so too changes in New York City's economy provide a partial explanation for the differences between the two groups. These changes, I will suggest, have affected not only the kind of jobs West Indians hold, but also the ways in which they are perceived and perceive themselves, socially and politically. These economic changes have fundamentally shaped the relations between the immigrants and the other groups in the city.

Over the years a popular mythology about West Indian business acumen has grown up in New York City. They have been called "black Jews" and described (inaccurately in my view) as a "middleman minority." In *Black Manhattan*, James Weldon Johnson summed up the popular stereotype of the 1920s: "They are characteristically sober-minded and have something of a genius for business, differing almost totally in these respects from the average rural Negro from the south" (1930:130).

This image of West Indians as ghetto entrepreneurs characterizes much of the academic literature as well. Of the slight academic attention that has been paid to West Indian immigrants, most has focused on the issue of economic success and the question (whether explicitly posed or not) of what this supposed success implies about the role of racism in explaining the continued high rates of poverty among native blacks (see, for example, Light 1972; Glantz 1978; Truab 1981; Arnold 1984). In their highly influential *Beyond the Melting Pot*, Glazer and Moynihan (drawing heavily on the work of Ira Reid, by then a quarter of a century old) summed up the prevailing view: "The ethos of the West Indians, in contrast to that of the Southern Negro, emphasized saving, hard work, investment and education" (1963:35).

The dual assumption that West Indians are more economically successful than native blacks and that this success is primarily due to cultural factors ("ethos") has been expressed forcefully by Sowell (1978; 1981; 1983). It has been challenged, both by those who question the fact of West Indian economic success (Allen and Farley 1987) and by those who question the cultural explanation for it (Steinberg 1981). At times this debate has degenerated into a numbers game, with observers providing differing analyses of the scant available statistics and proving, more than anything else, the inadequacy of the decennial census (the only major source of data) in answering such questions. The issue merits further examination.

In several books Sowell offers the statistic that, in 1969, households headed by West Indians (i.e., immigrants and their first generation of U.S.-born descendants) had incomes that were 94 percent of the national average, while those of native African Americans were only 62 percent. This figure means less than it appears at first glance. While Sowell sees West Indians as comparable to entrepreneurial minorities such as Jews and Japanese Americans, this statistic actually places them closer to African Americans, for the incomes of Japanese and Jewish Americans were, respectively, 132 and 172 percent of the national average. Whites of foreign stock generally have higher income levels than native whites, and Sowell himself reports that virtually all white ethnic groups have household incomes higher than the national average. In other words, if West Indians look like immigrants when compared with other blacks, they still resemble other blacks when compared to white immigrants.

Taking the logic of multivariate analysis somewhat further, Farley (1986) has argued, using the 1980 census, that once location, family type, and education are controlled for, the gap between African American and West Indian incomes narrows considerably and within occupational categories it actually reverses.[1] Yet this finding in and of itself only begs Sowell's "culture" question: if a propensity toward education and two-income families is not cultural, what is?[2] However, Farley's work does point out which aspects of West Indian life account for their economic position: his finding that the gap between foreign- and native-born black household income is far wider for female-headed households points to the particular importance of the high rate of the West Indian female labor force participation and will be discussed below. On the whole Farley's analysis quite convincingly supports his conclusion:

> West Indians are more extensively educated than native blacks but their attainment does not equal that of native whites. The unemployment rates of all groups of blacks were high in 1980 compared to whites. With regard to occupational achievement, black immigrants who have been in the country a decade or more and . . . [the children of immigrants] were clearly a step ahead of native blacks but lagged behind native whites. (1986:15. See also Allen and Farley 1987)

Yet what is striking about both Sowell and his critics is the ahistorical quality of their work. While Sowell offers analysis of the 1970 census to support a cultural argument, his representation of the culture itself draws on much earlier sources. Both Sowell and Farley (and most other observers) rely heavily on Ira Reid's rich but unsystematic observations about high rates of West Indian entrepreneurialism *in the 1930's*. Farley notes that both income and rates of entrepreneurialism and professionalism are higher for pre-1970 immigrants than post-1970 immigrants and higher still for U.S.-born children of West Indian parents, but he gives little consideration to how much of this is due to historical rather than generational factors.

To understand the economic life of West Indian immigrants, or any group for that matter, we must examine their experience in a

---

1. That is, a college-educated African-American professional living in the North is statistically predicted to have a higher income than a college-educated West Indian professional living in the North. An African-American machine operator with two years of high school living in the South would be expected to have a higher income than a West Indian machine operator with two years of high school living in the South, and so on.
2. An additional problem with Farley's analysis is his use of 1980 census data to counter Sowell's arguments made on the basis of 1970 census data. The number of foreign-born blacks in the United States tripled during the 1970s and obviously a much higher proportion of West Indians in the 1980 census were very recent immigrants.

historical context. In the case of West Indians in New York, the two large immigrant cohorts confronted quite different situations upon arriving in the city. The immigrants of the first three decades of the twentieth century, whatever their cultural propensities, were profoundly affected by the fact that they were part of a massive expansion in New York City's black population. The immigrants who came to New York following the 1965 Hart-Cellar immigration reforms have had their life chances shaped by another economic transformation: the restructuring of New York's role in the global economy from an industrial city to an international center of service sector activity.

The Enclave Economy: Ghetto Capitalism

The stereotype of West Indian "genius for business" is based, both in the academic literature and the popular imagination, on the experience of the first immigrant wave. Even then it is something of an exaggeration. Little economic data is available, but the fact that few West Indian businesses from this period have survived implies that they were neither plentiful nor greatly successful. Reid (1939), whose description of West Indian businesses in Harlem is often cited by later observers, noted that most West Indian immigrants had menial jobs as waiters, elevator operators, factory hands, and unskilled workers, particularly in the garment industry. Herbert Gutman's (1977) analysis of jobs held by blacks in New York in the twenties also concludes that while immigrants were somewhat better off than natives, both were largely restricted to low-wage labor, and that self-employment rates among West Indian immigrants were low compared to other immigrant groups.

Nevertheless, the notion of the West Indian as entrepreneur was not totally without basis. As early as 1901 West Indians were disproportionately well represented among New York black business owners (Foner 1979), and the establishment of rotating credit associations in Harlem during the next two decades gave West Indians a small leg up on African Americans in obtaining business capital (Bonnet 1982). By the mid-1920s West Indians were also engaged in cooperative business and home-buying schemes in Harlem, financed by pooled savings (Reid 1939; Johnson 1930).

How much of the economic position of West Indians of the first

[93]

immigrant cohort can be ascribed to traits and skills they brought with them? Some observers attributed their interest in small business to their fabled quest for personal autonomy (Domingo 1926; Du Bois 1920). Others maintained that West Indians were better educated than their African-American neighbors. Though an examination of the premigration occupational status of the immigrants indicates that education levels were probably not tremendously high, most of the immigrants do appear to have possessed what Johnson described as "a sound common school education" (1930:153). Calvin Holder's (1987) analysis of Immigration and Naturalization Service (INS) Annual Reports indicates that of adult black immigrants arriving in the United States between 1900 and 1932, 89 percent were literate, a higher rate than for most of the West Indian territories at that time.

Holder's work also indicates that immigrants were atypical in terms of occupational status. Only about 3 percent of the adult population was professional, but 34 percent was skilled workers (and Holder suggests that many of the 20 percent who listed no occupation were their wives). Agricultural workers made up the bulk of the West Indian labor force of the period, but they were underrepresented among the migrants; Reid (1939) notes that of those foreign-born blacks emigrating before 1930 who reported a premigration occupation, less than 15 percent were in agriculture.

Culture, education, and occupational background may have provided the potential for West Indian economic success, but it was the massive growth of New York's black community in the 1920s and 1930s that provided the opportunity. With this growth a black consumer market developed in New York. Unwelcome in white establishments, this population required stores, barber shops, beauty parlors, real estate agencies, bars, and restaurants. Most of those who capitalized on this growing market were white. Indeed until the protests of the 1930s many stores on Harlem's 125th Street did not even hire black workers. But in both Harlem and Brooklyn a number of West Indians were able to get a foothold in small retail and personal service businesses.

Others served the informational needs of the growing black community. The 1920s saw an expansion of black-oriented publishing, and many of its leading lights were from the islands. Still others addressed different needs. The first major kingpin of the Harlem numbers racket, Caspar Holstein, was a Virgin Islander, and "policy" remained a largely West Indian enterprise until it proved so profitable as to draw the attention of white mobsters (McKay 1940).[3] Democratic ward politics in Harlem also attracted a number of West Indians, who, not sharing the residual Republican tendencies that characterized African-American politics prior to 1936, were able to take advantage of Tammany's occasional attempts to reach out to the growing black community.

In addition to becoming retailers, entrepreneurs, publishers, and politicians, West Indians would make an even greater mark as the community's doctors, dentists, lawyers, and other professionals. Reid estimates that by the 1930s one third of New York's black professionals were from the Caribbean (1939:121). In addition to the 3 percent of immigrants who arrived with professional qualifications, many West Indians gained higher education in the United States, either at black colleges or at City University. While discrimination certainly limited educational opportunities during this period, it is fair to say that access to higher education was considerably easier than access to business capital. Thus for motivated and literate young islanders the professions, along with local politics, were probably the surest route to economic success.

Even more than in the retail trade, a growing black population provided these professionals with a ready market. In the United States native whites are often reluctant to service blacks; the very idea cuts to the core of what race and servility have historically meant in this country. In retail trade this role was sometimes filled by West Indians, but more often by "ethnic" whites—"middleman minorities"—who, however hostile towards their customers, are not bound by the same taboos of racial propriety that limit white natives. In ghetto retailing, the better financed white ethnics tended to domi-

3. It may have been Holstein's dramatic kidnapping in 1928 that brought West Indian domination of the numbers racket to an end. Seized on a Harlem street by a group of whites disguised as policemen, Holstein apparently came to an accommodation with his abductors; he was released some days later and although four men were eventually brought to trial for the crime, Holstein claimed to be unable to identify them. Yet the amount of the ransom—rumored to be $50,000—and Holstein's apparent ease in raising it drew the attention of federal authorities to the lucrative nature of the business, and soon several of Harlem's leading policy "bankers" were indicted for income tax evasion. This evidence of profitability also drew the attention of Dutch Schultz and his confederates, who ultimately wrested control. Holstein retired rather than deal with Schultz, but maintained considerable real estate holdings in Harlem and was highly influential in Virgin Island politics during the 1930s and 1940s.

nate, but in the professional services they were less able to do so because of limited English proficiency and the lack of American credentials.

West Indians, by contrast, possessed English language skills generally exceeding those of most white immigrants and southern-born blacks, and so they quickly moved into the professions. Allen and Farley (1987) note that in 1980 the male U.S.-born children of West Indian immigrants were over 30 percent more likely than post-1970 immigrants and almost twice as likely as African Americans to be professionals. While these figures may reflect second-generation assimilation, they may also show a residual effect of the professional orientation of the earlier immigrant cohort.

This market opportunity for black professionals was limited, however, to one very small and very poor niche within the economy, for very few whites of the prewar era would have chosen a black doctor, dentist, or attorney. Thus West Indian and other black professionals found themselves organically tied to and economically dependent on the predominantly African-American communities they served.

The same holds true for West Indian retailers, publishers, and especially politicians. The black community provided both their social position and their livelihood. Whatever they might have thought privately of African Americans, this economic position made them part of the black community and gave them an interest in expanding the opportunities available to that community.

West Indians in the Growing Service Sector

The post-1965 wave of Caribbean immigrants came to New York as part of a larger influx of foreign workers to the city. By 1980 New York was truly an immigrant city once more, with 24 percent of its population foreign-born, the highest proportion in half a century. But these new immigrants have entered the United States not at a time of unprecedented growth and economic expansion, as in the early twentieth century, but at a time of decline.

Between 1970 and 1980 total employment in New York City fell by 8.5 percent (Waldinger 1987b) and the number of manufacturing jobs dropped by 35 percent (Sassen-Koob 1984). How can the city absorb large numbers of new immigrants at a time when traditional sources of immigrant employment are in decline without creating massive unemployment (and social unrest) among native workers? The traditional answer that immigrants simply work harder and create their own opportunities through small business enterprise, is, as Marcia Freedman notes, "not so much wrong as too simple" (1983:96). In the case of West Indians hard work certainly does play a role, as does a reluctance to take public assistance. "Why you think I come here, for the weather?" one informant asks. "If I wanted to sit around on welfare, I would have stayed home!" On the other hand self-employment and the creation of new businesses play only a minor role—less than for earlier Caribbean immigrants. The story of how West Indians have fit into New York's economic structure has less to do with the jobs they have created than with their ability to fit into the growing sectors of a changing economy.

Whether or not the image of West Indians as a ghetto elite was ever an accurate picture of the first immigrant cohort, it certainly does not describe the situation of the post-1965 immigrants in New York today. Their economic position differs from that of their predecessors because of two major developments. First is the expansion of opportunities for the more educated sector of the black population to move into the mainstream economy in the wake of the civil rights movement. Second, and perhaps even more crucial in shaping the job market for the immigrants, is the reorganization of New York City's economy, especially the massive expansion of the service sector that occurred during the 1970s.

The results of the first development have been well documented (see, for example Wilson 1987). The opening of black educational opportunities in the 1960s and the increase, under political pressure, of public- and (to a far more limited degree) private-sector employment created opportunities for some blacks (including some West Indians) to move into the economic mainstream. As a result both ghetto politics and ghetto capitalism lost much of their appeal for a generation being offered a wider range of opportunities.

At the same time, ever larger numbers of blacks found themselves at the margins of the mainstream economy. The out-migration of the more advantaged blacks caused a further decline in ghetto institutions that were already suffering from large-scale financial disinvestment. As these ghettos collapsed socially and physically, still more of their populations fled. By the 1980s many traditionally black areas were abandoned by all but the poorest residents. The institutions that remained, such as Harlem's great churches and the few remaining restaurants, found themselves serving an aging population made up largely of weekend commuters (Wilson and Green 1988). An older Jamaican activist recalls: "I still attend a large church on 119th Street in Harlem, but now almost nobody in the congregation lives in that area. Most are older folks, like me, who come in from Brooklyn. The few young folks are all from Queens or Westchester or Nassau. They never see Harlem except on Sunday. It's that way with a lot of churches, clubs and so forth."

Under such circumstances the economic niches open to West Indians in earlier periods became less appealing, and in some cases, ceased to exist. In an increasingly impoverished ghetto professional services, while perhaps more needed, were less in demand. Ghetto retailing was increasingly difficult as the potential market shrank and a new wave of Asian immigrants replaced both white ethnics and older Caribbean blacks, competing for the dollars that remained. Finally, a new generation of African-American politicians who had come of age in the confrontational politics of the civil rights and community control movements replaced the older, largely Caribbean black Democratic leadership in the wards.

At the same time, other spheres were opening for the post-1965 migrants. Open enrollment at City University and affirmative action programs at many schools increased educational opportunities. Both public- and private-sector enterprises found themselves under political pressure to hire more blacks after the late 1960s, and West Indians seem frequently to have been the preferred choice. Of even greater importance in creating opportunities for new immigrants in New York was a precipitous decline in the number of white workers. This little appreciated fact effectively made discrimination in hiring both more difficult and more expensive.

The economics of job discrimination, as illuminated by sociologist Stanley Lieberson (1980), can best be understood if racism is thought of as creating a hiring queue. Certain groups, in this case whites, are preferred, other groups, in this case Asians and other non white immigrants, may be further back in the queue, while native African Americans and Puerto Ricans are in the rear. If the numbers of a preferred group declines, the price that group is able to charge for its labor increases and the cost of not moving down the queue and using less preferred workers goes up. As Roger Waldinger (1987b) points out, whereas total employment in New York City declined by 8.56 percent between 1970 and 1980, employment for both native and foreign-born whites declined by nearly twice that percentage. The reasons for this include increased suburbanization, the movement of jobs to the Sunbelt, and the aging of the white population. As white labor became scarcer and more expensive, groups further back in the queue gained ground.

Controlling for the change in the size of the labor force, Waldinger shows that native whites lost 13.8 percent more jobs than would be expected if the losses were evenly distributed, and foreign-born whites, an aging population comprising largely the pre-1924 immigrants, lost 15.7 percent more than expected. The largest gainers were foreign-born Asians, whose share of the job market increased by an astounding 257 percent. But the second highest gains were among foreign-born blacks, whose share increased 215 percent. Foreign-born Hispanics came next (+63 percent), then native-born Asians (+39 percent), with native Hispanics (+4.9 percent) and native blacks (+3.9 percent) gaining least (1987b:376–77).

While this huge increase in the West Indian share of New York City's job market is important, it may also be misleading because these figures reveal only that large numbers of West Indians work, not where they work. Though foreign-born blacks, Asians, and Hispanics all made substantial gains in their share of New York's jobs in the 1970s, they did so in markedly different areas. Asians have filled the traditional immigrant role, concentrating in small retailing and the professions (particularly in areas serving blacks). Hispanics have a growing share of the declining manufacturing sector. An examination of the economic role West Indians now play in New York reveals that their relative prosperity is less a result of entrepreneurial activity than of their ability to adjust to economic and social change by filling the lower rungs of New York's emerging service economy.

There are, to be sure, some classic immigrant entrepreneurial success stories in the West Indian community, mainly in the food and entertainment industries. One active community group, Brooklyn's Caribbean American Chamber of Commerce, runs a series of well-attended seminars aimed at developing small business skills. Yet on the whole West Indians are not concentrated in small business and generally do not dominate even the small retail businesses of their

Table 11. Percentages of Americans 16 and over reporting nonfarm self-employment income, 1980

	Men		Women	
	Foreign	Native	Foreign	Native
Black	3.4	2.9	1.1	0.9
White	9.7	8.4	2.3	2.5
Hispanic	5.3	3.8	1.4	1.1
Other	8.3	6.4	2.5	2.8

Source: Walter Allen and Reynolds Farley, *The Color Line and the Quality of Life in America* (New York: Russell Sage Foundation, 1987), p. 397. © 1987, The Russell Sage Foundation. Used with the permission of the Russell Sage Foundation. Original data source: 1980 U.S. Census of Population.

Table 12. Occupational characteristics of recent immigrants (1970–1980) and natives, New York State, 1980

	Jamaican	Dominican	Korean	Native	Total employed persons
Percentage of self-employed in civilian labor force	1.7	1.6	16.6	5.4	5.5
Occupation (% of employed persons 16 + years old)					
Managerial, professional, and specialty	11.0	3.9	32.3	26.4	25.7
Technical, sales, and administrative support	30.9	14.7	37.0	34.7	33.5
(clerical)	22.8	8.7	9.3	21.8	21.0
Service	33.3	19.7	9.1	13.0	13.9
(private household)	6.1	0.5	0.2	0.5	0.6
Farming, forestry, and fishing	0.3	0.6	0.0	1.4	1.3
Precision production, craft, and repair	9.9	10.5	6.5	10.1	10.4
Operators, fabricators, and laborers	14.5	50.8	15.1	14.4	15.2

Source: 1980 U.S. Census.

Table 13. Economic characteristics of recent immigrants (1970–1980) and natives, New York State, 1980

	Immigrant (post-1970)			Native		
	Jamaican	Dominican	Korean	Black	White	Total
% of age 25+ who are:						
high school graduates	58.4	24.4	83.5	57.8	69.9	67.5
college graduates	8.2	2.4	45.7	9.0	24.0	22.2
% age 16+ in labor force						
total	69.9	60.1	60.4	58.0	59.9	59.5
male	74.7	74.3	74.3	64.8	73.8	72.5
female	66.0	48.0	48.9	52.8	47.7	48.2
in civilian labor force, unemployed	10.0	12.0	5.3	11.3	6.4	7.1
Median family income ($)	15,727	9,117	17,762	13,026	21,672	20,180
% of families below the national poverty level, 1979	16.2	38.3	15.2	27.0	7.5	11.7

Source: 1980 U.S. Census.

own neighborhoods. Despite the "black Jews" mythology, West Indian rates of self-employment are low, as Table 11 indicates. While black immigrants were marginally more likely than native blacks to report non-farm self-employment income in 1980, they still show self-employment rates far lower than other immigrant groups—and lower than native whites as well. In fact the difference between black immigrants and natives is smaller than the difference between white immigrants and natives. Allen and Farley (1987) note that for American-born men of Caribbean parentage the self-employment figure was somewhat higher: 4.5 percent, still far below that of whites.

Recent immigrants are particularly unlikely to be involved in entrepreneurial activity. Comparing Jamaican immigrants, the largest Anglophone Caribbean immigrant group, with Dominicans, the largest immigrant Hispanic group, and Koreans, an Asian group whose size, time of arrival and urban concentration is roughly comparable, reveals much about occupational niches. As Table 12 indicates, very few Jamaicans or Dominicans who have arrived in New York since 1970 were self-employed by comparison with natives and especially with Koreans.

On the other hand, as Table 13 indicates, overall Jamaican labor force participation is high; especially for women it is much higher

[101]

than in comparable immigrant groups. Table 13 also reveals that Jamaican immigrants are remarkably close to other black New Yorkers in terms of education, and their unemployment rate, though slightly lower than that of native blacks and Dominican immigrants, is about twice that of Korean immigrants or of whites. Yet their incomes are higher and their poverty rate is far lower than that of native blacks (close to that of Koreans). The key difference seems to be the higher rates of labor force participation, particularly for women.

Table 14 implies that this high rate of labor force participation is true for other West Indians as well. In 1980 the median income for West Indian-headed families was $15,645, higher than that of native blacks or Dominican immigrants, although lower than that of native whites. Perhaps more noteworthy is the low percentage of West Indian families receiving public assistance, as compared to Dominican immigrants and natives. Allen and Farley (1987) report similar findings nationwide. Both foreign-born blacks and American-born blacks of Caribbean ancestry in 1980 reported unemployment rates slightly lower than those of African Americans, but much higher than those for whites. However, to be counted as "unemployed" one must be in the labor force, and Farley demonstrates that both black immigrants and their children have higher labor force participation rates than African Americans. For men the rate is still lower than for whites, but the rate of female labor force participation is higher than for natives of either race.

It is also necessary to examine what sort of jobs immigrants hold. In a few cases these jobs are based in their own communities, where

Table 14. Economic characteristics of immigrant and native families, New York City, 1980

	West Indian head	Dominican head	Native head
Median family income ($)	15,645	9,681	17,361
Median income of female-headed families	10,971	5,933	7,625
% families receiving public assistance	6.7	23.8	13.3

Source: Evelyn S. Mann and Joseph Salvo, "Characteristics of New Hispanic Immigrants to New York City," New York City Department of City Planning, 1984. (Original data source: 1980 U.S. Census)

much of the relatively small level of entrepreneurial activity is located. Though the growth of West Indian neighborhoods obviously created some small business opportunities—a demand for Caribbean bakeries and restaurants, shipping companies and travel agencies and, of course, entertainment services of various kinds—these small businesses, while they help support the Caribbean work force, do not themselves provide large amounts of employment.

More important for West Indian employment has been the growth of the service sector in the city in general. Even while New York lost manufacturing and some of its largest corporate headquarters during the 1970s, it was becoming a center for management services in an increasingly transnational economy. The expansion of financial activity, the growth in corporate support services that no longer needed to be physically near those they service, the decentralization of management, and the influx of foreign capital, plus the growth in medical, educational, and entertainment services, have all changed the complexion of New York's labor force.

The phrase "service sector economy" suggests highly paid white-collar employment, but that is only part of the story. The growth of financial services creates jobs not only for stockbrokers and investment analysts, but also for messengers, secretaries, and countless data entry personnel. Corporate headquarters employ maintenance workers, drivers, and a multitude of low-level clerks. The expansion of white-collar employment also created a surge in personnel and entertainment services, ranging from night clubs and gourmet food outlets to a host of businesses offering "designer" goods that require not only highly paid designers but also less well paid crafts people and their helpers.

In addition to these growth areas, other sorts of consumer services expanded as the role of the state declined in New York following the fiscal crisis of 1975 and the subsequent reorganization of the city economy after the election of Edward Koch in 1977. As city services were cut back, the private sector took up some of the slack in transportation (the growth of the taxi industry), education (private schools), and police protection (private security guards).

The ability of West Indians to fit into this growing but generally low wage sector is no doubt partially attributable to immigrant drive and to the versatility that is engendered by the very small societies of the Caribbean. Their success is also explained by a mastery of the

Table 15. Major occupations of employed West Indians age 16 and over, New York City, 1979

Female		Male	
Nursing aide	12,640	Machine operator, assembler,	
Secretary, typist, office clerk,		welder, cutter	3,700
data entry	10,640	Guard	2,200
Nurse	7,900[a]	Janitor	2,080
Servant, cleaner, maid or		Taxi driver, Chauffeur	2,060
housekeeper	7,460	Houseman	1,820
Welfare service	2,500	Auto mechanic	1,760
Bookkeeper	1,900	Manager	1,640
Sewing machine operator	1,860	Nursing aide	1,620
Cashier	1,320	Office clerk	1,440
Machine operator	1,220	Shipping clerk	1,440
Other	16,640	Accountant	1,340
		Carpenter	1,120
		Production supervisor	1,020
		Other	51,380
Total	64,080	Total	74,660

Source: 1980 U.S. Census. *Public Use Microdata Sample* (recomputed).
[a]Includes licensed and registered nurses.

English language that, to the ears of many New Yorkers, is superior not only to that of other immigrants but also to that of many natives, and by the high rate of female labor force participation in an economy that increasingly relies on low-wage female labor.

As Table 12 indicates, West Indians of both sexes appear to be concentrated in low-level service sector and clerical occupations. Over 22 percent of recent Jamaican immigrants (but only 8.7 percent of Dominicans) were in the census' "Administrative Support" category, which includes low-level clerical jobs. By contrast, even among these recent immigrants only 14.5 percent of the Jamaicans fell into the declining blue-collar category of "Operators, Fabricators and Laborers" (where over half of the recent Dominican immigrants are employed). Also noteworthy are the comparatively large number of Jamaicans employed in private household occupations.

Table 15 indicates that this concentration in service jobs is not restricted to either Jamaicans or recent immigrants. Particularly worthy of note are the large number of West Indians in health care occupations, 32 percent of New York's West Indian women being either nurses or nurse's aides, more often the latter. In addition, a large number of West Indian women were in clerical, keypunch, and data entry positions.

[104]

This economic concentration tends to perpetuate itself; compatriots tend to follow one another into certain positions, leading in some cases to the virtual monopolization of certain jobs by members of the same ethnic group. For West Indian New Yorkers the concentration in service jobs is far greater among women than among men, who tend to predominate in the more self-consciously ethnic political groups.

The creation of these ethnic niches within the labor market is highly dependent on the dynamics of the labor market as a whole. Even in the worst paid occupations, West Indian employment reflects recent social and economic changes. One example particularly worthy of note is child care and household employment. The marked increase in labor force participation by middle-class women during the 1970s created a huge need for household workers. In New York West Indian women have most often filled that need, particularly in the case of live-in child care. Though these occupations accounted for only 9 percent of West Indian women in the labor force according to the 1980 census, the actual numbers are surely far higher, as these are areas where undocumented aliens are concentrated. Increased numbers of middle- and upper-middle-class women working outside of the home during child-bearing years has been made possible in part by the importation of English-speaking Caribbean child care workers, and it is noteworthy that U.S. immigration policy encourages household employment as one of the few available legal routes to a green card.

Prospective employers may legally sponsor an alien household worker if they are willing to attest that no citizen or legal resident can be found to fill the job "at the prevailing wage." In New York as of 1985 this wage was considered to be $200 for a 44-hour work week. The employer is under no obligation to pay the prevailing wage, however, and even the minimum wage is seldom enforced for household workers. Shellee Colen reports that many live-in household workers make less than $100 per week, often less than they had made in the Caribbean. The payoff is that at the end of sponsorship period, usually about two years, they may be able to receive a green card and become a legal resident, at which time they generally leave for other areas of employment (Colen 1989, 1990; Bolles 1981).

Another area of West Indian concentration, one dominated by men, is cab driving, particularly "gypsy" cab and nonmedallion car

[105]

service operation. As this is also an area where the undocumented are concentrated, the official statistics presented in Table 15 almost certainly underestimate the numbers involved. Mass transportation service declined precipitously in New York following the fiscal crisis of 1975, and the use of hired cars of various types grew accordingly. Immigrants from many nations have gone into the legal medallion taxi service, but the strictly limited number of medallion taxis (frozen since the 1930s at 11,787) has driven the price of a medallion above what many can afford. As demand for taxis increased, however, medallion cabs were able to limit their activity to Manhattan almost exclusively, leaving the outer boroughs free for community car services and gypsies. The general reluctance of the yellow cabs to pick up minority passengers who might be headed to dangerous and distant neighborhoods of the outer boroughs inspired the bumper sticker now displayed by many gypsies: "We're not yellow, we go anywhere!"

By 1986 *The New York Times* estimated that 20,000 community car service vehicles were on the road, supposedly responding only to radio calls but many functioning as gypsies and picking up people on the street, in addition to at least 10,000 outright gypsies cruising the streets of minority neighborhoods. Also some 5,000 "black cars" serving large corporations on a voucher system were working in Manhattan.[4] Since these cars are shared, the number of persons employed is considerably higher than the number of vehicles. In areas of the outer boroughs such as East Flatbush and East New York, gypsy cab activity has expanded to directly compensate for declines in mass transit service. Caribbean immigrants now operate illegal jitney-style cab routes, a sort of private bus service making regular runs along underserviced bus routes and other main thoroughfares. These jitneys generally charge the same fare as the buses, and have been known to accept subway tokens as payment.

Thus the economic role that West Indians play in New York is directly tied to the recent transitions in the metropolitan economy. To the extent that West Indians have been successful, it has probably been due to skills and attributes that are particularly useful in the lower rungs of a service economy: notably mastery of English and high rates of literacy—and to high female labor force participation.

4. *The New York Times*, 3 December 1986.

But these low-wage jobs generally do not lead to capital accumulation nor do they give immigrants the control over resources and the ability to help their countrymen that small business ownership does. While most West Indian immigrants are able to rely on the help of family and friends to get them through hard times, some appear to be "falling through the cracks" into poverty. Though the rate of public assistance was low as of 1980 (limited both by cultural taboos against welfare and the inability of undocumented aliens to receive it), anecdotal evidence and the media point to the presence of recent West Indian immigrants in the city's homeless shelters. The decline in New York's economy after 1987 appears to have impoverished many others. With minimal unionization the service sector is uniquely vulnerable to economic downturns, and the community's internal resource networks, already strained by the increasing immigration, might well break down under additional pressure.

Why African Americans have benefited less directly from the expansion of the service sector is not clear (and beyond the realm of this study), but not only have black unemployment rates increased steadily since the late 1960s, black labor force participation has declined (Wilson 1987). An examination of the poorest segment of the black community, female-headed households, suggests some key differences between black immigrants and natives.

A number of observers of the first cohort of West Indian immigrants reported greater family stability and what Osofsky (1963:134) called "the orthodox respect for family ties" than was seen among African Americans. However, among the post-1965 immigrants (a group that is predominantly female to begin with) female-headed households are common. The 1980 census reported 29 percent of black immigrant families headed by women, less than the 38 percent of native black families, but still far more than the 11 percent of native whites or the 22 percent of native Hispanic families. In addition, these immigrant female-headed households were poor: their 1979 mean income, Allen and Farley report, was $12,300, as compared to $20,990 for families headed by foreign black males. However, they were not as poor as families headed by native black women, whose mean income was only $10,260. The incomes of foreign black male-headed households averaged 82 percent of those of white natives, and those of native black male-headed households, 78 percent. Foreign-born black female-headed families, poor as they were, did slightly better in comparative terms, making 83 percent of what native white female-headed households did. In contrast, native black female-headed households had average incomes only 69 percent of white female-headed households (Allen and Farley 1987:404). It appears that once again high rates of West Indian female labor force participation in low-wage jobs accounts for much of the difference between the two groups.

It is also noteworthy that during the 1970s and 1980s the proportion of jobs held by African Americans declined in most sectors of the New York job market. As Roger Waldinger points out (1987b), this decline was particularly severe in blue-collar employment. In the lucrative construction industry, for example, the share of jobs held by whites actually increased during the 1970s, despite highly publicized affirmative action efforts and a declining white share of the total labor force. This, Waldinger maintains, was the result of the efforts by white ethnic groups to monopolize these jobs and the lack of substantial private business ownership among African Americans.

Since the late 1960s African Americans have made substantial gains in public sector employment. This ethnic concentration in government jobs is, of course, not unprecedented. In the latter half of the nineteenth century the domination of public sector employment was a key economic resource of the Irish, a group whose extreme poverty and castelike oppression in their rural homeland is perhaps comparable to that faced by blacks in the United States. Yet, lest this comparison engender too much optimism, we must note with caution that despite their early politicization the Irish took longer to move into the American middle class than any other white ethnic group. Further, many of the methods the Irish used to partially monopolize public employment are no longer available because of the expansion of civil service and a century of municipal reform. Also the Irish political machines had seized a public sector that was expanding, while black politicians in New York and many other American cities are inheriting municipal governments in an era of public sector decline (Erie 1988).

For West Indian immigrants the establishment of ethnic niches within the labor force, like the creation of neighborhoods, reinforces ethnic identity. Such economic niches are the classic bottom-up way in which groups create ethnicity. Yet for black immigrants, work experiences inform ethnic identity in complicated ways. While being

[108]

West Indian has a great deal to do with what jobs people get, it is often being *black* that structures the dynamics of the job situation. Low-level service sector jobs bring West Indians into direct, and in the case of household workers, intimate, contact with whites (see Colen 1987). Basch and Toney note: "Since the majority of immigrants live and socialize in black—if not West Indian—communities, the average person first meets white Americans at work. These relations are almost always asymmetrically organized: whites are the supervisors and managers—i.e. the bosses. The work context is perhaps the first arena in which the West Indian's position as a racial minority is sharply felt" (1988:5).

Thus West Indian concentration in the service sector cuts two ways. The creation of economic niches apart from the rest of the black community helps to solidify West Indian distinctiveness, but the conditions of service sector employment and what many perceive as its racially created limits on advancement heighten West Indians' sense of commonality with all blacks.

This interplay of ethnic and racial identities is further complicated by the awareness that white coworkers are themselves divided along ethnic lines that often dictate their employment opportunities. Informants speak of a "Jewish mafia" or an "Irish mafia" dominating certain positions and limiting the chances of "black people" to "get ahead." Yet they are divided as to whether the best strategy is to attack this monopolization of positions, or to emulate it.

The economic roles played by West Indians and African Americans have become more separate over time. The concentration of West Indians in the rapidly growing service sector, though it does not necessarily bode well for the long-term economic advancement of the group, does permit an independence that early generations of immigrants may not have had. In a more segregated city, the position of earlier West Indian immigrants was inextricably linked to a black community of which they were not only a part, but were often leading members. Despite their relative (and far from universal) prosperity within the black community, their advancement was limited by the limits placed on the entire black community.

During the 1970s and early 1980s, changes in the New York City economy and the nature of its labor force, along with the partial success of civil rights and affirmative action movements, had created a different structural situation for the new Caribbean immigrants. The movement of West Indians out of the declining economy of the ghetto and into the growing if often low-wage service sector permitted more latitude in their relations with African Americans. On the one hand it has decreased the direct economic ties between the immigrants and the African-American communities. On the other it has brought Caribbean blacks into direct contact and often competition with whites, which may increase their awareness of racial discrimination and produce a stronger ideological identification with African Americans. To what extent such an identification may lead to common action remains an open question.

Economic changes do not necessarily cause changes in how people think about ethnic or racial identity. But the bonds between West Indians and African Americans (or for that matter, between middle- and lower-class African Americans) may become more subjective, ideological, and subject to redefinition as a result of such changes.

[4]

Community Organizations

People always say Caribbean people are not well organized.
Caribbeans are the best organized people in the city, probably. There are halls like Tilden Hall where every Saturday
night there will be like 1500 people gathering to party, to
dance. And not just Tilden Hall; there is Trinity Hall, Rainbow Terrace. A slew of them: maybe a dozen of these places
in Brooklyn and Queens where Caribbeans meet on weekends. But this organization never becomes political.
                                    —West Indian Political Candidate

Immigrant voluntary associations and social groups have long
played political roles in U.S. ethnic politics, particularly in New York
City. Since the nineteenth century immigrants have come together
for socializing, mutual support, financial assistance, and protection,
and these associations have often provided their first entry into the
formal political structure (Bayor 1978; Hannerz 1974; Lyman 1974;
Glazer and Moynihan 1963). Political actors often express the hope
that the traditional organizations of New York's West Indian community will provide the basis for political mobilization. But the network
of black Caribbean social clubs, sports clubs, and mutual benefit societies which have been active in New York since the turn of the century, and which have proliferated in recent years, generally have not
been a springboard into New York-based political activity.

The number and diversity of Caribbean voluntary associations in
New York today is striking, particularly in light of the relative pau-
city of such organizations in Great Britain and in the Caribbean itself
(Basch 1987, Rex 1982; Pearson 1981; Rex and Tomlinson 1979;

Miles and Phizacklea 1979).[1] Basch (1987) identifies three distinct functions that these associations serve for migrant communities. The first (often noted in early sociological literature on European immigrants to the United States) is an instrumental role: providing information and assistance with the problems of housing and employment and offering limited assistance in times of financial crisis. The second is to provide a context for "ethnic" activity; the associations become, particularly early in the history of a migrant community, the locus where the culture and status hierarchies of the home country can be maintained. No doubt this has important psychological benefits for those who have lost traditional or professional status by migrating. (The survival of cultural traits under the new circumstances invariably reflects a reworking of culture within the context of the host society.) Finally, recent work (Basch 1987; Georges 1984; Kim 1981) emphasizes a third role that voluntary associations play: connecting the migrant to the home society and influencing the politics and culture of those societies.

West Indian voluntary associations, particularly benevolent societies and sports clubs, were established in fairly large numbers by the first major migrant cohort during the first decades of the century; at least thirty such organizations associated with various West Indian territories existed prior to World War II (Reid 1939; Flager 1954; Ottley and Weatherby 1967; Bonnett 1982). Several of these early groups, such as the Grenada Benevolent Association, the Sons and Daughters of Barbados, and the Jamaica Benevolent Association Inc., survive to this day. According to Reid's description, these organizations held regular meetings, heard political speakers, and organized charitable activities as well as social events, outings, and sporting activities. Groups from individual territories remained divided, how-

1. Basch notes the striking contrast between the large number of associations among Vincentian and Grenadian migrants in New York and the lack of comparable groups among their counterparts in Trinidad. She attributes this to the different position in the ethnic and political structure that Vincentians and Grenadians play in the two societies. In the United States, ethnic voluntary associations help to distinguish the immigrants from other African Americans as well as to maintain political ties to their newly independent homelands. In Trinidad, however, where the central social cleavage is between the Afro-Caribbean population and an Indo-Caribbean population of approximately equal size, black West Indian immigrants are quickly assimilated into the Afro-Caribbean population, which seeks to maximize its numbers vis-à-vis Indo-Caribbeans. Native Afro-Caribbean Trinidadians thus tend to minimize the cultural differences between themselves and the immigrants (Basch 1987).

ever, from each other and from the wider black community, and this was a source of some frustration for black political activists of the day. In Ottley and Weatherby's account of prewar Harlem these organizations are referred to by the Yiddish term *landsmanschaft* (an interesting reflection of New York City's lingua franca of the period); they note that these groups "usually remained independent and did not cooperate with other similar groups. The chief bar to unity was the existence of little known antagonisms between West Indians from different islands" (1967:194).

The main thrust of community political activity during this period seems not to have been from the benevolent societies but rather from pan-African groups, particularly those associated with Garvey's United Negro Improvement Association (UNIA). Though UNIA groups were, at least in New York, often dominated by West Indians and were at times accused by their opponents of being "foreign" in membership, they espoused the unity of all black people and opposed differentiation between Caribbean and American blacks, much less between the various island groups. The benevolent societies tended to serve individual island communities, and many of the more politically active migrants avoided these groups, which remain largely apolitical and socially conservative.

For some migrants, these groups, with their elaborate officers' titles and formal procedures, may provide some psychological compensation for the loss of premigration status, or at least help to keep alive alternative systems of self-evaluation from that of the dominant culture. Their conservatism, however, is a source of frustration for many of the younger political activists in the new migrant community. One activist says: "You go to these old benevolent meetings, and the older heads, they think that you are crazy for bringing up any of these ideas. . . . These benevolent associations these [older] guys are involved with, you know why? They got nothing else to do. It's a monthly social thing. They go there and meet their friends from home. They get together maybe once a year and party. I don't have time for that."

During the late 1930s, new types of voluntary associations emerged in New York that were directly engaged in political activity in the home countries, generally as advocates of independence. These groups were often led by some of the most prominent members of the community and in many cases were directly associated with political parties in the Caribbean. For example, the largest of these organizations in New York, the Jamaica Progressive League (JPL), was founded in 1936 and joined forces with the newly founded People's National Party (PNP) in Jamaica in 1941.[2] It has served for many years as both an immigrant association and an overseas representative and fund raiser for the PNP.[3] Such organizations also serve many informal social functions, but their dominant purpose tends to be political. Though these groups do occasionally deal with U.S. issues affecting the community, particularly immigration-related matters, these are notably secondary areas of concern.

The emergence of such groups during the late 1930s reflects historical changes in both New York and the Caribbean. In New York the decline of the Garvey movement and the ebbing of the cultural influence of the Harlem Renaissance produced a climate where the parochial issues of the specific West Indian territories became more acceptable concerns for the intellectual leadership of the West Indian community. In the Caribbean, labor unrest and pro-independence agitation mobilized and created spheres of political activity for the black majority. Generally speaking, in both New York and the West Indies the influence of the more millenarian aspects of pan-Africanism and Garveyism declined as specific nationalist political goals, principally universal suffrage and independence, became perceived as viable. Of course these issues reemerged forcefully during the 1960s and 1970s.

The career of the Jamaican activist and writer W. A. Domingo serves to illustrate the historical pattern. Domingo, who had known Garvey in Jamaica, came to New York in 1912. He was active in the early days of the Garvey movement, although he was also a member of the Socialist party. In 1919 he broke with Garvey and during the 1920s he was associated with various pan-Africanist groups and eventually the Communist party. While he continued to be involved with Communist-led activity in Harlem during the early 1930s, he shifted his focus from racial and economic issues to Caribbean concerns, be-

2. As is often the case in Jamaican society, the presence of a PNP institution called for the creation of a parallel institution affiliated with the rival Jamaica Labor Party (JLP). Thus in the 1950s the Jamaica Freedom League, a pro-JLP, pro-independence, New York-based voluntary association, was established.
3. During the Manley administration the JPL leadership, long-time Americans all, were required by the U.S. Justice Department to register as foreign agents.

coming a leading spokesman for Jamaican self-government. In 1936 he was one of the founders and the first vice president of the JPL. In 1940 he returned to Jamaica to work full-time for the PNP and was immediately interned for twenty months by the colonial authorities. He ended his career as an ardent nationalist (Hill 1983; Lewis 1968).

Both political and social-benevolent organizations, as well as sports clubs and the women's auxiliaries associated with them, grew during the middle period of immigration, when the West Indian population was in decline. Basch (1987) notes, for example, that several Grenadian and Vincentian organizations had over five hundred active members during the 1940s and 1950s, and the JPL's dues-paying membership ran into the thousands during this period. But the concerns of many of these organizations seem to have turned to narrow lower-middle-class interests. Their parochialism as well as their striving spirit was captured by novelist Paule Marshall, whose depiction of a meeting of a prototypical benevolent society of the period, the thinly distinguished "Barbadian Homeowners Association," appears in *Brown Girl, Brownstones*:

> A banner and the American flag draped the platform where the officials sat, their dark, sharply planed faces set with an almost funereal seriousness, their watchful eyes fixed on the audience. And the audience of perhaps three or four hundred reflected the officials' gravity and subjected them to the same rigid surveillance. . . . It was an installation meeting for new members and [the speaker] was telling of the Association's accomplishments and aspirations, his voice rising and falling with the rich cadence of Barbadian speech. He spoke with fervor of the "fund" to which all members contributed and which in turn made loans to members. . . . "But we got bigger plans," he shouted, and [his] high nose caught the light, "we looking now to set up our credit system under government protection. When you hear the shout we'll have our own little bank. Then watch us move. . . .
> . . . After going on for some time he bared the gold etched teeth in a smile, "C'dear, we ain all business . . . we does break down sometime and play little bridge maybe on a Sat'day night. Oh, nothing like how those big-shot white executives does play in their exclusive clubs—all the while drinking the best scotch and smoking the finest cigars. No, we don have none of that. We ain white yet. We's small timers!" he cried in sudden fury. "But we got our eye on the big time. . . .
> ". . . This then is the Barbadian Association. Still in its infancy. Still a little fish in a big white sea. But a sign. A sign that a people are

[115]

banded together in a spirit of self help. A sign that we are destroying the picture of the poor colored man with his hand always long out to the rich white one, begging: 'please, mister, can you spare a dime?' It's a sign that we has a *business* mind! I thank you!" (1981 [1959]:220–21)

But all is not well in the association. A member rises to decry the exclusion of the other blacks of the community: "We got to stop thinking about just Bajan. We ain' home no more. It don matter if we know a person mother. . . . Our door should be open to every colored person who qualify. . . . I ain gon return till I see that word *Barbadian* strike out and *Negro* put up in its place. . . ."

The speaker is shouted down. "Look how that man want us to let in every sammy-cow-and-duppy for them to take over," one woman complains. "He's nothin but a *commonist*." This leads to heated discussion of the mostly African-American roomers living in the houses owned by the Barbadians. "I does still feel sorry enough for them sometime, y'know. . . . Even though they ain Bajans they's still our color," announces a woman. "I ain sorry for blast," replies another, "I had to get mine too hard. Let the roomer struggle like I did. . . ." Marshall's protagonist, a rebellious daughter of the community who is overwhelmed by the narrowness and stifling propriety of it all, offers a harsh judgment of the group:

"Your Association? It is a band of small frightened people. Clannish. Narrow minded. Selfish. . . . Prejudiced. Pitiful—because who out there in that white world you're so feverishly courting gives one damn whether you change the word *Barbadian* to *Negro*? Provincial! That's your Association." (Ibid.:222–27)

A more charitable view of the political role of such organizations is offered by a former president of the JPL, who notes the practical assistance they offered the independence struggle and the psychological support they gave for expatriates who were far from home during these struggles:

When it come to the fourth Sunday [meeting day], I really looked forward to being here, because this is where you come to hear about things in your own country. You discuss it. And that feeling of sadness or pride or whatever, take hold of you and you say, 'gee, what am I doing here?' . . . But you see, just to sit and talk about it give you a sort of a feeling of cooperation. . . . And then, on the other hand, if you can help in any way, it give that pride, to be able to say, well at least I was here, talking about the problems of the country and maybe doing *something.*

The huge increase in West Indian immigration starting in the 1960s had a profound effect on the voluntary associations. The total number of such associations has greatly increased, though most of the older associations have lost members. A few, principally Trinidadian fraternal groups serving recent immigrants, have grown to enormous size. Yet newer groups tend to be smaller than those of the pre-1965 period. Basch estimates that most organizations in the Vincentian and Grenadian communities during the mid-1980s attract between twenty-five and fifty active members, far fewer than during the late 1950s. These new organizations are also narrower in scope and more sharply differentiated. Charitable groups raising funds for specific projects in the home countries have been on the increase, as have professional and cultural groups.

There are several reasons for these changes. Some of the older groups have declined for simple generational reasons. The former JPL president, for example, sees West Indian organizations as a dying phenomenon: "The organizations . . . were very strong in the 1950s and '60s. . . . Now it is on a more limited scale. Since the migration to the suburbs . . . children grow up and move away, old people die and it is the same thing with the organizations. They are there in name only and for the few faithful who come and keep up the tradition."

More important, however, both the older political groups and benevolent societies may have outlived their original functions. Political groups founded before the 1960s generally had independence as their primary focus, and once independence was achieved or was clearly imminent they were faced with the problems of goal displacement, compounded in some cases by the return of key activists to the Caribbean. In the case of the JPL the goal of independence was partially replaced during the 1960s by the goal of returning the PNP to power.[4] But while the goal of independence could be counted on to unite a broad segment of the immigrant community, supporting particular political parties engaged in the day-to-day politics of the var-

4. The PNP, which under Norman Manley had controlled the autonomous pre-independence government of Jamaica, lost power in a referendum on the eve of full independence in 1962. It was returned to power in 1972 under Manley's son Michael.

ious independent Caribbean nations was certain to create divisions. By the time the PNP did come to power in 1972, much of the JPL's middle-aged, middle-class Jamaican-American leadership was decidedly uneasy with the party's leftward drift—a problem that deepened as relations between the Manley government and Washington became strained during the late 1970s.

This group, like many other political organizations of the period, attempted to tone down its politics and turn its attention to U.S. concerns, addressing, as one activist recalls, "the needs of Jamaicans, where they now live." He notes that "most of us who came in the '40s and '50s are now U.S. citizens, and when you have children here, they grow up as U.S. citizens, so naturally your concerns turn to what's happening here." Yet as the registered agent of a foreign political party, the JPL was reluctant to take strong local stands. Finally, as the political and economic situation in Jamaica deteriorated, interest in Jamaican affairs among older migrants waned along with the dream of return. By the mid-1980s the JPL membership had reached its lowest point in decades, and the organization was financially in the red. The former president notes: "People got turned off to us, as part of being turned off to Jamaica in general. People used to believe they were going back. . . . They would work hard in New York, save their money and retire to Jamaica. Now they save their money and retire to Miami."

The older benevolent groups also found their original reasons for existence increasingly irrelevant to the newer immigrants. With the size of the community increasing and post-1965 U.S. immigration policy emphasizing family reunion over labor requirements as the criterion for admission to the United States, newer immigrants were, as Basch (1987) notes, more likely to look to family members rather than compatriots for support and financial assistance. The growth of a thriving insurance industry within the West Indian community, as well as the availability of health and life insurance through many of the jobs held by immigrants, has left them less vulnerable to personal catastrophe.

Paradoxically, the small size of the newer organizations may be a result of the massive growth of the community. The West Indian community today is more differentiated in terms of its educational, occupational, and class backgrounds than it was during the pre-1965 period. As Fischer (1976) notes, the critical mass of a large group coming together in a city promotes internal differentiation of a degree impossible for a smaller group, and intensifies subcultural identities through contacts with other subcultures. Thus Barbadian nurses, former Vincentian teachers, former Jamaican fireman, folk dance enthusiasts from Carriacou, and other West Indian subgroups of various ages, social classes, tastes, and political persuasions all have their own associations. Some of these groups have formed alliances, usually based on national identities. These organizations, such as the Council of Barbadian Organizations and the Trinidad Alliance, often work closely with the consuls general of their respective nations and bring the community together around Independence Day celebrations, the visits of officials from the home country, and natural disasters back home.

By the mid-1980s literally hundreds of new West Indian voluntary organizations had sprung up in the New York metropolitan area. They vary in size, function, and nation of origin, but nearly all are associated with a particular Caribbean nation or territory. In 1985 the "Caribbean Guide" published by *Everybody's* magazine listed 158 such groups. Despite the magazine's attempt to be inclusive, even this is not a complete listing.[5] Organizations with formal ties to governments are not included, although it should be noted that in the case of small countries considerable functional overlap exists between diplomatic and expatriate associations.

The Guide lists thirteen explicitly political organizations, including groups that are attempting to influence the politics of the home country as well those trying to improve the lot of West Indians in the United States. In addition to political activity these groups sponsor social affairs such as fashion shows and beauty contests. Also listed are fifty-two fraternal, social, and mutual benevolent associations. These make up the largest share of the organizations, although many of the older mutual benevolent societies exist more in name than in fact. The largest and fastest growing organizations in the community are the predominantly Trinidadian fraternal groups. Like the old benevolent societies these groups bring recent immigrants together for

5. For example, the Guide included listings for only fifteen Vincentian associations in the metropolitan area whereas Basch's fieldwork turned up eighteen. Further, the Guide listings do not include Panamanian associations, yet my own fieldwork indicates that several of the Panamanian associations in New York are dominated by West Indian, not Hispanic, Panamanians.

camaraderie, but they also provide forums for alternative status hierarchies, where the good talker, the skilled dancer, the outstanding disk jockey (not necessarily the professional or the entrepreneur) are the "natural" leaders. Such groups often bring together people of different social standing who would probably not socialize together in the home country.

Unlike the benevolent groups of earlier times, many of these clubs are not formally oriented towards economic assistance of the members. Their primary purpose is (aggressively) social; they sponsor a hectic calendar of weekend outings, dances, huge parties in various Brooklyn and Queens meeting halls, and other social events. They also engage in charitable endeavors both in the home countries (raising funds for schools and hospitals) and in New York (setting up scholarship funds) and sponsor a seemingly endless stream of awards dinners and beauty contests. These "photo opportunities" are dutifully covered in the community press, which in recent years has stimulated the interest of community political activists and black and white non-West Indian politicians in serving as awards presenters or recipients. In 1985–86 a few such organizations moved, albeit hesitantly, toward more formal political activity.

The twenty-two sports clubs, mostly for soccer and cricket, also provide reversals of normal status hierarchies, particularly for younger immigrants. As they compete against one another, they are among the few organizations that provide at least tentative links between groups. They are also increasingly branching out into other areas of activity. For example, the West Indian-led Brooklyn Soccer Association sponsored a series of Carnival weekend shows in 1985 and has become involved in charitable affairs, and its young leader has been actively courted by political aspirants.

Everybody's also lists twenty-two professional and occupational groups. Some are geared towards occupations the members hold in New York, and these fill both social and professional networking functions. Perhaps more sociologically interesting are the organizations based on positions held in the old country such as the ex-police, ex-firemen's, and ex-teachers' associations. These groups maintain ties with professional associations at home, and they also preserve the former statuses of members, many of whom have experienced a decline in occupational status upon immigration. The twelve university and secondary school alumni organizations also reaffirm premigration status by bringing together "old boys" and "old girls" who, regardless of their present positions, share both educational background and social rank in the Caribbean context.

In this respect the voluntary association reflects the temporal crisis faced by many immigrants, who have sacrificed the present for either their own or their children's future. These organizations articulate their hopes, but when the dreams and chimeras of the future are not enough to fill the void left by the death of the present, the association helps bring the present back to life. The immigrants thus cease to see themselves as immigrants—persons caught between two points—and become "ethnics," and thus members, although perhaps marginal ones, of the host society. As time goes on it is not surprising that the voluntary associations have started to express this ethnic identity.

Voluntary Associations and Political Life

By their nature, voluntary associations tend to span the gap between private and public activity. At various points these organizations will serve as semiprivate extensions of peer groups and friendship networks, or they will emphasize formal and public activity; often the two realms cannot be neatly separated. But the dominant trend in New York's West Indian voluntary associations since the resumption of large-scale immigration has been away from the internal or private concerns of group members and toward external or public concerns in both New York and the sending societies.

For earlier immigrants mutual benevolent societies addressed members' direct personal needs for emotional, informational, and financial support in the new country. This is not to say that they were apolitical; far from it. But both in the United States and the Caribbean it was race rather than national or ethnic identity that defined their social and political positions and structured their political identities. In the United States they perceived their public interests as blacks, not as immigrants, and despite frequent local conflicts with native-born blacks, it was this identity that dominated their political expression, first in the Garvey movement and other pan-African organizations, and later within the Democratic party.

For the post-1965 immigrants the first function of voluntary associations, support of group members, is less important, as it is being largely addressed now by other institutions. On the other hand, the more public role of the groups in promoting ethnic activity has grown. Voluntary associations have become a means of reproducing ethnic distinctiveness. Their many activities—dinners, dances, outings, beauty contests, sporting events—emphasize culture as a central factor in public identity. Intentionally or not, such activities tend to differentiate West Indians from African Americans (Basch 1987).

The other chief role of voluntary associations, maintaining connections to the sending society, has tended to wax and wane over the years. For many older migrants the complex politics of Caribbean nations that did not exist as such when they left is less and less relevant for their lives. For others, however, the creation of the Caribbean micro-states during the past two decades has increased the opportunities for political influence. Key positions including consul generalships and United Nations ambassadorships have gone to New York-based community activists who are members of voluntary associations. Many of these associations have developed strong reputations in the Caribbean, thanks to their political and charitable activities. Professional groups based in New York are also widely respected in the Caribbean, and their newsletters are frequently circulated there.

Though the voluntary associations have become more assertively "ethnic" in recent years, they have taken only small and tentative steps toward becoming involved in New York political affairs. Community political activists have long seen in the growing network of voluntary associations a potential source of strength, but for the most part their attempts to capitalize on that potential have been frustrated. The parochial island-based form of ethnic identity articulated by the voluntary associations has generally proven ill-suited to the needs of New York-based political actors.

Thus by the early 1980s many individuals and institutions saw the building of a pan-West Indian identity as imperative. The community press needed the entire West Indian community if it was to grow beyond the level of small newsletters. Cultural groups needed a broader constituency to maximize their impact. Would-be politicians and "ethnicity entrepreneurs" needed a pan-West Indian power base to maximize not only their appeal but also their negotiating clout. For all of these groups and individuals the voluntary associa-

[122]

tions may have provided a first step into public life, but the limitations of such organizations had to be overcome by a reformulation of ethnicity within the New York context. In the second part of this book I will address the political aspects of this reformulation, starting with the one event that suspends the normal organizational context almost completely. That event, which is simultaneously the most "Caribbean" and the most "New York" statement of identity made by the community, is the annual Labor Day Carnival.

Eastern Parkway, Labor Day 1990 (photograph by Ernest Brown).

Women from Guadalupe arrive at Ellis Island, 1911 (photograph by Augustus Sherman, courtesy of the National Park Service, Ellis Island Immigration Museum).

Multi-ethnic retailing in Flatbush (photograph by Philip Kasinitz).

Housing in Flatbush (photograph by Philip Kasinitz).

Carnival, 1990 (photograph by Ernest Brown).

"Kiddie Carnival," 1990 (photograph by Ernest Brown).

Caribbean and African-American leaders at a Brooklyn meeting in the early 1980s. From left to right: former State Senator Waldaba Stewart, the Reverend Herbert Daughtry, *New York Carib News* editor Karl Rodney, Ambassador Lamuel Stanislaus, F. Donnie Forde (photograph courtesy of Caribbean American Media Services).

Community activists distributing naturalization material on a Brooklyn street (photograph courtesy of Caribbean American Media Services).

State Senator Martin Markowitz and challenger Maurice Gumbs (center) on the campaign trail, 1986 (photographs by Philip Kasinitz).

PART II

The Politics of Ethnic Identity

[5]

Carnival: Community Dramatized

Celebration does not resolve or remove ambiguity and conflict, but rather it embellishes them. It locates these social
facts . . . in a performance context in which they can be
thought about, acted upon and aesthetically appreciated. The
celebrants' hope . . . is that the rhythm of performance will
find an echo in life, if only for the moment.
—FRANK MANNING, "Symbolic Expression of Politics"

In the preceding chapters I have examined the roots of West Indian ethnicity in the everyday experiences of Caribbean New
Yorkers. Ideas about racial and ethnic identity are shaped in neighborhoods, on the job, and in social organizations, as well by contacts
with African Americans and with whites. Nevertheless, public expressions of racial and ethnic identity do not spring automatically
from these experiences. They are fluid, creative responses to situations that are themselves often in flux.

The event that most clearly embodies the conflicts and ambiguities
of being West Indian in New York is the annual Labor Day Carnival,
held since 1969 along Brooklyn's Eastern Parkway. By the early
1980s the Carnival throng numbered as many as 800,000, bringing
together much of New York's West Indian community as well as
West Indians from other cities in the United States and Canada. The
event is a self-conscious mixture of the traditions of the islands and
the needs of the ethnic enclave. It is the source of conflict and continuing reinterpretation, for it is in this celebration that the question
of "who are we in this society" is annually raised—and never entirely
resolved.

Carnival is a dynamic arena in which various ideas may be put forward in the playful guise of celebration. Like its diaspora cousin the London Carnival (see Cohen 1980a, 1982), it is a "contested terrain," a unique space in which social and political reality are subject to redefinition. As a sphere in which the potential for both conformist and oppositional politics is always present simultaneously, Carnival is not merely a reflection of politics; in a very real sense it *is* politics, a moment when new ideas about power relations may be articulated in the context of a public drama.

The Brooklyn celebration is modeled after Trinidad's Carnival, which is also the model for West Indian celebrations in Toronto and London. Though several southern Caribbean islands with Catholic planter classes developed Carnivals independently, Trinidad has been the primary source of Carnival traditions that have spread to St. Vincent, Antigua, Dominica, and other islands. Even in staunchly Protestant Barbados the Trinidadian Carnival tradition has recently been incorporated into the modern "Crop Over" celebration (Manning 1984). Yet it is important to note that the Labor Day Carnival is a New York event, not an attempt to recreate a Trinidadian custom. Trinidadians are the second largest West Indian national group in New York, but the majority of New York's Anglophone Caribbean population comes from islands with no Carnival per se. In New York, Carnival has become a pan-West Indian event, and has been an important factor in the development of a pan-West Indian consciousness.

At times the Carnival's organizers see the event as a political expression of ethnic unity and are quick to make comparisons to other groups, the Irish and the Puerto Ricans in particular, who have used parades and public celebrations to make political statements. Yet while Carnival is in some ways analogous to these events, its own internal dynamics often subvert the efforts of political activists (and its own organizers) to use it in an overtly instrumental manner. Though it plays a central role in defining and changing group boundaries, it has not thus far been successfully employed to project or promote a specific group cadre. The event remains so fecund with political possibilities, however, that every year those who would be leaders of the community devote a good deal of time, energy, and serious thought to it.

The Carnival Tradition

Although thoroughly Africanized in the nineteenth century, the. Caribbean Carnival tradition traces its roots to premodern Europe. Pre-Lenten festivals of the flesh that suspend normal social relations and rules of decorum are a feature of many Christian cultures. In the late medieval and Renaissance periods this time of ritual role reversal was often a source of what Victor Turner has termed a "lampooning liberty" for the popular classes (1983:104). Described by one historian as a "high season for hilarity, sexuality and youth run riot—a time when young people tested the social boundaries" (Darnton 1984:83), Carnival nevertheless went beyond the mere extension of behavioral norms. It provided, at least temporarily, an alternative view of reality. In a world where social distinctions were presumed to be rooted in the nature of things, Carnival allowed people to play with that most radical of ideas: the possibility of a different social order. In *Rabelais and His World*, Mikhail Bakhtin describes the European Carnival tradition as the "chorus of laughing people," a chorus charged with creative ambiguity. He warns us not to be taken in by the frivolity of the Carnival, for "the people have used these festive comic images to express their distrust of official truth, and their highest hopes and aspirations. . . . [Carnival] was the thousand year old language of fearlessness, a language with no reservations and omissions, about the world and about power" (1968:269).

Of course the rebelliousness of the Carnival tradition was temporally contained. The festival ended predictably in the reassertion of "normal" social arrangements. In many Renaissance versions the social order was symbolically restored on Shrove Tuesday (Mardi Gras) with the execution of a straw mannequin before the taking of the ashes and the coming of Lenten seriousness that marks the return to everyday life. Thus it could be argued that Carnival distracted the poor, draining off energies that otherwise might have gone into more substantive challenges to social hierarchy.

But if the inversion and mocking of social norms and authority can be seen as a "safety valve," it was (and is) a dangerous and unpredictable one. On more than one occasion late medieval carnivals could not be contained within their ritual boundaries and became occasions for mass violence (see Ladurie 1979). However, the power of Carnival lies less in its outward challenge to any given order or official truth than in its questioning of the very *idea* of order or official truth. Lynn Hunt has noted that in sixteenth- and seventeenth-century France local populations used Carnival masks to oppose the power of bishops and local nobles and that by "the end of the old regime such battles lost their edge." However, "the revolution revived them with an infusion of new political content. In the eyes of some disgruntled locals revolutionary ideologies and republican notables had simply taken over from the bishops and the landowners" (1984:67).

Not surprisingly, in 1797 revolutionary authorities banned Carnival, the wearing of masks, and the wearing of "clothes of another sex than one's own." In explaining this edict, a commissioner of the Departmental Executive Directory of the Gironde at Bordeaux noted: "It is under the mask that one gives oneself over to the last degree of imprudence in those unrestrained games that bring ruin and desolation to families" (quoted in ibid., 1967).

The commissioner would have found much agreement in late twentieth-century Trinidad. There Carnival protests fueled the independence struggles in the 1950s and the People's National Movement (PNM) took a Carnival slogan, "All o' we is one!", as its rallying cry. Yet once in power, the PNM would also have to deal with Carnival's implicit challenge to authority. Eight years after independence, it too would consider banning the event when the "black power" movement nearly toppled the government during Carnival week of 1970.

In European societies the Carnival tradition has largely died. The modern Germans and Italians who play the roles of Rabelaisian peasants during Carnival celebrations are bawdy folklorists attempting to recreate part of a lost world. The use of archaic costumes and the general museumlike quality of contemporary European Carnivals underlines this loss of purpose. The tradition long ago ceased to be a living part of the culture, and hence it falls within the domain of the folklore enthusiast. Thus departures from traditional costumes and forms (that is to say, innovations) are seen as inauthentic.

But Afro-Creole Carnivals of the New World, including their diaspora incarnations, are living traditions. While in recent years they have felt the impact of commercialization and the tourist industry, these events have continued to grow and change, and their content remains highly charged and (in the best sense) vulgar. Originally the festivals of Catholic slave owners, Carnival traditions evolved along parallel lines in Trinidad, Brazil, and Louisiana. In each of these places Carnivals developed under white domination in the early nineteenth century (even as they were dying in Europe), and the festivals of role reversal were fueled by the tensions inherent in a slave society.

In all three cases the festivals were fundamentally changed after emancipation, when they came to be dominated by blacks. In these postslavery Carnivals, the European traditions of temporary sexual license and role reversal were joined to West African traditions of masking and magical transformation. This combination (albeit in different proportions in the different societies) of the European tradition of masquerade as satiric commentary on the social order and the West African tradition of masquerade as a source of fantasy and power produced potent Carnivals that stood in opposition to established order.

In the Brazilian Carnival the anarchic impulse continues to dominate. If Carnival seldom leads to real revolutionary activity, it is even less likely to serve as an affirmation of the social order. While highly organized, the Brazilian Carnivals maintain a structure that is contrary to, and at times a mirror image of "normal time" social life. Maria Goldwasser writes: "In *Carnaval*, men can dress as women, adults as babies, the poor as princes and princesses and, even more, 'what means what' becomes an open possibility by a magical inversion of real statuses and a cancellation or readjustment of the barriers between the social classes and categories" (1975:82–83).

The most important of these "readjustments" involves the issue of race. The Brazilian Carnival draws participants from all sectors of the society, yet "Blacks and mulattos form the very core of *Carnaval*, since they provide the organization of every samba school, while white celebrities clamor to be allowed into the *desfile* . . . " (Turner 1983:114). Thus the racial stratification system of this highly caste-conscious society is inverted, with blacks temporarily dominating the social order.

It is probably no accident that Carnivals have continued with such vitality in racially stratified societies. While nominally open class-based stratification systems generally maintain the myth of meritocracy, racial systems of stratification are conceptually based on biological metaphors ("blood," "stock") and must masquerade as expressions of the natural order of things. In these societies the reversal of the social order and the suspension of the normal rules of social life has tremendous poignancy, even when done ostensibly in jest. Carnival, the leveler, provides the space in which these fixed rules of social relations can be challenged.

Thus the New World Carnivals continue to exist as a vital part of their cultures, as evidenced by the fact that, in contrast to Europe, they have continued to grow and change. Industrialization and development have influenced the Caribbean and Brazilian Carnivals, yet during the twentieth century they have become more, not less, important. Carnival has become a forum where people confronted by the forces of sudden and uneven development have expressed their feelings of dislocation. The folklorist may be struck by the modern themes and materials in Brazilian Carnival costumes, the fusions of mass media references with traditional symbols in Trinidadian Carnival art, or the replacement of live bands by mobile sound systems in London and New York. These Carnivals, ever changing, are modern, or perhaps "postmodern," phenomena. They express the real-life situations of contemporary people. The Port of Spain slum dwellers who created their distinctive Carnival music out of the leavings of multinational oil companies are a splendid case in point.

Carnival in Trinidad

As in Brazil, Carnival in postemancipation Trinidad came to be dominated by the black poor, developing into a "symbol of freedom for the broad mass of the population" (Hill 1972:24).[1] Gordon Lewis writes: "There is no need to accept the pleasing local myth that Carnival 'breaks down the social barriers' to see in it the brief annual revolt of the Trinidadian masses against a society which, for the rest of the year, has held them captive" (1968:32). From the late nineteenth century on, the fete was marked by masquerades, the ritualized violence of calinda stick fighting, and satiric calypso music. On

---

1. As Hill (1972) notes, however, the pleasures of Carnival also continued to hold a strong attraction for many members of the local white elite, despite the disapproval of the colonial government.

several occasions during that century it was also a time of violent confrontations between the poor and the authorities (Pearse 1956).

In the mid-twentieth century highly competitive neighborhood steel bands, a sort of cross between dance orchestras and street gangs, became the central organizing force of the Carnival (Brown 1990; Aho 1987). At the same time the island's business leaders sought to use the focus on music to gain control of the event, sponsoring calypso and steel drum contests and repressing the more rebellious elements (Powrie 1956).[2] After independence in 1962 Carnival also became a source of the symbols of nation-building (Hill 1972), producing the paradox of a status-conscious elite taking its cultural cues from the poor and converting their symbols of equality into expressions of national unity.

Yet elite domination of the basically proletarian fete remains partial and uneasy. "All o' we is one" has taken on a new meaning—that despite racial division Trinidad is one nation. Yet the older meaning, the egalitarian cry of the leveler, while submerged, was never completely forgotten. Thus while the Carnivals of the immediate post-independence period tended toward uncritical patriotic celebration, since 1970 political criticism has reemerged as a central theme (Roehler 1984).

Trinidad is the cultural and economic center of the eastern Caribbean and traditionally a source of employment for persons from smaller islands. Over the years the forms and traditions of Trinidad's Carnival were spread by returning migrants both to islands with native Carnival traditions and to predominantly Protestant islands, where they merged with other masquerade celebrations. The Carnivals of many of these Protestant nations are not held during the pre-Lenten season, and the African elements of the tradition tend to dominate over the European ones.

The Trinidadian version of Carnival has also been carried by West Indian migrants to the metropoles of the English-speaking world. It now symbolizes group identity for West Indians in London and Toronto as well as in New York (Manning 1984; Cohen 1980a, 1982). In this respect Carnivals may bolster the position of those who would serve as brokers between the immigrant communities and the state.

2. This period in the development of the Trinidad Carnival is marvelously.captured in Earl Lovelace's novel *The Dragon Can't Dance* (1979).

This function is generally approved of by authorities of the host nations, and all three of these Carnivals receive some form of state funding. In supporting the Carnivals despite the objections of nativists in London or rival ethnic groups in New York, the authorities make clear their commitments to some form of cultural pluralism. At the same time, these diaspora Carnivals provide a forum in which the social hierarchy *within* the immigrant enclave can be temporarily suspended and perhaps permanently called into question. Carnivals may also challenge the normal state of relations between the authorities and the enclave. This has been particularly true in London, where the Notting Hill Carnival has often been the scene of violent confrontations between West Indian youths and the police.

Carnival in Brooklyn

Unlike the typical ethnic parade, Brooklyn's annual West Indian–American Day Carnival is largely ignored by the city's press, yet it is one of the largest regularly scheduled street events in North America. Held during the Labor Day weekend, the festival consists of four nights of concerts, steel band contests, and children's pageants on the grounds of the Brooklyn Museum, and climaxes with the huge Carnival procession on Eastern Parkway on Labor Day. These "official" Carnival events are accompanied by dozens of affiliated dances, concerts, and parties in West Indian neighborhoods around the city.

Carnival was first celebrated in New York by migrants from Trinidad and neighboring islands in the 1920s. These celebrations were privately sponsored indoor dances. Held in the pre-Lenten period, the dances were originally attended primarily by migrants from islands with Carnival traditions. Similar parties continue to be held in private clubs and ballrooms in Manhattan and Brooklyn each February, but they remain small in scale and nostalgic in tone compared to the huge New York-oriented Carnival on Labor Day. In 1947 Jesse Wattle, an immigrant from Trinidad, organized the first street Carnival on the Caribbean model that was held on Labor Day, a time more suitable for outdoor celebrations than February. This Carnival ran along Seventh Avenue in Harlem, then the heart of New York's black community. The event had the endorsement of Congressman

Adam Clayton Powell, and its reputation soon spread via calypso, the "poor man's newspaper," back to the Caribbean.

> Labor Day I felt happy,
> Because I played Carnival in New York City
> Seventh Avenue was jumpin'
> Everybody was shakin'
>
> From 110th to 142nd,
> We had bands of every description . . .
> This is the first time New York ever had
> Carnival on the streets like Trinidad.
>
> (Lord Invader, "Labor Day," Folkways Records 1956)

While based on the Trinidad model and dominated by Trinidadian organizers, this street Carnival was from its inception self-consciously pan-West Indian, and Caribbean unity (albeit on Trinidadian terms) was a central theme. The sheer numbers of people involved in such a highly visible event helped to promote a sense of group identity. One of the current organizers of the Carnival recalls attending the 1947 event while he was a student living in Washington, D.C.: "It was quite something for me. I was amazed to see the numbers of either West Indians or people of West Indian extraction that participated."

Scheduling the event on Labor Day helped to break the always tenuous connection to Catholicism of the pre-Lenten Carnival and facilitated the participation of West Indians of all religions. New York's West Indians also avoided the more overtly pan-Africanist statements made by their counterparts in London and Toronto, who scheduled their Carnivals for early August, traditionally the time when emancipation is commemorated in the Anglophone Caribbean.

In 1964, following a small disturbance, the parade permit for Carnival in Harlem was revoked. Rufus Gorin, a Trinidad-born amateur band leader who had "played mas" (i.e., joined the Carnival) in New York since 1947, attempted to organize a new Labor Day Carnival in Brooklyn, where large numbers of West Indians had settled. The small ad hoc committee he headed initially met resistance from the city, which was hesitant to sponsor a large street gathering of blacks during that riot-torn period. Gorin was even arrested one year for parading without a permit. Then in 1969 Gorin's successor, Carlos

[141]

Lezama, obtained permission to hold Carnival on Eastern Parkway, Frederick Law Olmstead's massive boulevard that runs through the heart of what are now Brooklyn's black neighborhoods, and that forms the northern boundary of Crown Heights. The Parkway, with its landscaped median strip and bench-lined double sidewalks, is uniquely suited to the huge event, although one can hardly imagine a use more distant from Olmstead's stately vision.

From the beginning the response to Carnival in Brooklyn was enormous, as one of the organizers recalls: "With the movement into Brooklyn, the Carnival took on a totally different flair, and people had a different attitude, because you saw masses now—huge numbers taking to the streets."

By 1969 the numbers of West Indians in New York had already begun to swell following the 1965 immigration reforms. Both the community and the event would grow every year until the present, and the area immediately south of Eastern Parkway became, over the years, the cultural and demographic center of West Indian settlement in New York. Carnival has been held in this location since 1969 (despite occasional attempts by local Hasidic Jews to get it moved), and the committee, still headed by Lezama, is now a permanent organization known as the West Indian American Day Carnival Association (WIADCA).

Scheduling Carnival on Labor Day had a number of unanticipated consequences. Many New York-based band leaders and costume makers attend Carnival in Trinidad, bringing back the latest in Carnival songs and fashions, and famous Caribbean entertainers frequently spend Labor Day in New York. This bidirectional influence on Carnival reflects the larger pattern of linkage between home and host societies that is an important feature of the Caribbean diaspora (Sutton and Makiesky 1975), and indeed of the post-1965 migration in general. Another result of the Labor Day date was that it virtually guaranteed that the event would be ignored outside the black community. On Labor Day the New York press focuses its attention on the parade on Fifth Avenue, traditionally the occasion for assessing the state of the American labor movement. Early organizers were unconcerned by this lack of attention, but the current leadership has made a major effort to court favorable publicity, though with only limited success.

The new location of Carnival has also been problematic. Many, including the tourist boards of several Caribbean nations, have opposed the Eastern Parkway site because it is a "ghetto" location, and a move to Fifth Avenue is often suggested. In 1982 a group of West Indian businessmen attempted to mount a "Caribbean Basin Festival" in Manhattan on Labor Day weekend. Though they maintained that the Manhattan festival would augment, not replace, the Brooklyn event, it was soon widely perceived as a more "respectable" and "professional" rival to the WIADCA Carnival. This festival, held on a pier on Manhattan's West Side, was organized as a series of formal concerts, with little of the participatory atmosphere of the Brooklyn Carnival. When the Manhattan festival failed it was considered a victory for both Lezama and the Brooklyn site.

By keeping the event on Eastern Parkway the leadership has helped to make an effective claim to turf, albeit at the expense of a wider audience. Carnival has helped to establish Crown Heights as the center of West Indian life in the United States, and since 1969 the neighborhood has become more of a center for Caribbean blacks demographically and culturally.

Even the resistance to the festival by Hasidic groups has helped the West Indian community make inroads with local politicians. For example, when plans for the event were challenged in 1983 and 1984, the local state senator, Martin Markowitz, intervened on behalf of the WIADCA. Markowitz then became a grand marshal of the 1984 and 1986 Carnivals. While this may seem a trivial bit of quid pro quo, it must be noted that Carnival was held one week before a Democratic primary in which Markowitz was to face a black opponent in a district that is 75 percent black. The value for Markowitz of being conspicuously associated with the largest assembly of nonwhite people in North America was no doubt clear to all concerned. It was something that he wanted and something that was in the power of the WIADCA to give. To the extent that WIADCA is seen as an "ethnic" leadership group, this sort of brokerage relationship becomes possible.

In sharp contrast to most of New York's numerous ethnic festivals, the Carnival lacks a centralized structure. The WIADCA obtains the needed permits and deals with city officials, yet its members are more coordinators than leaders. The other half of Carnival, the dozens of dances, shows, and parties that go on throughout the city, are all run by individual promoters who operate independently of the

[143]

WIADCA. The various steel bands and their accompanying retinues of elaborately costumed followers are also privately organized and their leaders are frequently at odds with the association.

These "bands"—some actually are steel drum bands, others are groups of costumed revelers that dance to recorded music in the Carnival procession—may number from several dozen to several hundred persons. They are loosely organized around themes that emphasize fantasy ("Galactic Splendor," "Splendors of the Far East," "Party in Space"), ethnicity ("Caribbeans Unite"), or current events ("Cry for Freedom," "Tribute to Bob Marley"). Historical themes, with costumes influenced by Hollywood epics ("Extracts from Rome"), are particularly popular, as are those that use popular culture references in bizarre juxtapositions. In 1990 one band used the theme "Ponderosa in Hell," with its masqueraders clad in black and red and wearing cowboy hats, toy six-guns, tin stars, devil masks, and wings. In general costumes are only loosely coordinated. In some bands all members are in costume, but in most only a few members wear elaborate outfits while the others simply wear matching T-shirts. All bands, however, feature at least one or two (and often a dozen) extremely complex and fantastic outfits that are not so much costumes as small one-person floats.

The leaders of these bands, most of whom hold full-time jobs in nonmusical occupations, invest a tremendous amount of time in Carnival preparations. Sponsoring a band is expensive, and while most of the leaders could be described as middle-class, none is wealthy. Most seem to harbor no political ambitions. Yet they frequently report investing thousands of dollars out of pocket for band expenses. Although some of this money is recouped through the sale of costumes, at best the bands break even, and they often lose money. The directors of the musical groups and the costume makers usually start to work in the early summer, with work reaching a feverish pitch in the month preceding the Carnival. Typically this work—men constructing the mechanical parts of costumes, women sewing—takes place in improvised "mas camps" located in storefronts, basements, social clubs, and private homes: One community leader complains about these drab surroundings: "When you look at the skill and artistry that goes into costume designing, it is worthy of a massive place, you know, where you have the room . . . [but] at the present time we lack the facilities."

Costume design has recently been subsidized by grants from the National Endowment for the Arts and the New York State Council on the Arts. Community leaders feel such funding is appropriate, and even consider it insufficient compared with other cultural events in the city, or with the large state-sponsored budget for Carnival in Trinidad.[3]

A new addition in recent years has been a tournament of steel drum groups. Many of these groups, whose members tend to be young, will rehearse intensely from the early summer onwards. In the weeks preceding Carnival a series of contests is held in Brooklyn high schools with the finalists performing at the Carnival shows.

In the actual Labor Day procession each masquerade band half marches and half dances around a flatbed truck that may carry a calypso group or a steel band or, more likely in more recent years, a huge sound system playing recorded music. The trucks display banners announcing the name of the band's leader, its theme, and its sponsors (usually local businesses). On occasion the vehicle itself is part of the display: in 1988 a local shipping company decorated its delivery van as a outrageous version of a cargo ship, complete with shipping barrels on the roof. The bands remain completely independent of and in competition with each other. Unlike the organizations that participate in most ethnic parades, the Carnival bands are organized explicitly for Carnival and are not representatives of ongoing political or social organizations (with the one exception of a prominent social club made up of Trinidadians). Hence while Carnival suspends normal organizational life, it also creates the possibility of reformulating ethnic identity.[4]

---

3. WIADCA leaders sometimes complain of being unfairly compared to the Carnival organizers in Trinidad. Although the two events are comparable in size, the Trinidad Carnival is produced by a state-funded agency, the Carnival Development Commission (CDC), which, in contrast to the WIADCA, maintains a full-time staff. This is something of an institutionalized irony. In contrast to the colonial administrations who repressed Carnival, the populist PNM government sought to institutionalize it and make it the basis of a "National Theater." Since the resumption of popular unrest in the early 1970s this has meant that the state must produce a festival that features stinging criticism of itself. During the 1980s leading calypso singers showed little reluctance to use Carnival as a platform for very real attacks on the PNM (see Roehler 1984).

4. This decentralized structure is particularly noteworthy when contrasted with the organizational dynamics of other ethnic parades. The New York Puerto Rican Parade, as analyzed by Estades (1980) and Herbstein (1978), provides a useful point of comparison. The Puerto Rican Parade was founded in 1958 and is thus roughly contemporaneous with the Carnival. The group it celebrates is also from the Caribbean and also has a longstand-

Strikingly absent from the Carnival are the numerous West Indian mutual benevolent organizations and voluntary organizations. Along the Parkway one does not see representatives of the JPL, the Sons and Daughters of Barbados, or the other island-based groups that are prominent in West Indian organizational life. This absence underscores the fact that Carnival is a special time, when normal associations and boundaries do not necessarily apply. Of course the members and even the leaders of these groups are present, but not in their organizational capacity. A number of pan-West Indian organizations including the Caribbean Youth Organization of America, the Caribbean Action Lobby, and several New York-based publications have set up information booths along the Parkway on Labor Day, but the only organization whose name figures prominently in the procession itself is the WIADCA,[5] whose members remain primarily a group of coordinators—and never completely in control of their own event.

A lack of central organizational authority is evident in the form of the Carnival procession. It starts with a collection of dignitaries, grand marshals (usually local business leaders, celebrities, and politicians), and city officials. They march, or rather saunter, down the Parkway at about noon. However, at that time the main body of the Carnival may be a mile or even two miles behind them, so few pay much attention to them. They are usually followed (as much as twenty minutes later) by a carload of beauty contest winners. They too are largely ignored. The real "action," the bands on flatbed trucks surrounded by masqueraders, may not make it down the Parkway for hours. The huge crowds that line the Parkway eating, drinking, and talking to friends show little interest in these parade elements that are grafted rather uneasily onto the Carnival form.[6]

---

ing ambivalent relationship to the black community. Yet the parade follows much more closely the model of white ethnic celebrations, the Irish St. Patrick's Day Parade in particular. Community organizations hold center stage, with hundreds of groups from antipoverty agencies to hometown clubs visually dramatizing the existing organizational structure of the Puerto Rican community.

5. While the Association's original and still primary *raison d'etre* is Carnival, it started to sponsor other cultural events in 1983, and since that time has increasingly become a year-round organization, partially in response to the expectations of the governmental agencies and politicians it works with.

6. Manning (1983b) notes a similar situation at the Bermuda National Cricket Championships where the "action" on the sidelines—gambling and the display of the latest fashions—often upstages the cricket games themselves.

Long after the dignitaries and beauty queens have made their way down the Parkway, the real Carnival begins, as more than a dozen large bands and their retinues start down Eastern Parkway. Theoretically they are in order, but the structure breaks down almost immediately. Bands stop, change direction, or take to the side streets. Most simply become bogged down in a dancing mass of humanity in which the distinction between participant and spectator quickly disappears. Many of the bands do not even finish the three-mile route in the allotted six hours. No matter. It is not a race, it is a Carnival. As a dramatic event Carnival is strikingly leaderless. There are themes and a certain ebb and flow, but no particular center or head.

The typical ethnic parade, by contrast, is based on a military metaphor and is largely *about* leadership. The dramatic structure of celebrations such as the Puerto Rican Parade or the St. Patrick's Day Parade serves to interweave the interests of the group with the careers of individual politicians. Hence, as Herbstein (1978) reports, aspiring Puerto Rican politicians invest great time and energy in obtaining Parade offices and visible positions in the event. The Parade presents the image of a unified people marching *behind* their leaders.

Carnival also draws those who seek recognition as community leaders, yet the event itself subverts notions of leadership, for it is essentially a throng of autonomous individuals. The centerless nature of the Carnival leaves the politicians and even the WIADCA officials at something of a loss as to where to be. How does one "lead" an event without a head or even a very clear direction? The grand marshals are barely recognized by the crowd; they are clearly not the focus of the event. Interestingly, neither of the two men who have dominated the WIADCA (Gorin and Lezama) have used this position to obtain higher office. Both have held respectable but rather modest jobs in their "normal time" lives. Yet during Carnival, when normal statuses are suspended, they become major figures in West Indian New York. They are recognized as such by representatives of the wider society who come to Eastern parkway to participate in the event.

As a leveling experience Carnival symbolically obscures social differences—hence part of the importance of masking. While the large bands all have themes, even they are often upstaged by individual masqueraders whose costumes may make outrageous satiric statements on recent events. The vendors who line the route and the constant stream of people in both directions along the side of the Parkway obscure any clear focus of attention. Near the Brooklyn Museum reviewing section the police attempt to keep people out of the middle of the Parkway, maintaining some semblance of a distinction between those in the procession and those watching, but further up the Parkway they generally do not even try and, in any event, the distinction becomes meaningless as the day goes on. Even the language of Carnival is participatory: one is not said to have watched a Carnival or even marched in the Carnival. Rather one "plays mas."

Carnival as a Generator of Ethnic Identity

No event is as uniquely identified with New York's West Indian community as the Carnival. It is by its nature a huge, peculiarly public, and (despite the lack of press attention) visible event, whose organizers insist that it makes an "ethnic" statement. "Ethnic" identity, however, is a feature of public life that functions on a number of different levels. Carnival clearly asserts a massive presence in New York, but unlike a parade, a Carnival cannot be easily used to make a strategic statement: it is too anarchic to be manipulated and too unstructured to lend support to a structure. Nevertheless, the message advanced is a message that Carnival is uniquely able to put forward: the simultaneous assertion of cultural particularity to the outside world and a leveling of "normal time" distinctions (particularly among nations of origin) within the community.

Politically, Carnival is more geared toward group mobilization than toward any particular issue or individual. During the 1980s several groups took advantage of the opportunity to register voters and to urge legal residents of the United States to take out U.S. citizenship. Yet their pamphlets and posters stressed only that there are huge numbers of West Indians in New York and that by participating in the United States these numbers could be converted into power. The overt assumption was that West Indians constitute a political group with clear and agreed-upon interests. The WIADCA in particular tries to get local officials to show respect for the Carnival and, by extension, to view the West Indian community as an "ethnic" group. As Lezama writes: "To West Indians, as one of the many ethnic minorities in New York, the need for social collaboration, the introduction of a feeling of community and brotherhood are variables critical to us in maintaining our existence within the wider sphere of other ethnic groups" (WIADCA souvenir brochure, 1983). A former Association officer puts it more directly: "We expect the powers that be to recognize Carnival as part of our culture, as the culture of any other group is recognized. We don't get that kind of recognition yet, but we are working towards it."

This notion, that West Indians are an ethnic group like other ethnic groups, implies the presence of clearly recognized political leaders to whom the "powers that be" can pay deference and who may serve as brokers between the state and the ethnic population. The WIADCA attempts to present itself as such a group, and toward that end it works closely and visibly with city and state officials. Yet Carnival subverts these goals, for in its satirizing of authority and hierarchy it tends to undermine the authority of its own organizers and the political officials from whom recognition is sought. Many people in the great throng do not know Lezama's name. The other WIADCA leaders are even more anonymous as they attempt to lead an event that stubbornly refuses to be led. It is the stilt walker, the devil man, the band leader, and the calypso musician who stand out from the crowd and who will be remembered—and only for their Carnival role, not for their "normal time" identity.

But if Carnival does not create group leaders, it does assert group boundaries. More than any other event it visibly embodies the emerging Pan-West Indian identity now evident in New York. As Hill and Abramson note: "Transplanted to Brooklyn, the great variety of dances seen in Island performances has dwindled to two or three steps suitable for moving down Eastern Parkway in a huge crowd. In New York City the local villager has a new identity: he or she is not just an islander, but a West Indian" (1980:83).

Because Carnival draws on the common elements of Afro-Caribbean culture, it has helped to form a conscious "West Indian" identity at a time when the politics of the Caribbean promotes differentiation among the islands. "Culture," one organizer notes, "can bring us together. Politics tends to separate us." The calypsonian Mighty Sparrow has expressed a similar sentiment:

You can be from St. Cleo, or from John John
In New York, all that done,
They haven't to know who is who,
New York equalize you.
Bajan, Grenadian, Jamaican, "toute monde,"
Drinking they rum, beating they bottle and spoon.
Nobody could watch me and honestly say
They don't like to be in Brooklyn on Labor Day!
("Mas in Brooklyn," Recording Artists Productions)

Here the old Carnival theme of leveling takes on a new meaning. To the symbolic reversal of class and caste differences is added the obscuring of differences of origin: "New York equalize you." The Carnival presents the imagery of a melting pot—not one that makes Americans out of immigrants, but one that takes "Bajans, Grenadians, Jamaicans," and creates *West Indians*.

The fractious nature of the West Indies is never completely forgotten, however. Insular nationalism often breaks through the surface of the common identity, in the privately organized parties and concerts that take place in conjunction with the "official" Carnival events. The Grenadian-born journalist Herman Hall writes: "Labor Day weekend Carnival shows are becoming more specialized as nationals from each island do their own thing. Parties organized by Guyanese are packed with Guyanese. The Haitians have their own shows, as do the St. Lucians . . . [E]ach group has its own fete" (1982:17).

Furthermore, to the extent that Trinidadian symbols have dominated the Carnival, the defining of this new West Indian identity takes place on unequal terms. Though the attempt is made to include people from throughout the Anglophone Caribbean and, more recently, Haiti,[7] the WIADCA, the steel bands, and the costume-making workshops are dominated by Trinidadians and Grenadians. Jamaicans, both the largest and fastest growing West Indian population in New York, are particularly underrepresented in Carnival organizations. In part this is because they lack a Carnival tradition; moreover, the Jamaican national musical form, reggae, is in many ways a rival to the Trinidadian calypso that dominates the traditional Carnival.[8] In

---

7. After the fall of Jean-Claude Duvalier in 1986, the Haitian presence became notably more visible, with Haitian flags, Creole posters, and Haitian bands increasingly part of the Carnival scene.
8. In Toronto reggae has become an important feature of the Carnival and reggae

New York, then, Carnival continually walks the line between its Trinidad heritage and its pan-Caribbean agenda. A Jamaica-born politician who marched in front of the 1984 Carnival puts it this way:

When you talk about Carnival, three or four different places come to my mind: Trinidad, Panama, Venezuela, maybe New Orleans. . . . [I]t's a worldwide thing. They [Trinidadians] transferred it here in their own image. I wouldn't want to take it away from them as such, you know, as being Trinidadian. And yet, you find that now it's blended. You have other groups in it. Any group you will check, you will find all other West Indians participating in it. It's not a Trinidad Labor Day Carnival, it's a Caribbean Labor Day Carnival.

The cultural tension between Jamaica and Trinidad, the two largest nations of the Anglophone Caribbean, is old. Trinidad, the home of the steel drum and calypso and a center for West Indian art, literature and dance, was clearly the dominant force during the early postwar era. During this period Jamaican popular music was largely derivative of both Trinidadian and African-American styles, and Jamaican culture in general was under the influence of the United States. The 1960s, however, saw the evolution of two distinctly Jamaican cultural forms—Rastafarianism and reggae music—that provided the language for a new flowering of Jamaican culture. By the decade's end both had burst forth from the slums of West Kingston to have an enormous influence on Jamaicans of all social classes, as well as on young people throughout the region and indeed the world. Though the split between advocates of calypso and reggae music in the London and New York Carnivals started as a Trinidadian-Jamaican conflict, it quickly came to symbolize generational splits within the larger West Indian communities.

Reggae is a mixed form. Its lyrics, shaped by Rastafarian philosophy, are militantly pan-Africanist, but its vocal harmonies and rhyth-

---

events are often among the best attended, a fact the Jamaican press reports with some pride, although this is in part due to large numbers of young whites who attend these events. In London the calypso/reggae split has divided Carnival along generational lines. Cohen (1980a) reports that since 1976 recorded reggae has come to dominate the event, although young West Indians seem to be mixing both Trinidadian masquerades and Jamaican music into a new synthesis. Cohen's (1982) article on the earlier period of the London Carnival illustrates how, beneath the presentation of unity, public festivals may be contested terrain between groups and subgroups.

mic use of electric guitars are strongly influenced by British rock music. The conspicuous use of marijuana (a sacramental plant for believing Rastas) by many leading reggae musicians also helped win acceptance of the rock audience. Thus while the respectable middle class of West Indian societies had long looked to Britain for their notions of cultural propriety, young people from the lowest strata of Caribbean society gained wide acclaim in Britain in part because they flaunted the most disreputable of lower-class Jamaican habits: ganja smoking.

By contrast, calypso and its recent derivative, soca, while older and seen as more respectable in the Caribbean, are less accessible to most European or North American listeners. The music is faster and more percussive, using blaring brass rather than guitars for rhythmic accents. While both reggae and calypso songs are often about sex, the latter tend to be bawdier and more humorous. Reggae's politics tend to be messianic and revolutionary, whereas calypso is topical and satiric, focusing on specific people and events.

My experience from 1983 to 1990 confirms Donald Hill's (1981) observation that young reggae fans tend to remain toward one end of Eastern Parkway and on side streets during Carnival, listening to recorded music, while Trinidad-style street "jump up" predominates in the middle of the Carnival throng. Not all of these young reggae fans are Jamaican, but it does seem that many young New York West Indians have taken to expressing themselves in this Jamaican mode, just as their elders tend to articulate their ethnicity in terms of Trinidadian origin.

In an attempt to include more Jamaicans and more young people in general, "reggae nights" were added to the 1983 festivities on the Thursday night preceding Labor Day. The reggae concert is both part of the Carnival and at the same time distinctly separate from the weekend's other events. "The Jamaicans," Lezama was been quoted as saying, "wanted their own night" (*Jamaica Weekly Gleaner* 1983). Given the association with Rasta, marijuana, and a more militant racial stance than the WIADCA usually assumes, the inclusion of the reggae concert represents a major, if tentative step towards a broader conception of Caribbean unity. A further step in this direction was taken in 1987 with the addition of a "Haitian Night," featuring Haitian music and dance, on the museum grounds.

At the same time, the Association continues to seek funding to train young U.S.-born West Indians in such skills as costume making and steel band music, thus promoting their own particular (basically Trinidadian) definition of West Indian culture. They have also sponsored an annual "Kiddie Carnival," held on the afternoons preceding the Saturday and Sunday night Carnival shows. In these events children compete for prizes for the best costumes and dance to calypso on the big stage as proud parents fawn and flashbulbs click. The WIADCA sees these events as ways to pass on "ethnic traditions" to the young, an idea which is very consistent with American notions about the role of ethnic culture, even if it co-exists somewhat uneasily with the bawdier side of Carnival.

It is not altogether surprising that the funding for these children's events has come from the government (specifically the National Endowment for the Arts and the New York State Council on the Arts). The acceptance of an "ethnic" self-definition led the WIADCA leadership to look to the state believing that their ethnic assertion should be supported as the cultures of other groups are recognized and supported. However, the very self-consciousness of this effort changes the nature of the events.

Carnival has helped to redefine ethnic boundaries and has provided a public forum in which the content of "ethnicity" is playfully worked out, but at the level of ethnic identity that relates to outsiders it has been only partially successful. Though WIADCA leadership projects an image of West Indians as an ethnic group and asserts rights based on that identity, members of other groups are generally not present at Carnival to sample West Indian culture. The audience is almost entirely black and overwhelmingly West Indian; most white Brooklynites are barely aware that the huge event takes place.

In terms of explicit political mobilization, the organizers walked a thin line during the 1970s. On the one hand, the attempt was made to keep Carnival from serving as a device to endorse specific candidates or programs. But on the other, the WIADCA solicited state sponsorship and sought the endorsement of the politicians, which they felt was their due. By the 1980s an apolitical Carnival had become impossible.

Carnival and Politics

In 1984 the WIADCA lost its political innocence. The selection of Senator Markowitz as a grand marshal constituted the virtual endorsement of a white politician fighting to retain a seat in what had become a 75 percent black district. This, in addition to the handling of Jesse Jackson's appearance at Carnival that year, opened a rift between the WIADCA and Brooklyn's dominant coalition of black political leaders.

The underlying ambiguity of the West Indian community's relationship with the rest of black New York comes to the surface in the Carnival. Despite frequent talk of black unity and allusions to Pan-Africanism, Carnival by its nature differentiates West Indians from other blacks.[9] For the earlier organizers it was important that these differences be defined as narrowly "cultural." Carnival provided an arena where they might be expressed more directly than they generally were in politics. In recent years, though, politics has come more openly into the Carnival. In 1984 the Reverend Jesse Jackson made an appearance, arranged by WLIB, New York's leading black radio station. WLIB is owned by former Manhattan borough president Percy Sutton, and has over the years fluctuated between generally black and specifically Caribbean programming. The Jackson appearance was arranged at the last minute (he was coming to town to make a number of campaign stops for Walter Mondale and to endorse Queens congressional hopeful Simeon Golar), and was approved by the WIADCA on the eve of the event. Jackson's plans were not announced to the public until Labor Day morning.

Jackson was driven in from behind the Brooklyn Museum to the reviewing stand at 5 P.M. Rather than appear on the reviewing stand where he would have been photographed with Markowitz, he spoke at a separate podium set up by WLIB. His speech was carried on WLIB and (in a McLuhanesque touch) broadcast to the crowd by thousands of individuals who turned up the radios they were carrying. Jackson seemed unaware of the Caribbean nature of the Carnival. After getting the crowd fairly quiet, the band sound systems turned off, and the music stopped (no mean task), Sutton introduced Jackson. Jackson in turn introduced Assemblyman Al Vann and a number of other non-West Indian black politicians. He did not introduce Lezama or the other WIADCA officials, nor did he make any

9. Even the invocation of pan-Africanism is often couched in terms derived from Garveyism and Rasta, which have special meaning to West Indians. Thus while the stated message is the unity of all black people, the form of presentation emphasizes Caribbean particularity.

mention of the Association. After his opening remarks Jackson surprised revelers by launching into his standard stump speech, culminating in his personally registering several people to vote. The immediate crowd, numbering a few thousand, were attentive, but the rest of the throng, numbering several hundred thousand, were uncomfortable and restless as they listened to the disembodied voice coming from hundreds of radios. Several times band sound systems suddenly blared on for a moment, then were quickly turned off. Jackson referred to the legacy of a number of black historical figures, but only the name of Marcus Garvey drew a major response from the crowd. After his lengthy remarks he ducked into a van operated by WLIB, where his photo was taken with a number of politicians including Carl Andrews, Markowitz's opponent.

Lezama and the other WIADCA officials were furious at what they regarded as a snub. But their anger was directed less at Jackson, who remains extraordinarily popular in the West Indian community, than at the local African-American politicians who stage-managed his appearance. A publisher and former member of the WIADCA says "It was really a disgrace and an insult to the Caribbean community the way WLIB handled it." Other community leaders reacted similarly. Interviewed a few months later, a leading West Indian journalist recalled:

It was an abortion. I mean here was Jackson speaking to the largest crowd he had ever addressed, and if ever they wanted an opportunity to do something for black unity, this was it. Instead they insulted people. . . . If they wanted to demonstrate unity, Rainbow Coalition or whatever, he would have had a Caribbean person introduce him, he would have had a picture taken with the Caribbean leadership, and there would have been a sense of recognition of the community. . . . I mean, if Jesse goes to Moscow, he is briefed, right? He knows who he is going to speak to and what to speak about! But with us no one saw the need to brief him at all. . . . It was a real insult.

A West Indian political candidate allied with Markowitz noted: "I was on the platform and I was just so mad, I thought, O.K. Jesse, well let's continue [motions as if turning a sound system back on] . . . not that we had anything against Jackson, but to express how mad we were about the way the thing was handled."

While the feathers ruffled on the Parkway that Labor Day were eventually smoothed over, the incident was not atypical of New York black politics in the mid 1980s. The native African-American leadership, inspired by the rhetoric of unity and the presence of a crusading national leader, took its West Indian component for granted. The Caribbean "leaders," particularly those whose leadership is largely restricted to Labor Day weekend, were quick to take offense at what was seen as a snub on the very day they celebrated West Indian distinctiveness. Carnival is an experience in which the question of "who we are" is annually raised anew and is of particular importance for Caribbean blacks who are all too aware that they are not generally perceived as distinct from the rest of the black community, neither by whites, blacks, nor (in many social contexts) even by themselves.

The WIADCA's immediate reaction to the events of 1984 was to promise that there would be no political speakers at future Carnivals. Yet by 1985 a number of politicians (only a few West Indian) had seized upon Carnival as an opportunity to get their message across and had undertaken partial sponsorship of "mas" bands so that their names would appear on the trucks. Thus signs saluting "City Councilwoman Rhoda Jacobs" and the "Greater Flatbush Independent Democratic Club," urging "Andrew Stein for City Council President" and "Roy Innis for Congress" (in 1986), and even "Free South Africa" hung alongside those naming Caribbean bakeries, shipping companies, and restaurants.

In 1988 Jesse Jackson returned to the Carnival under very different circumstances. Jackson had galvanized New York's black community during the city primary several months before, and his popularity among West Indians had soared. He had also carefully mended fences with community leaders during the intervening four years. Jackson spoke from a small platform in the middle of the Carnival route and was sponsored by the Caribbean Action Lobby. He spoke on Caribbean issues, made no attempt to stop the main procession, and mingled with the crowd.

Having reversed their "no political speakers" policy, the WIADCA was careful not to take sides in a politically contentious year. It also invited Mayor Koch, who used the opportunity to snub labor union leaders with whom he was feuding by going to Eastern Parkway instead of the Labor Day Parade. Koch spoke to a small group at the museum end of the Parkway early in the day, long before the main body of the procession arrived. Careful crowd control allowed only a small minority of the Carnival throng anywhere near the speaker's platforms, and Jackson and Koch (whose relations were strained, to say the least) scheduled their appearances so as not to be in Brooklyn at the same time. The organizers also allowed two of New York's most controversial African-American activists, C. Vernon Mason and the Reverend Al Sharpton, to march with the other dignitaries. While supporters of Mason and Sharpton (a mix of native and Caribbean blacks) heckled Koch, all of the politicians were kept far from the main body of the event. Most of the crowd never saw any of them and were probably not aware of their presence.

Several younger Caribbean politicians and political aspirants feel that Carnival should embrace a political position more pointed than this all-inclusive neutrality. They see the event as an opportunity that has not been sufficiently exploited. One noted in 1985:

> Informant: You look at the West Indian Carnival, it grows bigger and bigger every year and it's going to get better. That is an instrument that those of us who are political have always wondered why it is not used in a more political way, and the reason why is that those who brought it into being were not really political animals. . . . [T]hey saw it as an art form. We see it as an assertion of the culture, but also as a shining instrument that should be used to galvanize political activity around it. Those of us who are political have more or less been kept away from it, or stayed away by choice. In due course we will take it over.
>
> P.K.: Specifically, what would you change?
>
> Informant: Well, you look at who becomes the head marshal, in the past they've used Cuomo, they've used Koch, last year they used Marty Markowitz, stuff like that. . . . [M]ore progressive thinking people might not have used Marty . . . but these are people they have a beholden relationship to for things like grants and the like.

This individual may underestimate the extent to which the "ethnic" parade model, including references to a "Jewish" or "Irish" road to incorporation into U.S. society made by Lezama and the other WIADCA leaders, *is* in fact a political position. To make a statement of cultural difference in a city where political goods are popularly seen as being distributed along ethnic lines is to make a claim for a type of equality, or at least for "ethnic" prerogatives. The statement says, in effect, "I am different, therefore I am equal, and thus I am

entitled to what the other groups get." Still, he is correct in saying
that Carnival has not been widely used as a forum for directly promoting Caribbean politicians or policies. In part this is due to the
organizers' attempting to cling to the fete's anarchic Trinidadian
form. Ironically some of the younger, more militant politicians propose a Carnival that would be closer in format to the typical American ethnic parade. Colin Moore, a *Carib News* columnist who is considered to be on the left wing of New York's Caribbean leadership,
puts it this way:

> [T]he organizers of the Carnival have not outgrown their parochial
> roots. The gentlemen from Laventille, Sangre Grande and Arima still
> view Carnival as an opportunity to "play mas." They could not per-
> ceive its broader cultural implications or political significance. As a
> result of this shortsightedness, this gerontocracy of aging "mas men"
> has been unable to impose the discipline, organization and creativity
> necessary to transform the Carnival from a Laventille affair into a Car-
> ibbean event, from a Brooklyn road march into a citywide media
> event, from a backyard bacchanal into a significant political event.
> (1985:15)

He goes on to propose a stronger sense of "discipline" and to urge
more participation by community organizations and politicians. He
notes that "A parade is not only a spectacle of people marching on a
street. A meaningful parade must also reflect the attitudes of the
sponsors about local, national or international affairs" (ibid., 15).

These activists urge a more assertive ethnic stance for West Indians, but they would have them take this stance by curbing the
unique features of the event and conforming more closely to the
standard ethnic parade format. But this sort of ethnic community-
building is in some ways less a challenge to the established order
than the traditional Carnival. Those who would formalize and "discipline" Carnival (both the old guard "mas men" like Lezama and the
more radical activists quoted above) would confine it to a form that,
though lacking in "creative ambiguity," could be easily understood
by the wider society. They take their model not from any Caribbean
experience but rather from the many existing ethnic parades in New
York. Both conservatives and radicals see acceptance of this model as
a sign of being "serious."

Given the antiauthoritarian nature of the event it remains to be seen whether these younger politicians will be able to channel it towards more formal political ends. Carnival is not a forum that can easily be turned into a promotional device, but it remains the place where the idea of a Caribbean community in New York can be put forward and dramatized. So long as its form remains in flux, it will continue to provide the social and temporal space in which notions of group identity can be played with. By participating in the Carnival, huge numbers of people are exposed to such notions. Thus a pan-Caribbean community becomes a reality, at least for Labor Day, and for the rest of the year, a possibility.

[6]

The Leadership

Who speaks for the Caribbean Community? . . . A friend suggests a method of determining who the true leaders are. . . .
(a) Invite all those who claim to be Caribbean leaders to a free
boat ride up the Hudson. A few boats may be necessary. (b)
Take on the boats one 500 pound sack of rocks for each self-
proclaimed Caribbean leader. (c) Anchor in deep water up the
river. (d) Bind each Caribbean leader hand and foot, attach a
500 pound sack to each one, and throw them all into the
river. (e) Wait patiently for the true leaders to break the surface of the water.

—MAURICE GUMBS, "Who Speaks for the
Caribbean Community?"

Twenty-five years ago dozens of West Indians occupied prominent political and economic positions in New York's black community, yet few would have claimed to be "Caribbean leaders." Today
dozens of persons have put themselves forward as such. They have
created a network of interlocking organizations and committees, most
of them *ad hoc*, that reflect their shifting alliances and rivalries.
Their activities fill the community press, which plays the role of
kingmaker among them but also depends on them for access to information. They spend a great deal of time giving each other awards
and creating "photo opportunities."

While these prospective leaders differ greatly in ideology and ability, they are united by two fundamental beliefs. First, they agree
that there is a West Indian community to be led. This means that
they must emphasize West Indian distinctiveness both in terms of
culture and group interests, while at the same time transcending the
traditional organizational infrastructure of the community, which is
based on separate nations of origin. Second, they appear to agree

[160]

that something is to be gained by being recognized as the leader of that community.

By believing in and seeking out a West Indian community, these leaders are at least partially responsible for inventing it. As John Higham notes, the amorphous nature of American civil society places ethnic groups in a tenuous position organizationally. "Ethnic groups," he writes, "lack either legal definition or a distinct assured territorial base. Unlike families, cities or universities, ethnic groups have no encompassing institutional framework" (Higham 1982:70). Nonetheless, ethnic groups are recognized as vital units in governing many American cities. Appeals for ethnic electoral support and the search for an ethnically balanced ticket are no longer conducted *sub rosa*. Ethnically based exit polling has made it possible to assess the success of such efforts on a group-by-group basis. But although ethnic groups are real, they are loosely structured, and to the extent that they function as interest groups they are largely the creations of a loosely defined leadership. Higham writes:

> If an amorphous social structure has tended to weaken and fragment ethnic leadership, it has also given ethnic leaders a special importance. To them in large measure falls the ever pressing task of defining the group. With certain exceptions, ethnic communities cannot take their existence for granted, so leaders must clarify what the social structure leaves indistinct or indeterminate. Leaders focus the consciousness of an entire group and in doing so make its identity visible (ibid.:70).

In New York's West Indian community the leaders and would-be leaders stand between two traditions of leadership. They bring with them an understanding of the highly ambiguous role that "leaders" play in the Anglophone Caribbean. They also have at least some idealized notion of the role that "ethnic" leaders have played for other groups in New York. In moving between these two traditions Caribbean leaders attempt to carve niches for themselves.

The interplay of these traditions can be problematic. One of the most striking features of the former slave societies of the Anglophone Caribbean culture is a deep suspicion of authority in general and political leadership in particular (see Pearson 1981; Wilson 1973; Singham 1968). In such societies, for a member of the black masses to make a claim to power is to leave himself or herself open to the charge of forgetting or perhaps betraying his or her roots. Such a person who obtains high office or even gains the attention of political officials is likely to be suspected of self-serving motives, even while being admired for gaining access to the institutional sources of power.

Peter Wilson, in his study of Provedencia, suggests that for black West Indians a complex relationship exists between "respectability," which often amounts to conforming to approved white standards, and "reputation" within the black community, which "prizes in particular those talents and skills which bolster self image by putting down, undermining and ridiculing respectability" (1973:223). Gains made by becoming more respectable are accompanied by a loss of reputation. The individual who is too successful in gaining respect may be pulling himself up at the expense of others. Yet for an aspiring political leader the rejection of respectable standards is also deemed inappropriate. And so the dilemma: leadership requires respectability, yet respectability undermines the tie to the community, and thus the legitimacy of leadership.

The conditions of the diaspora community further complicate this relationship. New York's political leadership, black and white, recognizes a community of considerable size and potential strength and seeks out those who could be spokespersons for that community. These would-be brokers are then torn between the need to shore up their position within the community and the needs of the political structure on whom they depend for recognition as "respectable" ethnic leaders.

A conversation I had with an informant at a mass meeting in Brooklyn that featured a Caribbean prime minister sums up much of the ambivalent attitude of the West Indian community toward its "leaders." As we waited for the prime minister's arrival our attention was drawn to one of the organizers of the rally, who was working the crowd. He was a handsome young man, wearing an impeccable suit with a red carnation in the lapel, greeting everyone. It was clear that he was very much the man in charge and also a bit nervous as the prime minister was more than two hours late. My informant, knowing I was interested in leadership, pointed him out to me and remarked:

Informant: Oh, there is [name]. . . . He is really movin' up. You see him everywhere now. Yes he is really doing all right.

PK: What do you think of him?

Informant: Well, he is one of a long line of this sort of politician, you know—a breed we have a lot of in the Caribbean. He is good looking and he talks real good, a good orator, but that is mostly what he is, you know, talk. This sort of fellow, I suppose they have the interests of the community at heart, but they also wear their ambition on their sleeve. Still, he may get something out of it. I wish him well.

Here the leader is seen as playing a game. He is admired for his skill at the game, and his value to the community will be judged in terms of his usefulness. His popularity is based on what he can deliver, but also on personal popularity and, in no small part, how good a show he can put on.

Given Caribbean ambivalence about leadership, it is not surprising that the man most frequently identified in the community press and by my informants as a leader of Brooklyn's West Indian community denies being a leader at all. "I am not a leader," he states with a bit of a smile, amused but not surprised that someone interested in group leadership should come to him. "I have never led any organization. I am studying to be a good follower. One of the problems of this community is that we have too many leaders and not enough good followers."

Since the late 1970s a number of distinct modes of ethnic leadership have been visible in New York's West Indian community. There is an "old guard": middle-class, usually middle-aged leadership group that maintains close, if paternal, ties to many in the Caribbean community and is connected to American political figures as well. For the old guard power is seen as an informal relationship to those they see as the source of power. They seek to be the patrons and the "kingmakers" of the community. They have generally been hesitant to offend the status quo in the United States and they make few demands on public officials; they seek primarily to be consulted and are satisfied when they have been granted access. For them it is enough to be conspicuously connected to those with power, perhaps winning for the community a sense of vicarious participation. Since members of the old guard prefer informal authority, they have founded few organizations.

In recent years this old guard has been joined by a new breed, generally somewhat younger, whom I term the "ethnicity entrepreneurs." These are people who make their living by bridging the gap between the polity and the Caribbean community. Unlike the old

guard they are "joiners" and they have produced a plethora of community organizations. They hold formal leadership positions (sometimes self-created) and are far more public than their elders in celebrating their ethnic heritage. Yet in many ways their position is less
dependent on the Caribbean community than on the sponsorship of
the political establishment. They capitalize on both the state's interest in supporting ethnic organizations and the needs of local politicians to make ties to the growing Caribbean community.

Finally there are those who actively seek public office, the politicians whose changing position I will explore further in Chapter 7.
Increasingly these people seek to use the Caribbean community as a
power base. At the same time they cannot afford to limit their activities to the community. Political aspirants must maintain a strong
identity with the community in order to avoid appearing to have
forgotten their roots, but they must also carefully avoid alienating the
members of other ethnic groups whose support may be necessary
later on. Thus they must juggle racial, ethnic, and ideological identities as they move through the ever more complex terrain of New
York politics.

The Old Guard

"The old middle-class leadership is still very much represented in
the totality of the Caribbean leadership today. Fortunately, we as
Caribbeans have a sophisticated mechanism for dealing with that.
We venerate them." Thus, with tongue slightly in cheek, a leading
political actor assesses the community's most prominent members.
The older Caribbean leaders, centered mainly in Brooklyn, differ
markedly from those younger men who came to prominence in the
early 1980s. Their backgrounds in the Caribbean were generally
middle-class and they often hold professional status in New York, a
fact that contrasts them sharply with the younger "ethnicity entrepreneurs," whose ranks include both intellectuals and individuals
whose Caribbean roots were decidedly proletarian.[1] Though their

1. By "proletarian" I mean skilled workers, small farmers, and low-ranking civil servants of the Caribbean. These individuals constitute the upper working class in societies
where to be "working-class" is a *relatively* privileged position. Yet their class position is

leadership is informal and highly clientelist, the old guard are an important factor in Caribbean-American politics, and few events of any significance are not graced by the attendance of their more visible leaders. Their significance is largely in the links they effect. They link the post-1966 immigrants with the more thoroughly incorporated pre-1930 immigrant cohort; the new immigrant communities with established politicians (with whom they have extensive though informal relations); and, increasingly, the U.S. immigrant community with governments back home.

The current old guard are actually an intermediate generation in the experience of New York's West Indian community. They are mostly from the smallest cohort of immigrants, those who arrived in the United States between World War II and the 1965 immigration reforms. Also included in the group are some of the U.S.-born children of the pre-1930s cohort, although most of these individuals made little of their Caribbean connection until quite recently.

Most of this group, who were in their early fifties to early seventies at the time of this research, were too young to have been shaped by the Harlem Renaissance, the Garvey movement, the expansion of the New York Caribbean community of the 1920s, and the heyday of Communist and other labor movement activity in Harlem during the 1930s.[2] At the same, unlike the younger activists, they came from a colonial rather than an independent Caribbean and had already come of age long before the "black power" movement's impact on the West Indies. Middle-aged and professionally established at the time of the

---

clearly different from the largely professional community leaders (often physicians) described in this chapter, and they would have little chance for association in their home countries with some of the old guard leaders or with the younger university-trained intellectuals they associate with in New York. This fact is often noted with some irony on all sides.

2. The few surviving members of the earlier generation of Caribbean activists are sometimes adopted as father figures by the current generation of Caribbean activists. Yet for the most part these individuals have made little effort to participate in West Indian ethnic politics and have chosen instead to continue activity through black political organizations or labor unions. Many continue to avoid publicity and warn of potential ethnic splits within the black community. Wesley McDonald Holder, the Guyana-born ex-Garveyite considered the dean of black Brooklyn politics, ran Mayor Koch's largely successful 1985 campaign in Brooklyn's black community despite being eighty-eight at the time, yet he sought and received almost none of the publicity associated with "Caribbeans for Koch." Holder went out of his way to help me contact other Caribbean political actors, but he politely and firmly declined several requests to be interviewed about his own past and present activities.

community's greatest growth, these leaders inherited a ready-made constituency. Yet they also found themselves very quickly at risk of being passed by a politically ambitious younger generation.

In the case of the most prominent member of the old guard, Dr. Lamuel Stanislaus, the transition from neighborhood patriarch, informal West Indian cultural broker, and Brooklyn dentist to Grenadian diplomat and New York City mayoral advisor belies the usual assumptions about the one-directional nature of the assimilation process. Stanislaus's increasingly formal roles in both New York City ethnic politics and in international politics have actually reinforced and facilitated each other. His situation illustrates the cross pressures that leaders his generation are subject to, and also the inadequacy of certain conceptual categories in the discussion of "assimilation" among contemporary immigrant groups.

Stanislaus was born on the tiny island of Petit Martinique, the smallest of the three islands that today make up the nation of Grenada. Son of the local schoolmaster, he nonetheless spent his early years in a cottage with no running water or electricity. His journey from this third world backwater to New York City took place in several stages. As a boy he had to travel from Petit Martinique to the slightly larger island of Carriacou, from which he took another boat to the main island of Grenada to attend secondary school. It was on these trips from Carriacou that he formed a friendship with his fellow "small islander," the future Grenadian prime minister Herbert Blaize. The friendship would continue for fifty years and shape the political futures of both men. Blaize and Stanislaus attended school in the city of St. Georges; a small capital of a tiny colony, it must nonetheless have seemed a bustling metropolis to the young men from the outer islands. After graduating Stanislaus moved on to work in the regional metropolis of Port of Spain, Trinidad. In 1945 he attended college and dentistry school at Howard University in Washington, D.C., and finally, in 1956, he moved to New York, where his father had migrated some years earlier.

This respectable but marginal background—a "good" family from an isolated region—is not atypical of the Caribbean migrants who made good in New York City in the postwar period. Though sometimes derided as "small island men" by comparatively cosmopolitan Jamaicans and Trinidadians, migrants from small territories were disproportionately well represented among the prominent West Indian

New Yorkers of that time.[3] Why they did so well at this period is a matter for speculation, but one might well hypothesize that the small islands represent a more extreme version of the conditions that force migration throughout the Caribbean. Constricted opportunity, poverty, and isolation force many, and particularly the talented and ambitious, to start seeking opportunities elsewhere at a very early age. Emigration becomes a normal, expected part of the adult life cycle, fundamental for both individual advancement and the economic survival of the community.

By the time Stanislaus left home the main flow of West Indian migration was headed for Britain rather than the United States. When he arrived in New York fresh from Howard in the 1950s, his profession made him a respected member of the small West Indian enclave in Brooklyn. The migrants of the first three decades of the century were already established within the broader black community, and the newer immigrants were comparatively few in number and modest in their expectations. In this community Stanislaus found a clientele in need of his professional services. His status, personal charm, and emphasis on West Indian camaraderie and mutual assistance, as well as a reputation for professional competence, quickly made him a success.[4]

This success led to invitations to take prominent roles in Grenadian and West Indian cultural activities. Like his schoolmaster father, Stanislaus soon found he had a talent for public speaking, and

3. Of course "small" in this case means small by Caribbean standards. Jamaica, with an early 1980 population of 2.25 million, or Trinidad with 1.2 million are indeed very small nations, but veritable giants compared with Grenada (110,000) or St. Vincent (115,000). All of these nations, however, are far larger than the tiny islands that make up the smaller parts of the new Caribbean nation states, such as Carriacou and Petit Martinique in Grenada (combined population of less than 10,000), Nevis in the nation of St. Kitts and Nevis (population approximately 12,000 of the 44,000 national total), or the British territories of Montserrat (12,000) and Anguilla (6,500).

Among the small islanders and their descendants who became prominent in New York are J. Raymond Jones, the first black Democratic county leader (St. Thomas), Bertram Baker, the first black elected to the New York State Assembly from Brooklyn (Nevis), long-time Harlem city councilman Fred Samuels (Montserrat), New York judge Bruce Wright (father from Montserrat), and former state senator Basil Patterson (father from Carriacou).

4. Ulf Hannerz has written about the role that professionals such as Stanislaus play in American ethnic communities: "Even when most of the membership of the group has been restricted to the positions in the lower strata originally assigned to them by the dominant group in the society, some members . . . [are] able to advance themselves through enterprises of this kind without becoming heavily dependent on the patronage of outsiders" (1974:54).

although he accepted no formal leadership role in the benevolent societies, he found that he was frequently called on to serve as master of ceremonies at their various functions. This prominence in turn enhanced his professional reputation.

Stanislaus's frequent contacts with community members made him a focal point: he was willing to sell a few tickets for an affair to his clients, or use his office as a distribution point for publications or political material he approved of. He also developed a reputation as a man who would help out his fellow immigrants, easing their transition to the new country, and eventually he emerged as something of a community spokesman. Though Stanislaus was financially able to move to the suburbs or to a fashionable neighborhood of Queens, he continued to live in Brooklyn and raised his five children there.

He cultivated the press, and his statements and activities frequently found their way into columns by fellow West Indians in the *New York Amsterdam News* and (on those rare occasions when it paid the community any attention) the mainstream press as well. When a West Indian press came into being during the 1980s he quickly became one of its favorite personalities. *Everybody's* magazine has twice named the dentist its "man of the year," placing him in the company of Nobel laureate Arthur Lewis and Congresswoman Shirley Chisholm. Yet despite this prominence Stanislaus displayed a West Indian preference for informal authority. He rejects the description of himself as a community leader and he has often taken informal and background roles in organizations officially led by people far less prominent and well educated than himself.

As is typical for West Indian activists, Stanislaus made his first contacts with U.S. politics through the parochial island benevolent associations:

I joined the Grenada Benevolent Fraternal organization shortly after setting up my practice in New York, and though the thrust was not political we can not get away from the fact that politics engulfs every phase of our lives and activities. Through some of my Grenadian brothers and sisters I got to see that there was an interest in our homeland, and naturally politics entered into that. Also a lot of them were talking about "letting down your bucket where you were," and taking an interest in affairs here.

Grenadian and U.S. politics were not mutually exclusive. In the early 1960s Stanislaus's stature in the Grenadian organization increased both because of his growing professional reputation in New York and his personal relationship with Herbert Blaize, then emerging as the principal opposition leader (and briefly colonial chief minister) of Grenada. In fact it was an island concern—a New York fund-raiser to build a high school on Carriacou during the mid-1960s—that brought Stanislaus into contact with Shirley Chisholm, then running for the state assembly. He recalls: "She was making her bid for elected office on the state level . . . and she asked for an opportunity to address the group, seeing as it was a Caribbean gathering. Blaize, who was then chief minister of Grenada, was there and we met Chisholm for the first time. She got me interested in local politics and after that I started to work with the Chisholm campaign."

Chisholm was born in Brooklyn, but her parents were from Barbados and she spent part of her childhood there. She was one of the younger members of the Unity Democratic Club, a group of black activists (many were New York-born children of West Indian parents) who were then challenging Brooklyn's white Democratic machine and its West Indian allies. Like the rest of this group (and for that matter many of their opponents), Chisholm identified herself publicly with black rather than specifically Caribbean interests. Still she was unusually emphatic about her Caribbean roots and made frequent contact with Caribbean organizations. Her outreach to this community won her loyal supporters and a source of funds.

Although he stayed in the background, Stanislaus became a fund-raiser and activist. He worked on Chisholm's campaigns for the assembly and Congress and, as he says, "one thing led into another." He was active in the Bedford-Stuyvesant Restoration Corporation, which brought him into contact with state and national political figures. He also became a behind-the-scenes figure in the WIADCA, in which he served as a broker between the Association and the various political figures it has contact with.

In 1977 Stanislaus took an unusually public stand in founding a group called "Caribbeans for Percy Sutton," which raised money for the former Manhattan borough president's run in the mayoral primary. The group is historically important for two reasons. First, it was the first time that a group of Brooklyn West Indians had given political support as West Indians. Although they were supporting an African-American candidate, they did so as a distinct constituency, a self-conscious interest group. Second, Stanislaus and his group came out of the primary with a less than favorable impression of many

African-American political leaders. Years later, when his own support of Mayor Edward Koch was being roundly criticized in the black community, Stanislaus would recall:

> You see [in 1977] I was telling my black brothers and sisters, some of them American, that Sutton is the man, that we have a beautiful opportunity and your ethnic pride should move you in that direction, [and] they were giving me a lot of reasons why they were not behind him. They were saying Sutton is too close to Jews and all kinds of nonsense. What the hell, you cannot win an election in New York without getting support of Jews and other ethnic groups: blacks alone cannot win a citywide election. And *I* spent a lot of time and *money*, because I thought I had the vision. So in supporting Koch, now, I make no apologies.

"Caribbeans for Percy Sutton" brought together, under Stanislaus's leadership, a group of middle-class West Indians who were beginning to feel ignored by New York's black leadership (some of whom were of Caribbean descent). Over the next several years, as the visibility of the Caribbean community increased and the number of West Indians holding elected office diminished, this dissatisfaction would become more pronounced. Although many West Indians maintained informal ties with many politicians through the political clubs, the replacement of many clubhouse politicians by insurgents made such ties less meaningful, a fact that became particularly obvious after Shirley Chisholm retired from Congress in 1982.

At the same time, "Caribbeans for Percy Sutton" had brought the West Indian constituency to the attention of City Hall. Stanislaus met Koch during the 1977 campaign and, while he continued to support Sutton, he was positively impressed. Over the next eight years he would continue to have contact with the Koch administration, and in 1985 he would head "Caribbeans for Koch." In 1986, when Koch appointed the Commission on Black New Yorkers (a group that included black executives, educators, and ministers but, conspicuously, no politicians), it was no surprise that Stanislaus was named a member. In the late 1980s some of the community's younger "ethnicity entrepreneurs" complained that holding West Indian events that involve the city administration without Stanislaus had become difficult because the Koch administration insisted on his involvement.

The 1980s also saw an increased formalization of Stanislaus's role as an ethnic spokesman. With an increasing number of West Indian organizations in New York, he was appointed, as the community's most visible member, to a number of boards of directors and advisory councils. He and members of his generation came to be increasingly venerated as a new generation sought legitimacy by placing prominent names on the letterheads of their organizations. Nevertheless, while Stanislaus was a frequent fixture on the dais at public events, he remained skeptical about the value of formal organizations: "Within the Caribbean community we have too many organizations. The proliferation is weakening us. I am for attempting to find an overall Caribbean organization that can speak with authority for the Caribbean community."

Yet when the Caribbean Action Lobby arose specifically to do this, Stanislaus, though serving as an officer, remained critical of its ability to overcome the ambitions of individual members. "I doubt seriously that the Caribbean Action Lobby will be able to unite the community," he noted in 1985, "because already within it, you see this strife for position and power."

Thus, despite his bemoaning the lack of formal West Indian organizational strength, Stanislaus (and many others of his generation) continues to see politics largely in terms of personal relationships to the sources of power. His support for Koch was justified on these grounds. "It's not good to always be confrontational," he said. "We need a liaison to power. The more we press for dumping Koch the greater will be the backlash. So we should support a variety of candidates, not put all the eggs in one basket . . . and as an old student of politics, I will tell you, the mayor is going to win."

Power is thus conceived in clientelist terms. Stanislaus's relationship to his people is based on respect and loyalty. "Some people are born leaders," he notes, "but others acquire leadership by virtue of their outreach in the community, by virtue of their contacts, by virtue of their support. You may not be a leader in the formal sense, yet you have this support." His own relationship to prominent politicians—the mayor, the borough president, members of Congress,—is seen in the same informal terms. Even when he formed "Caribbeans for Koch" his role was that of a facilitator: he hosted meetings, made introductions, solicited contributions. In his few public statements on the matter, Stanislaus spoke more of the political value of the

Koch connection and Koch's "strong support for the culture of the Caribbean" than of matters of policy. His is a politics less of issues than of access.

The changing politics of the Caribbean formalized Stanislaus's role in that arena as well. The Grenada he left was a small colony with a limited franchise and was ruled by the conflicting interests of distant London, a tiny local elite of white and "near-white" planters and an emerging but still small minority of "brown" professionals (Smith 1965). After he left, Grenada introduced universal suffrage, became self-governing, joined the West Indian Federation and saw that federation collapse, voted to be united with Trinidad and Tobago (only to be rebuffed by Trinidad), had its self-governing status revoked by Britain and later reinstated, and finally, in 1974, became an independent nation. In each of these changes, the expatriate community played a role, and the increased level of political activity heightened the politicization of the Grenadians in New York. As the United States replaced Great Britain as the power most influential in Grenada's national life, Grenadians in the United States occupied an increasingly strategic position for influencing Grenada's politics. Thus, for immigrants of Stanislaus's generation, the 1970s brought both increased incorporation into American life and increased influence over affairs in the islands.

Stanislaus's connection to Blaize helped keep him prominent in opposition circles during the long reign of right-wing populist Eric Gairy. As might be expected, Blaize's largely middle-class, "respectable" Grenada National Party (GNP) was a leading force among Grenadians in the United States, even during the years when it was consistently losing elections to Gairy's Grenada Labor Party (which despite its name drew most of its support from poor black small farmers and farm workers). Independence increased the New York community's importance as a source of funds and electoral support.[5]

In 1976 Blaize and other middle-class oppositionists formed an electoral alliance with the New Jewel Party, a group of young radicals, many of whom had studied abroad and been deeply influenced

5. Few modern societies have received as much social scientific attention per capita as tiny Grenada. Sources on its class structure and politics were surprisingly plentiful even before the events of 1979–83. See, for example, Singham (1968) and Smith (1965). For a review of this literature in light of later developments, see Segal (1983), and for later events see also Lewis (1984).

by the American civil rights and black power movements as well as by Marxism and the African socialism of Julius Nyerere. As the Gairy regime was more and more perceived as an embarrassment (the problems of flagrant corruption being compounded by its leader's increasingly erratic behavior), the alliance drew broad support in the New York community. It was narrowly defeated in an election in which fraud was widely suspected. After three years of further economic deterioration and abuse of power by Gairy and his "mongoose gang" of political thugs, members of the New Jewel Movement seized power in 1979 in a bloodless takeover, in which Grenadians in New York and Washington, D.C., had a hand.

Stanislaus, who had not been back to Grenada in many years and was a U.S. citizen, was offered the New York-based position of consul general by the new prime minister, Maurice Bishop. But after learning that Blaize and the old GNP would have no role in the new government, he declined. Over the next several years both Stanislaus and Blaize distanced themselves further and further from the Bishop government. After Bishop's assassination in 1983, Stanislaus, like many New York-based Grenadians, supported the U.S. invasion (he prefers the term "rescue mission"). In the U.S.-sponsored election that followed he led a New York support group for the newly formed New National Party (NNP), a coalition led by Blaize that was clearly the choice of the Americans. Thanks in part to an infusion of funds raised in the United States, the NNP soundly defeated both Gairy and the decimated remnant of the Bishop wing of the People's Revolutionary Government, now rechristened the Maurice Bishop Democratic Movement.

After the NNP's November 1984 victory it was widely reported in the New York press that Stanislaus was to be offered the ambassadorship to the United Nations by his old friend Blaize. Stanislaus remained publicly "undecided" and the post remained unfilled until after the "Caribbeans for Koch" Organization was well under way. In May of 1985 he formally accepted the U.N. position.

The appointment of the Brooklyn dentist raised some opposition in Grenada and caused some amusement in the American press. Stanislaus had, after all, left Grenada almost forty years before and had visited only a few times since. He was a U.S. citizen and active in U.S. politics. What is more, the Reagan administration chose to allow Stanislaus to keep his citizenship despite his being a diplomatic representative of a foreign government, a fact that led opponents to question his independence and credibility. *The New York Times*, taking an unusually patronizing tone, reported on 18 October 1985, that Stanislaus's dental clients had filled the galleries at his first address to the General Assembly and were both extolling and displaying the evidence of his dental skills.

Neither Stanislaus's lack of previous diplomatic experience nor his New York connections are unique, however. In small nations such as the micro-states of the Anglophone Caribbean, it is common for professionals to assume political roles late in their careers, and other Caribbean nations have appointed long-time New York residents to diplomatic and consular posts. While Stanislaus's appointment to the UN and his continuing involvement in the politics of New York City is only perhaps the most extreme example of a general pattern; indeed when he stepped down following the NNP's electoral defeat in 1990, he was replaced by another long-time New Yorker.

Thus the independence of Caribbean nations has not forced West Indians in New York to choose between the politics of home and host countries. Quite to the contrary, the increased politicization of life in the West Indies has led to increased political participation in the United States. Sometimes this relationship is direct, as when West Indians seek to influence U.S. policy towards their home nations. The most obvious examples of this are the pro-Caribbean stances of Trinidad-born congressman Mervyn Dymally and Brooklyn congressman Major Owens (an African American in an increasingly Caribbean district). There is also a more indirect political relationship between the mobilization and formalization of political influence at home and the use of the same organizations and networks to influence affairs in New York.[6]

One reason for this interplay is that the Caribbean notion of nationality, at least for members of Stanislaus's generation, is highly flexible. The increasing rate of West Indian naturalization does not mean that Reid (1939), Foner (1983), and others were wrong in concluding that West Indians are hesitant to give up allegiances to former countries; rather it suggests that citizenship is no longer seen as an important indicant of national loyalty. Furthermore, many West

6. For other examples of the interaction between New York and the Caribbean in terms of political ideology and activity, see Sutton and Makiesky (1975) and Basch (1987).

Indians seem to feel that loyalties to two nations are not inherently contradictory.

This dual loyalty is not surprising when one considers the recent history of the West Indies. Though Stanislaus is quick to assert his paramount loyalty to Grenada, his native country's political identity is an extremely recent construction. Like most of the small islands, Grenada developed in tandem with the rest of the region, and a long history of intra-Caribbean migration has spread many families throughout territories that became, in the 1960s and 1970s, separate independent nations.[7] Stanislaus's beloved Grenada National Party for years attempted to submerge Grenada's national identity in a West Indian Federation or a union with Trinidad and Tobago,[8] and it also recognized the right to military intervention of the Association of Eastern Caribbean States in 1983—hardly the usual approach to issues of sovereignty.

Today many West Indian nations (and their nationals in New York) revel in the symbols of nationhood. Advertisements for bakeries in the New York press display the lyrics of national anthems, and store fronts on Nostrand Avenue display the flags of Caribbean nations. This has at least something to do with the comparative newness of such symbols. Issues of national symbolism and national boundaries, long taken for granted in much of the world, have a currency in the Caribbean that reminds the observer that such things are recent political constructions.

At the same time, the constructed nature of nationality is so obvious in the West Indies that it is taken, perhaps, a bit less seriously than in other places. The result is a fairly selective use of the idea of

7. It should also be noted that among Grenadians who came of age after independence and who lived through the highly politicized late Gairy years and the 1979–83 revolution, the sense of national identity seems considerably stronger than among their elders.

8. The GNP's hesitation about independence was perhaps justified in light of subsequent history. Since the introduction of universal suffrage in 1951, Grenada had been the scene of almost constant struggle between the colonial authorities and Gairy's class- and race-baiting populism. The middle-class GNP had little use for either side in this conflict, but at least during the 1951–74 period each could be relied upon to curb the worst excesses of the other. Federation with larger West Indian territories would have greatly diluted Gairy's strength (his highly personal style of leadership does not travel well) and allowed the GNP to unify with other parties of the middle class. Independence, however, not only erected an artificial international boundary between Grenada and its traditional markets and chief sources of employment, it left Gairy totally unchecked, and after two and a half decades of pandering to the rural poor, he could hardly be expected not to engage in wholesale plunder in their name.

national loyalties. In this atmosphere Stanislaus's dual roles as Grenadian diplomat and advisor to Koch are not seen by West Indians as fundamentally in conflict. The usual assumption that incorporation into U.S. society implies the lessening of ties to the home society seems to be wrong for West Indian immigrants, in part because it is based on an inappropriate model of what national loyalties are.

Thus the old guard such as Stanislaus and his generation have reversed the usual direction of the "assimilation" process. They have moved from the position of being vague cultural brokers into roles as diplomatic intermediaries for their home nations, while at the same time becoming more formally involved in ethnic politics in New York. They remain, however, primarily interested in informal political influence and do not see their role as building new organizations. Their style of leadership stands in conflict with the up-and-coming generations of Caribbean activists who migrated to New York during the 1960s and 1970s. Activists of this generation, whom I have called the "ethnicity entrepreneurs," were shaped in part by the politics of the independent Caribbean nations, but also by different assumptions about the nature of ethnic politics in the contemporary United States. The politics of these new activists is thus more Caribbean in style but far more American in form than that of the old guard. They continue to venerate their elders, but they seek to create a politics in which the old guard's personal approach will give way to a more formal notion of community leadership.

The Ethnicity Entrepreneurs

Ethnicity is the *raison d'être* for a number of groups and organizations in New York's West Indian community today. The mostly male leaders of these groups (who in some cases constitute virtually the entire active membership) represent a new style of leadership. Less well known in their community than the old guard leaders, and less well regarded by white intellectuals than the community's radical activists, they have nevertheless been more successful than either when it comes to building ties to New York's political establishment. They are, or perhaps hope to be, a subspecies of the type John Mollenkopf calls "political entrepreneurs": actors who seek to create "new governmental bases for exercising new powers" and who thus "are always looking for ways to use governmental authority or governmental revenues to build up supportive constituencies" (1983:4–5). Their activities have been more restricted to the realm of ideology than the relatively nonideological (and far more powerful) figures Mollenkopf describes, and in this respect they are more reminiscent of the advocates of certain positions concerning public morality that Howard Becker (1963) terms "moral entrepreneurs." Hence I refer to this type as the "ethnicity entrepreneur."[9]

The ethnicity entrepreneur serves two quite distinct constituencies: the ethnic community whose interests he claims to advocate, and the representatives of the polity and the larger society. The latter are largely politicians, black and white, but also include representatives of publicly active corporations and academic institutions. It is to these constituencies that the ethnicity entrepreneur turns most often for financial support. The ethnic ideology the entrepreneur puts forward must reflect the balancing of the needs of these two constituencies. Despite their dependence on outsiders these men are important voices of the community as far as the wider polity is concerned.

From where does the entrepreneur's "leadership" actually arise? The leader of one of New York's best-known West Indian organizations is quite candid on this matter. In a sparsely attended public meeting of well-known figures from a variety of Caribbean groups he noted:

All of us are basically self-appointed leaders and we should not apologize for being self-appointed leaders. Most leadership is self appointed. Change does not take place as a reflection of the masses. Elites change, and the elite will then change the group. That's why I think [another leader who had previously spoken] is right about focusing on middle-class professionals. I am tired of apologizing for not being the leader of a mass movement. The masses have no voice, except us. And if we are out of step with the masses, believe me, they will let us know.

9. The term "ethnicity entrepreneur" should not be confused with "ethnic entrepreneur," which has been used to mean an entrepreneur who is ethnic. The "ethnicity entrepreneur" is an actor who deals in the political marketing of ethnicity.
I should acknowledge that in a recent public statement, the late Professor A.W. Singham used the phrase "professional community leaders" to refer to some prominent New York West Indians (1985:19). If I understood him correctly we are talking about the same type of leader, and probably about some of the same individuals.

[177]

In fact there are few occasions for assessing an ethnicity entrepreneur's true strength in his community. Electoral behavior is one, but except on those rare occasions where he himself is running for office, such assessment is limited to the issue of endorsements and the number of votes an entrepreneur can deliver. And it is a question whether a particular endorsement is true leadership or rather sensing where the crowd is heading and getting there first. Another test of strength is how many people an entrepreneur turns out at a given event, but that too is complicated by other factors. In fact, with the exception of rare moments of mass political involvement, the entrepreneur is very much the man in the middle. His relationship with the wider polity depends on his being a recognized advocate of his community, yet his position in the community is at least partially based on his relationship with the broader polity.

It is ironic, but not really surprising, that access to political leaders increases the entrepreneur's credibility within his own community. By sitting on the dais at public events, by receiving various awards in recognition of his "community service," by having meetings with prominent officials, and, most important, by getting into the newspapers, the entrepreneur establishes visibility ("the highly visible Mr.——" or "the well-known Mr.——" are community press appellations for actors who lack more concrete titles or offices). His visible connections with well-known political figures may be seen as evidence of his clout. Thus he becomes known as a "power broker," a "guy who can deliver."

How much the entrepreneurs actually deliver is a matter of some debate. Critics are quick to point out that "photo opportunities" such as the well-publicized meetings of West Indian "leaders" with the mayor or declaration of a "Caribbean-American Awareness Day" by Brooklyn's borough president are among the least expensive favors that these politicians could grant. "It is not surprising," one critic noted, "that the professional Caribbean leaders found no difficulty in meeting with the mayor. . . . Gracie Mansion becomes for some members of the English speaking (Caribbean) elite in New York City, synonymous with the governor's house which they left behind" (Singham 1985:19). It is certainly true that the demands put forward on such occasions are generally modest. Most amount to community "recognition," a word that is frequently used but seldom concretely defined. Yet the importance of recognition should not be underestimated. Attaining a place within the political structure implies some commitment by politicians to treat the community as they do other communities, even if that place is not yet programmatically specified.

Perhaps more important than gaining recognition for the group, such political occasions help the ethnicity entrepreneur establish a reputation within the group. In sharp contrast to the "old guard," who are linked to segments of the West Indian community by ties of patronage and obligation, the ethnicity entrepreneur lives according to Hobbes' dictum: "Reputation of power is power."

This reputation may be translated into conspicuous displays of community support, which in turn can be utilized to gain further access to politicians and perhaps more tangible political rewards. For example, one Jamaica-born leader of a Central Brooklyn political club described his group's successful efforts to pressure then congresswoman Elizabeth Holtzman into introducing immigration reforms, which were subsequently passed:

> I would like to feel that the pressure we put on her to do something helped lead to this bill. . . . Because we used to have meetings up at the——Society, you know, up on Eastern Parkway . . . and I think what grabs an elected official is walking into a room and there was standing room only! I mean, we got out hundreds of people. She loved to come talk to me after then. At first it's "I have introduced, last week . . . ," then the next week she comes back and it's "I have got you a bill."

The visibility of the ethnicity entrepreneurs is increased by the close relations many enjoy with white politicians. This simultaneously enhances their status and calls into question their loyalty to the community. Between their dependence on the polity and their need for popular support the ethnicity entrepreneurs dance with varying degrees of skill, guile, and integrity. They balance the needs of their two constituencies while carving out a niche for themselves. In so doing they also articulate notions of group identity that come to take on a reality of their own.

Some ethnicity entrepreneurs make a reasonable living from their efforts. Kenneth Burke once noted that a man's occupation may become his preoccupation, but in the era of the block grant it is more likely to happen the other way around. A few have been "selling" ethnicity for many years; others have only recently drifted into this from other lines of work. Despite the inevitable criticism, often voiced by rivals, few could be fairly described as "in it for the money." Most are quite sincere in their desire to help their people and also candid about the role that ego plays in their claims to leadership. For some, money is no doubt part of the attraction of public life, but it is probably not as important as the status and recognition to be gained. They work hard, and even those who make their living from these activities could probably do as well or better in other fields.

More important than the question of personal gain is what their activities mean for the West Indian community. Since their position is dependent on relationships between the West Indian community and the government, ethnicity entrepreneurs have a central interest in two propositions. First, while the West Indian community may be part of the broader black community, it is sufficiently distinct in terms of culture, geographic location, and political interests to require its own leadership cadre. Second, it is important that this leadership group be strident enough to retain at least minimal credibility within the community, yet not so militant as to preclude working relationships with the political establishment.

The Caribbean identity the entrepreneurs seek to create stands in opposition both to the parochial concerns of the various national clubs and mutual benefit societies and to claims that West Indian interests are identical to those of U.S.-born blacks. The entrepreneurs are often well aware of the synthetic nature of these group boundaries. The apparently contradictory stand they must take, opposing both the broad definitions based on race as well as the narrow ones based on national origin, is usually explained on the grounds of pragmatism. As the president of a prominent pan-Caribbean organization puts it:

> All political definitions are definitions of convenience, and we happened to luck upon the convenient definition of English-speaking Caribbeans of African descent. . . . I tell you a little funny one that is going down now. The other day a fellow came up to me, white fellow, and says "you leaving me out." Turns out he's a white Caribbean. But remember, the political definition is one of convenience. You conveniently recognize it or you conveniently oppose it. . . . Now if at some point, if white, Dutch-speaking Caribbeans achieve a critical political mass, we will have to address ourselves to a change in definition. In the meantime I am not concerned about any sub-, sub-, subgroup that may arise in theory because they only become a point of concern when they become a demographic political mass.

The entrepreneurs generally see nation-of-origin organizations as inconvenient and impractical for participation in U.S. politics. Privately, some voice frustration with the backward-looking nature of such groups, but nevertheless they provide an important organizational infrastructure for community activities. Many ethnicity entrepreneurs see their own memberships in such groups as the beginnings of their public life, and their roles as spokesmen in the broader Caribbean community by no means preclude involvement in the politics of their nations of origin.

What follows are accounts of the careers of two ethnicity entrepreneurs active in New York today. While their specific activities differ, both are very involved in formulating the content of West Indian political identity. Both are fairly typical in the types of connections they maintain between their community's social and political organizations and the government. While not seeking political office themselves, these men form a vital bridge between those who run for office and the organizational base of the community.

Roy A. Hastick is a figure of increasing prominence in Brooklyn's Caribbean community. Born on Grenada, Hastick emigrated to the U.S. Virgin Islands as a young man. Like many ambitious young blacks lacking professional education, he took the civil service route to upward mobility and became a police officer. In 1973 he returned to Grenada and joined the police force there in the months preceding Grenadian independence. In 1975 he emigrated to Brooklyn, and not long after arriving in Crown Heights he became simultaneously involved in both Brooklyn and Grenadian exile affairs. He recalls: "When I first came here, living in the Crown Heights district, I found the neighborhood was in terrible shape. You saw a lot of boarded up buildings, potholes, abandoned cars, crime. So what I did was, I organized a block association which was the Clarkson Ave. Block Association. I am the founder of that."

From this modest beginning, Hastick was soon leading an immigrant social group and making ties with other sophisticated Caribbean immigrants who had experience in organizing:

I also realized that there were quite a lot of ex-policemen, from the Caribbean—not only from the Caribbean, but from Grenada . . . living right there in Brooklyn. So I sort of said to myself, "why don't we pull them together." The guy who really pushed me into that was a guy . . . [who] used to be the president of the Barbados Ex-police

Association and he got me involved in getting the constitution together, incorporating, tax-free status, and all that.

Hastick went to work for the Port Authority. There he became friendly with a commissioner, who became aware of Hastick's community involvement. This helped to pave his way into political activity: "I used to talk to this guy, you know, the commissioner, I used to talk to him all the time about my neighborhood, and he said 'look, you're involved with the ex-police and all, why don't you get in touch with your local politician, and see if he can help.' So I contacted my local politician, who at the time was [City Councilman] Ted Silverman."

Silverman, a Jewish politician in a district where demographics had turned against him, would be the first of a number of politicians with whom Hastick would work closely. After being involved in a number of small projects, Hastick was appointed by Silverman to the voluntary but politically powerful Community Planning Board in 1979.[10] Though the board's youngest member, Hastick was soon elected to chair its public safety committee. He also went into business as a private security consultant, a field that allowed him the flexible schedule needed for political activity and put him in a position to make full use of his growing political connections. Over the next few years Hastick was appointed to a number of highly visible Community Board committee positions, and in 1983 he was elected first vice president.

Hastick continued his involvement with the ex-police and founded a community newspaper, *The West Indian Tribune*. While the *Tribune* itself did not last long, the Tribune Company became the umbrella organization for Hastick's other activities. Hastick took an of-

10. In 1973, in a move toward decentralizing political decision making and increasing local control, New York City was divided into fifty-nine community districts. Each is represented by a voluntary community board of fifty local members, which reviews all land-use decisions made in the district. While these boards have only advisory authority, their recommendations on local issues are often accepted. Their mandate to hold public meetings on land-use issues gives them considerable power to publicize, question, facilitate, or obstruct new projects. Members of these boards are appointed by the borough president, with half of the members being recommended by the area's city council members. Unofficially these bodies often serve as a bridge between these elected officials and various constituencies. As a grassroots form of political organization, they are used by city officials as both a sounding board and a forum for building support. In this respect they have taken on many of the functions once filled by members of political clubs.

For an account of the structure and problems of the community board system, see "Community Boards: How are We Doing?," a special issue of *New York Affairs* 6, no. 1 (1980).

fice across the street from Brooklyn's Borough Hall, the center for local Democratic party activity, and while still taking on security contracts he began to work practically full-time as a self-described ethnic "ombudsman."

R.H.: I have this thing in me where I try to deliver services for my people. I happen to know how the system works. In fact I learn it the hard way. It's like for me, you do something for somebody, they going to do something for you. So, I got several results. Like the Crown Heights Youth Festival, I did that. . . . People call me with things, they want to get things to the mayor's office or the borough president's office. They need somebody to serve as an ombudsman.

P.K.: Do you view yourself as an ombudsman for Grenadians?

R.H.: Not really Grenadians, I'm really a Caribbean person. I don't look at myself as a Grenadian. I really work for several groups. I was very instrumental in helping the St. Vincent ex-police group get started. I was instrumental in helping the Caribbean-American Art and Cultural Link, I worked with the Labor Day Association, I have worked very closely with other groups, Guyanese groups. . . . I see myself as . . . I'm not bragging, but I'm in a position to help.

Although he has been associated with a number of fellow Grenadians in various organizations, Hastick had little direct involvement with Grenadian politics during the Bishop years. Perhaps because of a feeling of being rejected by Grenada, perhaps because the political situation made return to Grenada unlikely, he became more involved during this period in local politics and the Crown Heights Caribbean community. "After years with the Grenada thing, I started to really concentrate on local politics. . . . [T]hat's really where it's at."

Here is a pattern that seems to hold throughout the West Indian community and perhaps in other New York immigrant communities as well.[11] As long as the dream of return home remains viable, there is hesitation to become involved in local politics and, in particular, to take out U.S. citizenship. But when the political situation deterio-

11. In her study of Dominican activists in upper Manhattan, Georges (1984) notes that many left-wing Dominicans in exile during the Balaguer regime showed little interest in U.S. politics except where it pertained directly to the Dominican Republic. After a moderate government came to power in 1977 many of these activists were able to visit home for the first time in years, and they discovered that the economic situation had so deteriorated that permanent return, however politically desirable, had become economically unfeasible, at least in the foreseeable future. Thus many began to see themselves less as exiles and more as part of the Hispanic minority in the United States. What followed was a notable increase in Dominican political activity in New York.

rates or economic problems make return less likely, there is often an explosion of interest in local New York politics. This shift in emphasis need not, however, be permanent, as Hastick's case demonstrates. After the U.S.-backed Blaize regime came to power in Grenada, a number of long-time Brooklynites who had had little recent involvement with Grenada became increasingly active. Hastick, a Blaize supporter, joined with Lamuel Stanislaus and others in forming the New National Party support committee in New York, and made himself available to the press as a spokesman for the group.

Still active on the local scene as well, Hastick attracted attention in early 1985 by calling a meeting in support of the Caribbean community press. Here the opportunity was provided by community dissatisfaction with the New York press's coverage of the sudden death of J. M. "Tom" Adams, the prime minister of Barbados, in March of 1985. Adams died unexpectedly on the same weekend as Soviet premier Chernenko, and his death was generally given little attention in the New York press, including the black press. Many community spokesmen, including some who had little sympathy for Adams's pro-U.S. politics, expressed shock at the lack of notice paid by Washington and the U.S. media to the passing of a strong regional ally (although Mayor Koch, whose foreign policy stands are dictated by rather different considerations than those of the federal administration, did send a well-publicized message of condolence). The controversy received prominent attention in the Caribbean community press, which had of course been the only New York media to cover Adams's death as a major story. When Hastick called a meeting to discuss ways to support the Caribbean media, that media naturally gave the meeting full coverage.

This gathering, calculated to achieve maximum publicity, and brought professed community leaders and office-seekers out of the woodwork. They called for more support from advertisers that do business with the Caribbean community and the New York press. The black press in particular was taken to task for past failings. Perhaps more important, the leadership was assembled, pictures were taken, and names were mentioned in the *Carib News*. Hastick was of course prominently featured.

The meeting exemplified the reciprocal relationship that exists between the community press and the ethnicity entrepreneurs. The entrepreneur does not exist without an audience, and the press is one of the primary ways in which an audience can be reached. The press can grant favored actors visibility and can link low-level operators with more prominent figures. At the same time, faced with the monthly, weekly, or even daily task of generating news stories, the press needs the entrepreneurs, who not only provide a huge volume of ready-made news with their numerous meetings and social events (not to mention their infighting, which usually makes for the best stories of all) but are vital sources of information.

Despite his Caribbean focus and his alliances with white politicians, Hastick did not sever ties to African-American politics. While he and the other ethnicity entrepreneurs have endeavored to play the ethnic card in their relations with the white political establishment, they have continued to maintain ties with at least some of the leaders of the African-American community.

In 1983 Roy Innis, the controversial leader of the Congress of Racial Equality (CORE), sought to reorganize the Brooklyn branch of CORE. Once a leading civil rights organization, CORE had lost many of its constituents when it turned sharply to the right under Innis's leadership. Innis, who had lost none of his militant style, had nevertheless become a Reagan backer and a leading black Republican (he would later become a regular guest on TV's nortorious "Morton Downey Show"). He had taken a number of public stances on issues ranging from the role of private enterprise in the black movement to subway vigilantism which had isolated him from the majority of black organizations. When the Brooklyn chapter of CORE sought to break away from the national organization, Innis, who is from the Virgin Islands, sought to reorganize the Brooklyn chapter along more conservative and Caribbean lines. After meeting a number of Caribbean figures through fund-raising efforts for a Caribbean cultural project, Innis appointed a prominent Anglophone Panamanian as chairman and Hastick as the president of the "recognized" Brooklyn CORE. While this organization did little besides granting Innis an occasional platform, it added an impressive credit to the entrepreneur's résumé and gave him a tie to a well-known—if lately in disrepute—civil rights organization. It also gave Innis, who was testing the waters for a bid for Brooklyn's Twelfth Congressional seat in 1986, a base in Brooklyn's Caribbean community.

In early 1985 a number of business and political leaders approached Hastick about organizing a Caribbean-American small business group. Advocating small business and self-reliance has a strong appeal in the Caribbean community, where there is a long tradition of support for black capitalism going back to the Garvey movement. It was also, in the Koch and Reagan era, smart politics. As Hastick notes, "federal cutbacks in financial and technical assistance programs have created a void for minority business owners." It was a void he would try to fill. Hastick was eventually sought out by the Brooklyn Economic Development Corporation, a joint venture of Brooklyn Union Gas, Consolidated Edison, Manufacturers Hanover Bank, and the Brooklyn borough president's office, to start discussions leading to the formation of a Caribbean American Chamber of Commerce. An announcement of a "networking session" for community business owners was sent out under Hastick's name on the stationery of the West Indian Tribune Company.

Hastick was soon able to parlay these discussions into a permanent organization, funded partially by member contributions and partially by grants from several corporations and local utilities. Creating the permanent Caribbean American Chamber of Commerce and Industry provided Hastick not only with a steady paycheck but also with a base for his other community activities. He assembled a board of directors consisting of a Caribbean ambassador, a judge, a local publisher, representatives of several corporate sponsors, and several other ethnic organization leaders. Only one of the ten original board members was in fact a Caribbean-American businessman. It was clear from the beginning that while business was the Chamber's nominal focus, politics was very much on the agenda. The Chamber's activities continued to have the conspicuous patronage of Brooklyn borough president Howard Golden and African-American congressman Edolphus Towns.

Within Chamber, Hastick has undertaken the publication of a Caribbean businessman's newsletter and sponsored a series of workshops on small business concerns such as locating credit and establishing trade with the Caribbean. Several corporations, particularly those who do substantial business with the Caribbean community, have participated and helped to finance these projects. The Chamber has been a cosponsor of Caribbean trade fairs and other activities designed to stimulate trade between Caribbean nations and the United States. Local utilities and government agencies rather than private corporations bought most of the space at these trade fairs, but the private enterprise ideology behind these events was sufficiently in tune with the Reagan administration Caribbean Basin Initiative to earn Hastick a personal letter of commendation from U.S. Secretary of Commerce Malcolm Baldridge. Naturally this was reprinted in the Chamber's newsletter.

One striking fact about the Caribbean American Chamber of Commerce is that there is little in its activities that is distinctly Caribbean. Despite the attempts at linkages to the West Indies, for the most part it expresses the interests of small businessmen. Some of its members are African Americans, it is politically sponsored by both Jewish and African-American politicians, and its funds come largely from white and African-American community relations officers in major corporations. Nor are its concerns unique to West Indians: loans, credit, Small Business Administration policy, the problems of commercial rents, and so on. As Yancey, Eriksen, and Juliani note, much of what passes for "ethnic behavior" in the United States is in fact the expression of class and community interest and "is ethnic only by coincidence" (1976:399).

On the other hand, it is politically significant that such organizations choose to see themselves in ethnic terms. That the leaders of the Caribbean American Chamber of Commerce share an ethnic tie and that they organize on the basis of that tie may help them build business relationships. Naturally, the fact that they share class and community interests reinforces the ethnic tie. It must be noted too that the sponsoring agencies, both private and governmental, have proven particularly receptive to this ethnic mode of organization, indeed probably more so than if they had organized using the vocabulary of race.

In February of 1986 the Caribbean American Chamber ambitiously announced its "first annual" Economic Development Awards Dinner, a $100-a-plate fund raiser (tables could be had for the bargain rate of $1,000). The featured speaker was borough president Golden, and the honorees were carefully chosen to include a white executive (chairman of a prominent brewing company), a trade specialist from the U.S. Department of Commerce, and both Caribbean and African-American local businessmen. The gathering was held not in one of Brooklyn's West Indian neighborhoods but in a posh hall in a white neighborhood often used for fund raisers and other political gatherings. Almost to the point of parody, the event adhered to the standard form of political fund-raising dinners and, except for the palm trees on the Chamber's logo, there was little that marked it as distinctly Caribbean. But if events such as this display little ethnic culture, they do reflect ethnic strategy: they not only show the entrepreneur's willingness to play by the dominant culture's rules, they also voice the ethnic community's demand to be taken seriously as players.

In many instances it is the representatives of the political establishment who contact the entrepreneurs and aid in the initial founding of their organizations. It clearly serves the purposes of many white politicians and executives to have a highly visible West Indian, which also means a highly visible black, at their side. It is not surprising then that when Stanislaus formed "Caribbeans for Koch" in 1985, Hastick became one of its members.

Though to some degree Hastick's career parallels that of Stanislaus, there are important differences. Stanislaus, the cultivated professional, has generally used his prestige to gain informal authority. He long eschewed positions in organizations until first he accepted the relatively genteel role of a diplomat. Hastick, a man of humbler origins, is by contrast an empire builder. He has founded one organization after another and constantly sought to expand his circle of contacts. His prestige (and his livelihood) is a result of this activity.

While Hastick occupies the space between government and the private sector, other ethnicity entrepreneurs have carved out a niche on the periphery of academia. Taking their inspiration from the numerous ethnic studies institutes that have been created in recent years, these men have formed research groups, information services, and consulting firms that provide information on the Caribbean community. In addition, such activists utilize these organizations—profit-making and nonprofit—to provide themselves both a living and a political base.

F. Donnie Forde is one of the most persistent of these activists. Controversial and sometimes contentious, he has nevertheless managed to keep his small media studies corporation solvent throughout the 1980s—no mean feat in the Reagan era—and has also gotten his share of political attention.

Unlike Hastick, Forde has no roots in the island-based mutual benevolent societies. Forde hails from Aruba, a Dutch West Indian dependency that, according to the 1980 census, has sent only about

1,100 nationals to New York. He emigrated to the United States in 1959 as a teenager and attended Northeastern University during the waning days of the civil rights movement. There he became peripherally involved in black politics, his involvement intensifying after he finished school and settled in New York. Here he worked in various capacities on behalf of a number of black political candidates and black causes. By the late 1970s he had begun a career as a free-lance journalist, covering both African-American and Caribbean stories and emerging as something of an expert on the Caribbean community for the African-American press. He also developed a particular interest in voter registration and the citizenship rights of West Indians.

In 1980 he founded Caribbean American Media Studies Inc. (CAMS), an organization dedicated to the study of and dissemination of information about recent West Indian migrants. Although the group had from its inception a large and impressive board of directors, Forde is the president and often the only full-time staff member. The bulk of CAMS' initial funding came from contributions from the community, primarily from a successful bakery owner. More recently, as Forde's political contacts have expanded, CAMS has received city and state funds for a variety of projects ranging from studies of undocumented aliens to programs for immigrant children in the public schools and consulting on the black immigrant role in the 1986 Statue of Liberty bicentennial celebration.

From the beginning CAMS was a multifunction organization involved in a variety of activities. Ford relates: "We, a group of us, decided that if we are going to have a strong community, we were going to have some strong institutions, you know . . . so at that time [Karl] Rodney started building the paper [*The Carib News*] and I started out with this here. We held seminars on a variety of things. . . . [O]ur real goal is to increase awareness of the rest of the city [about the Caribbean community] and helping migrants, you know, help them become citizens."

This last activity, aiding naturalization, has been CAMS' major focus since the mid-1980s. It distributes information on the naturalization process and on which Caribbean nations recognize dual citizenship, and in leaflets, flyers, and press releases it encourages West Indians to become U.S. citizens, reminding them that they can never expect a fair share of political clout until they do so. CAMS also runs naturalization and voter registration activities in conjunction with several churches and political groups, and its volunteers man naturalization information tables in several locations around the city. During the amnesty period for undocumented aliens during 1988–89 it greatly expanded its operation to include the processing of approximately 1,000 amnesty applications.

Amnesty and citizenship are attractive issues for organizations like CAMS. Since all citizens are potential voters and since political participation is one reason West Indians become citizens, activity on these issues draws the cooperation and support of West Indian politicians as well as the interest of non-Caribbean politicians. In addition CAMS remains dedicated to wider cultural and social-scientific purposes. Questionnaires are distributed to each person CAMS helps naturalize in an effort to build a data base on the community, and the organization seeks within its limited means to serve as an information source on the Caribbean community for researchers, friendly politicians, and the press.

CAMS' organizational goals are loosely defined, which permits a wide range of activities depending on what Forde sees as important at any one time. Its constituency, non-Hispanic Caribbean blacks, is something of a synthetic construction, as Forde himself points out:

> What really happens, you know, is even though they call us West Indians, in a sense, we have certain cultural commonalities which are a legacy from slavery, but we only become real West Indians in exile in that we are united. When we come onto one land mass, with no ocean to divide us . . . we come here, you know, and you can walk from Jamaican to Barbadian territory, we go to each other's parties on Saturday night. . . . The true West Indian, strictly speaking, is a West Indian American or Caribbean American . . . whatever you want to call it.

Forde's thinking on this has been influenced by what social scientists have said about the role of ethnicity in urban life. The first of a series of endorsements that appeared in CAMS' initial brochure came from Daniel Patrick Moynihan, who not only wished CAMS success but took the opportunity to remind readers that he had called attention to the importance of West Indians twenty years before in his and Nathan Glazer's *Beyond the Melting Pot*. We see here a sort of feedback loop between the academy and the polity. Forde, in setting up an ethnic organization, is influenced in his thinking by

Moynihan the scholar, and thus helps to put forward an idea about ethnic identity based in part on Moynihan's observation of previous periods. In response, Moynihan behaves much like the politicians he wrote about in promoting the ethnic organization. His endorsement is then used to promote the position of Forde, as the entrepreneur angles for legitimacy.

However, because Forde is not a social scientist the social-scientific arguments he quotes take on a different meaning. When Glazer and Moynihan wrote about the persistence of ethnic politics they were attempting, at least ostensibly, to describe reality. For the ethnicity entrepreneur, such arguments are not descriptions but references to the dominant political ideology. Thus they become claims of entitlement, as ethnic political assertion is presented as "the way things are supposed to be." If a new immigrant group is not represented adequately, then something must be corrected, and it is the responsibility of the state to correct it.

Not surprisingly, political officials and ethnicity entrepreneurs like Forde tend to seek each other out. Forde is naturally cautious about establishing too close a relationship to these politicians, pointing out that his affiliation with them does not imply an endorsement. "I'm not a politician," he explains, "so I don't have to play those games." Still, the sort of ethnic recognition he seeks (and makes his living from) must come from the government. The politicians themselves, moreover, routinely employ ethnic symbolism and make claims to legitimacy based on their service to ethnic constituencies. Thus Forde and the politicians need each other.

From its beginnings CAMS was caught between two rival groups of Brooklyn politicians: those allied with Brooklyn borough president and Kings County Democratic leader Howard Golden and the group of black politicians allied with African-American assemblyman Albert Vann in the "Coalition for Community Empowerment." In 1985 Golden, running for reelection against Vann, was in need of black support. At stake was more than the borough presidency; a clear Golden win would solidify his position as county leader and heir to the powerful party boss Meade Esposito. A Vann victory, on the other hand, would establish an insurgent as the city's preeminent black leader and indicate to one and all that the days of the Brooklyn machine were over. Vann was strongly supported by Jesse Jackson, whose 1984 New York primary campaign he had led, registering thousands of new black voters in the process. If these voters could be delivered as a voting block, Vann would clearly be in a position of extraordinary influence, not only in New York but nationally.

It was thus critical for Golden (who also faced two rival white candidates) to divide the black vote. In part this was done on the basis of old loyalties. Early on he secured the endorsement of one of the borough's two black congressmen, Edolphus Towns, a long-time Golden ally although a nominal member of Vann's Empowerment group. The other road to division was ethnic: Golden sought allies in the West Indian community.

Hence when Forde, looking for publicity for CAMS, suggested in early 1985 that Golden proclaim a "Caribbean-American Awareness Day" to honor prominent community members, he found a receptive audience. As an elaborate photo opportunity the event promised Forde publicity and a way to make further contacts (community leaders being usually receptive to events in which they will be honored). But, the event held the danger of appearing as an endorsement of Golden by West Indian leaders, many of whom preferred Vann or Golden's chief white rival, state senator Martin Markowitz.

What occurred was a mutual dance of attraction and avoidance. A ceremony was held, a proclamation was read, Golden presented Forde with a plaque, and CAMS presented one to Golden. Both men brought in their own photographers so that the event could be immortalized in accordance with their own agendas. Golden neglected to invite African-American politicians allied with Vann. Forde invited them on his own only to have them snubbed by Golden. Golden attempted to create the impression that Forde was endorsing him. Forde tried to create the impression that he and Golden met as equals. Both men displayed a great concern about where they should stand when the cameras clicked. "Power," as Meade Esposito, Golden's considerably more colorful predecessor "is done with mirrors."

A few days later Forde would conclude that his own image-management skills were not quite yet a match for Golden's: "We tried not to make it look like an endorsement of anybody. . . . I am not completely aware of all these political games yet, but you know, I am learning."

While such events as the "Awareness Day" may appear to be a

vacuous exercise in ego-stroking, at least some in the West Indian community take them seriously, because they do afford "recognition" to those who often feel politically invisible. But they can also place politicians in a difficult position. In this case, not to participate might appear as a snub to the West Indian community, and to participate might appear as an endorsement of Golden.

The *New York Daily News* gave the event prominent coverage. The *Carib News* praised Forde and editorialized that the event was "very refreshing," though it also expressed the hope "that this recognition carries with it some substance and not just a public relations gimmick" (1985b:15). Thus while many in the community are skeptical about the value of ethnic symbolism and were cynical about Golden's motives, they would also have been deeply offended if such recognition had not been forthcoming. As far as Forde is concerned, he was clearly suspected in some quarters of having too cozy a relationship with white politicians, but at the same time the publicity increased his prominence in the community.

Events such as "Awareness Day" may also be used to reward supporters. In 1986 the event, now apparently annual, was held at City Hall, with Mayor Koch presiding. Awards were given out to the editor of a New York-Panamanian newsletter, the reporter who covers the Caribbean community for the *Daily News*, a prominent cleric, and a caterer who, in addition to being a CAMS contributor, had provided the refreshments. Several hundred people received elaborate invitations to the Board of Estimate Chamber for the ceremony, and though many were certainly cynical about the mayor and his interest in the Caribbean community, even some of his sternest critics attended. Thus the politics of ethnic symbolism tends to draw in even its critics, for who can risk offending the "Caribbean community" by not showing up?

During 1985 and 1986 Forde's amicable relations with Golden (who easily won reelection) continued and those with Vann deteriorated. Though he and his organization carefully avoided making endorsements in the 1985 elections, Forde used the press to attack Vann in a number of forums. While not endorsing Koch, Forde attacked those who attacked the Caribbean leaders who did endorse him, stressing that membership in the black race did not require denying the "sociological partitioning" into ethnic communities anymore than divisions between Jews, Italians, and Irish meant that they were "relinquishing their membership in, or for that matter, their obligations to, the white race" (Forde 1985).[12]

But like Hastick, Forde seeks to retain his ties with many African-American leaders (including some generally perceived as quite militant black nationalists). He emphasizes that in the long run the Caribbean community is part of a broader black community, whatever strategic alliances with white politicians its leaders may make while asserting their independence:

> Caribbean people are definitely part of the black community and we want to be. We also feel that this community should be led by a native-born black American. But we will not work with leaders who are xenophobic and who can't work with us. We must have some say. . . . Sociologically, culturally, we have some differences with black Americans, you know, some different interests, we all should recognize that. But some people will exploit those differences and try to create divisions. That can be very destructive. We have to be very careful of that. Hell, my kid was born here. He's a black American. . . . [W]e have a lot more in common, really. So a lot of people are suspicious of the overtures made by the mayor and some other politicians.

It is also true that African-American politicians, including those allied with Vann, have made efforts, albeit inconsistently, to appeal to Caribbean ethnic sentiment. In a much publicized development in 1985, Assemblyman Roger Greene, a Vann ally, secured funds to open a Caribbean Research Center at Medgar Evers College, a branch of City University located in Crown Heights. The center sought not only to study the Caribbean, but to provide information on the New York Caribbean community. The Center had been proposed by CAMS as well as other groups, and Forde was named to its board of directors. Forde, however, was not satisfied with the arrangement and accused the college president of seeking to appoint a center director who was pro-Vann, a charge that was vehemently

---

12. Of course virtually no one talks about "obligations to the white race" anymore; the whole phrase has a distinctly archaic ring to it. Today, taking pride in "race" in the biological sense is increasingly unacceptable, whereas ethnicity in the cultural sense is considered a valid basis for group identity no matter how dubious the claim of ethnic identity may be. Thus—Klansmen aside—whites rarely speak of pride in being white, but rather in being Italian, Jewish, Polish. "Black" in this discourse represents not racial but ethnic identity. "West Indian" also represents ethnic identity, which overlaps but is not synonymous with "black." Herein lies the problem for men like Forde.

denied. In the ensuing weeks charges and countercharges flew, with several activists vying for the position and making accusations. At least one local politician wrote in the *Carib News* that the whole affair exemplified the poverty of the community, in that such a small grant ($100,000) could elicit so much squabbling: "If we have to fight at all, let's wait to fight over millions of dollars, not over a few thousands" (Gumbs 1985b).

In the end the directorship was filled by a respected academic with a left-of-center perspective but not clearly associated with any New York political clique. Yet it is not surprising that an ethnic research group, even if founded by solid academics with the best of intentions, would inevitably be politicized. Ethnicity, whatever else it may be, is to a large extent a political strategy; how ethnicity is presented implies specific political positions. This is not to imply that ethnicity is in any sense unreal, or not deeply felt, but merely to emphasize that the public use of ethnic ties is a consciously chosen act that in large part emerges from the relations between the ethnic group and the government.

The Ideology of the Entrepreneurs

It is important to note that men such as Hastick and Forde hardly represent the full spectrum of political opinion in New York's West Indian community. Indeed their relative conservatism and ties to white politicians have evoked scorn in the community's radical and intellectual circles ("semiperipheral hustlers" is how one Caribbean academic describes them). As we will see in Chapter 7, Caribbean political aspirants who seek to win office for themselves rather than simply make alliances with existing officials are often critical of such men's limited vision and sometimes speak of them as "sellouts." Even in the network of several dozen full- and part-time ethnicity entrepreneurs now functioning in New York, Hastick and Forde are probably more conservative than most.

But even though militant activists claim that the version of ethnicity put forward by men such as Hastick and Forde actually has few adherents in the community at large, this version has gained considerable governmental sponsorship in New York. Thus many who may disagree with the ethnicity entrepreneurs' approach often find themselves working with them. Others work out accommodations with

[195]

other politicians that parallel those of the more conservative actors: overtures to the West Indian community by Howard Golden and Marty Markowitz, for example, produced similar overtures from Al Vann.

Ethnicity entrepreneurs have produced nothing like a West Indian political program, but they share a common view of their own activity, which is first and foremost intended to promote the idea of a West Indian community. This becomes important when one remembers that the majority of Caribbean organizations and social clubs in New York are based on national identities. The ethnicity entrepreneur is thus trying to create something beyond the consciousness of most of his constituents. In so doing he must take his cues at least partially from the milieu in which he operates—New York City. Ethnic assertion is, paradoxically, a mode of assimilation, drawn at least in part from the host nation's political culture.

Virtually all of the ethnic entrepreneurs I have interviewed profess a deep belief in pluralist democracy, although in a form that is perhaps more pluralist than democratic. They accept as a given the notion that ethnic groups are interest groups and that group representation is good for its own sake. Ethnic pluralism is seen as one of the strengths of American political life. At times this is expressed in purple terms that seem borrowed from American "Statue of Liberty" mythology. One activist notes: "This country is great because of the acceptance of each other's cultures. . . . [T]his is the process of acculturation, the respect for recognition of each other's culture. It tends to make this city, this state, a beautiful mosaic." Another states that Caribbean political mobilization "is good for the city. It adds vitality to the city. The new immigrants were Jews, Irish, Italian. Now it's Caribbean people. We are the force that will be felt. There can be no ifs, ands, or buts about it." More often it is voiced in more pragmatic terms:

Look, what is good for you may not be good for me. What is right for you is not right for me. . . . We feel that we have paid our dues, we feel that we have contributed, and we feel that we need people of our own to represent us. This is not saying that you are not good enough to, but [there] is that feeling. We have learned that everybody has their representatives. Jewish people have theirs, they back them all the way! The Italians do it, the Irish do it. Nothing wrong with us wanting to do it. . . . We need it.

Most of the younger West Indian activists in New York today came to the United States at a time when arguments for cultural pluralism had already replaced notions about the "melting pot" as a legitimizing myth. This is not to argue for or against the conclusions of works like those of Glazer and Moynihan, but simply to note that once such conclusions are accepted as "the way things work," they will have an important effect on the way groups mobilize. Thus, a young East Flatbush lawyer and political candidate expresses his appreciation for the process of ethnic competition and succession in terms that show his practical grasp of pluralist theories:

> We should represent ourselves and speak for our interests. We need to control our own areas, that is how the thing works. If I were to accept your representation, when the select job comes, why would you give it to me? You give it to yours, which is what you are supposed to do. But don't you see what happens? Every community is supposed to generate its own leadership. Every community is like a little village. You, as a person growing up in the synagogue or wherever, who do you know? Who is your running mate? Your running mate is not me, it's "Itzy,"—you say, "hey, Itz, I got a job here, you want it?" Now you not necessarily doing it because you hate anybody, you doing it because you reach for somebody you know. Now, that's what I say we should be doing.

This emphasis on the control over the affairs of one's own community has an affinity with ideas brought from the Caribbean, from Garveyism to the various twentieth-century independence struggles. As one popular Brooklyn cleric asserts, "It is better to govern oneself badly than to be governed well." Furthermore, the idea of helping one's own kind and using politics as a way of creating economic opportunities is quite consistent with the clientelist political style that dominates much of the Anglophone Caribbean today.[13]

Clientelist politics is far from unknown in the United States, particularly in the last bastions of urban political machines such as Brooklyn, Queens, and the Bronx. Thus, in the New York context, at a time when what Jim Chapin has called the "myth of machine empowerment" (quoted in Sleeper 1985:9) is in full flower, ethnic mobilization is far from rebellion but rather an example of playing by the rules. It is seen as a way of emulating those groups perceived as

13. See, for example, Stone 1980, and Singham 1968.

currently dominant. That the effectiveness of such a strategy for minority groups has always been dubious in no way diminishes the power of the mythology.[14]

This belief in ethnic mobilization as a strategy for immigrant groups is shared by many of the white politicians with whom the ethnicity entrepreneurs come in contact. In the words of a campaign strategist for a Jewish member of the state assembly representing a predominantly black and increasingly Caribbean district, one hears not only the expectation of Caribbean ethnic mobilization but the implied belief in an immigrant timetable for political empowerment: "They [West Indians] are beginning to come together as a block, you know, vote as a block and act as a block politically, like they are supposed to. . . . But it's slow. They are still not as organized as they should be by now. It's tough but it's coming."

Generally the efforts of West Indians to play ethnic politics have thus far benefited white politicians at the expense of black empowerment. Many militant activists, both African-American and Caribbean, accuse these white politicians of using a cynical "divide and conquer" strategy that the ethnicity entrepreneurs are playing into. The entrepreneurs are sensitive to this charge, and even members of Stanislaus's "Caribbeans for Koch" proclaimed loudly that "there will be no divide and conquer game here; we are too sophisticated for that." However, it would probably be a mistake to attribute too much calculation to the white politicians who help to promote West Indian ethnicity. Immigrant/ethnic mobilization is wholly consistent with the world views of such politicians. They too see this as the way things are "supposed to be," a natural consequence of the immigration process.

Many West Indian activists also profess a belief in what might be termed the "twenty-year myth." This idea, briefly stated, is that any immigrant group takes approximately twenty years to pass through the largely personal trials of making their way in their new country.

---

14. Jim Sleeper (1985), for example, questions the wisdom of seeing the political machine as a model for the empowerment of blacks. He notes that the Irish, the white American ethnic group that practiced patronage politics more effectively than any other, were also the slowest to achieve middle-class status. Historian Steven Erie has questioned the popular notion that Irish-American political machines responded to later waves of immigration by incorporating members of these groups, maintaining that the limited political capital of the machines prohibited wide distribution of rewards and that non-Irish groups gained little apart from symbolic incorporation (Erie 1985, 1988).

For the first twenty years, it is asserted, immigrants are preoccupied with basic economic survival, putting their children through school, adjusting to the new culture, and establishing the internal networks of their community. Only after this, presumably, do groups tend to turn toward political mobilization. As an education-related ethnicity entrepreneur (and rival of Forde's) puts it,

> If one goes back and studies migration patterns, particularly in New York, which is the mecca of migration, one would find that [with] the migration wave that took place at the turn of the century, it took the groups approximately twenty years to anchor some kinds of roots. And . . . after those roots have been anchored the result is that the community starts to be involved in civic issues, in community political issues.

An Afro-Panamanian activist elaborates this theme further:

> You really can't separate out the Caribbean immigration process from any other immigration process. I perceive what I call a twenty-year cycle in the immigration process. . . . Now the immigrants who came after 1960 were mostly your hard-working, poor folks . . . which are no different than the Italian or Irish immigrant. Their main concern during the first ten years is to survive and succeed, and that did not mean involvement in the political process. . . . It meant success of the children. . . . That is chronologically important because it takes fifteen, twenty years for the children to succeed . . . and that brings us up to the 1980s. So that even if a [his own name] did not exist to articulate those needs, I suspect that somewhere around 1980 to 1985 you would have a spontaneous coming forward and articulation on a political level would take place on the part of middle-aged Caribbeans, whose children had succeeded.

The questionable historical accuracy of this twenty-year myth for previous immigrant groups notwithstanding, the political implications of this view for the West Indian community are clear. Large-scale immigration from the Anglophone Caribbean resumed in 1966. In the mid-1980s the twenty-year myth is a way of asserting that "our time has come."

A variation on this theme, also borrowed from social science research on immigration, is what one activist terms "an ethnic critical mass theory." The assumption here is that the combination of numbers, length of stay in the United States, and geographical concentration naturally produces increasing political and cultural assertiveness.

This activist explains: "In any group, unless you are a lunatic—and we do have some of those—but unless you are crazy, you do not come forward and manifest your identity as a badge of honor unless, within the society your group . . . has achieved that level—notice I don't give a number—where it is perceived that the group can protect its members."

Another puts it thus:

> It's not that there was no consciousness before, but there was no base. Look, if I am a homosexual and I am an isolated individual, I stay in my closet and I function as an accountant. I move to San Francisco, then I function as a homosexual. It's not in my interest to do other-wise. You don't see no yarmulkes on the street in, uh, Yuma, Utah [*sic*]. So it's not that folks did not conceive of themselves as Caribbean before; they did, at home . . . but now they have a community base.[15]

Thus, like many political actors, the ethnicity entrepreneurs of New York's West Indian community have developed an ideology that depicts as historically inevitable an outcome that they are working hard to bring about. The twenty-year myth not only portrays political power as an entitlement, it also ties the entrepreneur to a process that is noble, quintessentially American (or at least quintessentially New York), and virtually assured as a victory. By drawing the analogy to white immigrant groups rather than making the more plausible one to nonwhite groups (many of which have been in the city far longer than twenty years and have long since achieved "critical mass"), they have produced an ideology that is both a compensation and a potential rallying point.

What if the promise of ethnic empowerment is not fulfilled? It is too early to know for sure, but it seems most likely that a failure by the ethnicity entrepreneurs to establish power bases analogous to those of European immigrant groups would be attributed to racism. Those in the community who are skeptical about the value of ethnic

15. Clearly these ideas draw not only on the political culture of the contemporary United States (and New York City in particular), but on the social sciences as well. It would be difficult, after all, to find anyone in modern society who is not somewhat influenced by what the "experts" have said about persons "like" him or her. The social scientist is involved in a multidirectional discourse that includes the persons who are being studied. Thus in assessing ideas put forward by political actors one must separate the role of an idea as an observation of reality from the role of that idea as political claim. At the same time, one must recognize that the actors may not be making this distinction.

assertion generally point to the obvious historical differences in how America has incorporated white and nonwhite immigrants. Future failure might well produce the feeling that America is, for racial reasons, welshing on its "Statue of Liberty" promises, and would in all likelihood produce a stronger identification with native blacks and other racial minorities.

Certainly there are substantial issues on the ethnicity entrepreneur's agenda involving Afro-Caribbean concerns that are clearly distinct from, if not necessarily at odds with, those of American blacks. Immigration is the most obvious of these issues. The Caribbean Action Lobby, which for a time in the mid-1980s united activists of a variety of political persuasions under one umbrella organization, was formed in the wake of the renewed debate on immigration legislation. Immigration policy not only divides the interests of black immigrants from black natives, but more surprisingly it has tended to separate them from Hispanics as well. Throughout the early 1980s New York Hispanic groups tended to join with Hispanics elsewhere in opposing immigration reforms that would penalize the employers of illegal immigrants; their opposition was a major factor in the defeat of the Simpson-Mazzoli immigration bill of 1984. Most West Indian leaders tended to support Simpson-Mazzoli and subsequent bills because of their amnesty provisions for undocumented aliens. This difference of perception could be seen in the language of the debate: in New York's Spanish-language press, Simpson-Mazzoli was the "*inmigracion*" bill, but in *Carib News* headlines it was "The Amnesty Bill."[16]

When members of the congressional Black Caucus, including Central Brooklyn congressman Major Owens, joined Hispanic legislators in opposing Simpson-Mazzoli, many West Indians were outraged. Owens's supporters and allies had a difficult time in selling this stand to their constituents, who saw it as ignoring their interests. Over the next several years immigration reform became a major unifying focus for the community. After the Simpson-Rodino Act was passed in 1986 (Owens was one of several black legislators who quietly broke ranks with their Hispanic allies and supported it), many ethnicity

16. Ironically, once a limited amnesty was passed under the 1986 Simpson-Rodino bill, Hispanics, particularly those on the West Coast, proved much more likely to take advantage of it than did West Indians.

entrepreneurs turned their attention to helping immigrants apply for amnesty, though some of the more left-leaning community activists criticized the program for not going far enough.

West Indian political actors also show an interest in, although far less unanimity on, American foreign policy as it affects the Caribbean. Owens in particular has been pushed to take stands concerning U.S.-Caribbean relations, and he has frequently been caught between factions in a community where not only every national group but also every political party in the region is represented. His strong opposition to the U.S. invasion of Grenada was seen as a mistake by many in the community, where opinion on the issue was fairly evenly divided. On the other hand Owens has won much Caribbean support by taking the lead on less controversial issues, such as supporting the overthrow of the Duvalier regime in Haiti.

There are rather few issues on which West Indian interests differ markedly from other black Americans, and Caribbean identity politics is as much a strategy for gaining access to government power as an expression of distinct community needs. Thus the ethnicity entrepreneurs often have difficulty in maintaining a credible following; their "top down" ethnic leadership is sometimes at risk of becoming disconnected from the community they supposedly lead. Many politically active West Indians reject the assimilationism of both ethnicity entrepreneurs and the old guard, but few have been as successful at securing patronage or building a support base in the community. The reasons for this lack of success highlight the dilemmas that ethnic political assertion poses for both the immigrants and for African-American politicians in New York.

The Militants: Black Power Advocates and Left-wing Intellectuals

A third loose grouping of community leaders in New York's West Indian community identify themselves with left-wing positions internationally and with the struggle for black empowerment in New York. At times when circumstances call for an African-American–Afro-Caribbean common front, such as during the weeks following the Howard Beach killing or when tensions between blacks and Hasidic Jews in Crown Heights or blacks and Korean merchants in Flatbush have flared, these actors often come to the fore. Yet they have been relatively unsuccessful at building a permanent leadership cadre.

There are a number or reasons for this. First, many of these individuals are directly tied to left-wing political groups in the Caribbean. Jamaican and Grenadian exile groups, for example, seek to play a role in the political struggle back home. They publish newsletters, raise money, hold meetings, and, like sojourners in earlier times, keep their attention focused on issues in the West Indies. Unlike the old guard, however, their Caribbean politics are radically nationalist and often anti-American. As a result it is much more difficult for such activists to balance roles in Caribbean and U.S. politics. They are, for example, less likely to consider becoming U.S. citizens. In general they tend to see their journey into the heart of the neocolonial power as a form of political exile, and this fact sometimes leaves them at odds with the majority of this community of economic migrants.

A greater limiting factor is parochialism. These activists bring to New York all of the divisions and factionalism of their home nations and sometimes find it difficult to work with countrymen with opposing points of view. Finally, as people of the left, they have less motive to become involved in U.S. politics than do other immigrants. Within the Caribbean context such persons may actually have significant influence. Their struggle has sometimes helped put sympathetic governments in power. But the natural U.S. allies of these groups have little to offer in the way of patronage or institutional support, and to join the North American left is to share its marginality.

Nevertheless, after some time in this country many such activists do put aside the narrowest of their concerns and become affiliated with other left-wing political groups under the banner of third world solidarity. This stance is particularly common among intellectuals, perhaps because the intellectual sphere is the only place in contemporary North American life where the left has an institutional foothold, tenuous as it may be. The intellectuals have taken a leading part in organizing lectures and community forums, and have brought the community into contact with many of New York's educational institutions. They contribute to both the white- and black-oriented left-wing press, can be heard on New York's "progressive" radio stations, and have generally helped to rejuvenate the city's political discourse. Their search for an institutional base often brings them into contact, indeed sometimes uncomfortably close cooperation, with the ethnicity entrepreneurs. Research centers and cultural institutions require political and corporate support, and more often than not it is the entrepreneurs who have access to such support.

Third world solidarity generally also includes a strong identification with African Americans. Within New York's West Indian community, advanced education and increased length of time in the United States seems to promote greater fellow feeling with American blacks (see Vickerman 1991; Foner 1987), and so New York-based West Indian intellectuals are among the leading advocates of black empowerment and black unity. (Often they express embarrassment at the less "progressive" attitudes displayed by many of their countrymen.) This association is reinforced by institutional ties: many Caribbean intellectuals teach in departments of African-American studies or write for African-American-oriented publications.

One prominent figure in the West Indian community today who combines many of the attributes of an ethnicity entrepreneur, a radical intellectual, and a black power advocate is Guyanese-born Colin Moore, who came to broad public attention as one of the young black lawyer-activists who helped organize community response to the killing at Howard Beach. He has also led demonstrations against the harassment of blacks by Hasidic security patrols and has been involved in many well-publicized court cases, including serving as attorney for a defendant in the 1989 Central Park jogger rape case and for the Haitian woman allegedly assaulted in the incident that sparked the Church Avenue boycott of Korean merchants in 1990.

Moore was well known in the Caribbean community long before he burst onto this broader stage in the late 1980s. Described by one knowledgeable journalist as "the left wing of the Caribbean leadership network," Moore was a founding member of the Caribbean Action Lobby (CAL) and has worked in a number of organizations with both ethnicity entrepreneurs and old guard leaders. In his regular column in the *Carib News*, which ran for several years in the mid-1980s, and on his weekly radio show, he continually urged closer cooperation between native and immigrant blacks. He has attacked Caribbean alliances with white politicians, such as "Caribbeans for Koch," but at the same time he has voiced frustration with

African-American leaders whom he sees as taking the Caribbean community for granted.

A student activist in the Caribbean, Moore came to the United States in 1970 and quickly became involved with African-American organizations in Queens, where he then lived. He recalls:

> I became involved with the United Democratic Club, I was a member of the executive board, I was a member of the Jamaica [Queens] NAACP. I was the president of the black lawyers of Queens. In actual fact my affiliation was with Afro-American politics, not Caribbean politics. I suppose the reason is that Caribbean people in Queens were not organized politically. There was no Caribbean organization there. But when I moved to Brooklyn, I became more identified with Caribbean issues, and that is when we organized CAL.

Moore cautions, however, that the expression of a specifically Caribbean agenda should not be seen as a break with the larger black community:

> The new leadership, who came in the 1960s, people like myself, we obviously have a difference in terms of orientation [from older West Indian politicians]. But even with this new sort of Caribbean nationalism, there is still an identification with blackness, with the African heritage. . . . [T]he problem is that we are under all kinds of cross pressures. [In Brooklyn] you have an Afro-American community to the north, . . . an ethnic white community to the south, an orthodox Jewish community south of Brooklyn College, and Hasidic islands right in the middle of Crown Heights. What has happened is that the community is caught between these different cultural pressures. The tendency has been to be played by one group against another. So some people say, "Now you aren't black. Well, all right, you're black, but you aren't the same as *those* folk, we can give you so and so. And the other is saying, "Yeah, you black, so blah, blah . . ." and you get a case of divided loyalties. . . . I think in terms of alliance with the progressive Afro-American community. But this may not be the consensus. It has not happened yet.

Moore has advocated black unity in Caribbean circles and has been at the same time the most prominent Caribbean in left-wing African-American circles. His writing and public speaking also frequently bring him into contact with white Americans concerned with immigration policy. In addition, he has served as attorney for many of the Caribbean political aspirants we will discuss in Chapter 7.

As the most prominent black power advocate within the Caribbean community, Moore frequently found himself outside the emerging West Indian organizational network as the 1980s wore on. Though his notions about the position of the West Indian community probably have no less grassroots support than those of the more conservative political actors (indeed, they probably have more), they clearly received less material support from outside the community. Political commitments have kept him from working closely with the city's predominantly white power structure, and in any case they have little reason to support him. On the other hand, Moore's "progressive" African-American allies have shown little interest in cultivating Caribbean organizations or in promoting an autonomous West Indian leadership cadre. Though individual West Indian activists, intellectuals in particular, were generally welcome in black left-wing circles during the mid-1980s, claims of Caribbean group entitlement were not. Thus Moore is very much a man in the middle.

Would it be possible for Moore to build an organization along the lines of those built by the entrepreneurs? Since he never tried (he abandoned his leadership role in CAL voluntarily), it is impossible to say. A successful attorney, he has never needed a patronage organization to provide himself with a paycheck. Yet it would be fair to say that New York's establishment has been considerably less receptive to his mode of ethnic leadership than to those of Stanislaus or Hastick.

During the 1980s, against a background of shifting racial and ethnic alignments, New York's West Indian leadership sought to define the community's identity. In so doing they introduced new vocabularies into the community's political discourse, vocabularies which, while ostensibly about ethnicity, are also very much about power. Yet in the broad and amorphous sphere of community leadership these vocabularies are often in flux, and the nature of leadership itself may shift from one context to another. In the narrower realm of electoral politics many of these issues come into sharper focus. It is to the history of West Indian involvement in New York's electoral politics that we now turn.

[7]

West Indians in New York Electoral Politics

> It is primarily the political community, no matter how artificially organized, that inspires the belief in common ethnicity.
>
> —MAX WEBER, *Economy and Society*

Though West Indians and persons of West Indian descent have been politically prominent in New York for many years, there was neither a recognized West Indian political constituency nor much talk of a "West Indian vote" before the early 1980s. The reason is that West Indian politicians have historically been considered—by themselves as well as others—as representatives of the broader black community. Identification with the interests of this broader community has been partly a matter of ideological commitment and partly a pragmatic matter of political demography. For the most part, however, it was a response to the overwhelming fact of racial categorization in the United States. It was race, not ethnicity in the cultural sense, that structured the life chances of West Indian immigrants. Thus it was race that conditioned their political responses, even to the point of their playing down ethnic identity in the interest of racial unity. One former state senator notes:

> I do not think you can say we had Caribbean leadership per se at that time [prior to 1970]. . . . [T]hat would not be an accurate assessment. There were persons of Caribbean background, myself included, who were elected officials with a one-hundred-percent identification of themselves as American black politicians. . . . Those political leaders of

the American black community who happened to be of Caribbean background were exercising a function as representatives of the broader American black community. In fact, most of them went out of their way to overcompensate and deny their Caribbean heritage. They did not speak publicly on any Caribbean issues—national, international, or local.

The history of West Indian participation in New York City politics appears, therefore, to defy the usual assumptions about how American ethnic groups utilize local political power. Functioning as representatives of a larger black community, Caribbean politicians started to come to the fore during the mid-1930s, at a time when the number of West Indians in New York was declining. By the late 1950s, when the West Indian proportion of New York's black community was at the lowest point in this century, West Indian individuals dominated New York black politics. But during the 1970s, as the size of the community swelled, the number of West Indians in elected office plummeted. By 1985 one activist, Ernest Skinner, would complain:

> The fact is that in Brooklyn, the borough which is home to more Caribbean residents than any place outside the homelands, there is but one elected official, an assemblyman, who is Caribbean. . . . What is interesting about this near vacuum of political leadership . . . is that it is so markedly different from the 1920s to the 1950s. . . . How do we account for this apolitical behavior from the kinfolk of the likes of Hulan Jack, . . . Constance Baker Motley, . . . and Bertram Baker? (1986c:8–9)

Of course Jack, Motley, and Baker never put themselves forward as specifically Caribbean representatives, but rather as representatives of the broader black community. Recently, however, we have seen West Indians put forward demands on a self-consciously ethnic basis. This new political style first came to public attention in 1977. It reached something of a watershed between 1982 and 1985 when it brought about sharp conflicts with other black politicians (which generally ebbed as the decade came to a close). How much appeal this ethnic politics holds for the community at large is unclear. It has not thus far delivered electoral victories, although it has shaped some electoral outcomes. It does, however, represent a marked change from earlier periods.

Black Immigrants in New York Politics before 1977

The expansion of New York's black population in the first two decades of the century brought with it a flurry of political activity. Both major parties sought to win the growing black vote, but neither was willing to make any concession that might alienate their white constituents, so alliance with the ideologically oriented leaders who arose from the labor movement or from civil rights groups was impossible. Such leaders could not serve the mainstream political parties if they were to question the foundations of the American caste structure, and they could hardly hold onto their core constituencies if they did not. Therefore both parties looked to more cooperative black associates who could get out the black vote and manage black discontent in exchange for control over patronage jobs. Ira Katznelson describes the arrangement this way: "[A] black "leader" handpicked by the white controlled machine delivered votes while avoiding contact with white voters in the area. In return the leader achieved prestige because of his influence with his white patrons and personal privilege or, at a minimum, protection from harassment. The black voters which the leaders mobilized were awarded a few menial patronage jobs to create an illusion of progress" (1973:68).

Progress was never more than an illusion, Katznelson maintains, for it provided individual mobility for only a few (usually very few) black brokers. Not only were these individuals unable to voice the interests of their constituents, but their one source of real power, patronage, was disproportionately small for the size of the community they represented.

Before the mid-1930s blacks in New York were further handicapped in their allegiance to the Republican party. The party of Lincoln had essentially abandoned its black supporters during the 1890s, but with no place else to go northern blacks reluctantly continued to support it, either out of habit or because it was seen as the lesser evil. Democratic cooperation with southern antiblack terrorism shaped the perception of that party for many African Americans, and as late as 1933, according to Harold Gosnell, Republican presidential candidates could count on 75 to 95 percent of the black vote nationally (1933). In New York the Republican connection served to politically marginalize the already socially isolated group. From Richard Croker's return from Ireland in 1897 to the election of Fiorello La

Guardia in 1933, New York was a Tammany town, and blacks could exert little influence on a Democratic machine. As a result, the black share in the spoils system was meager.[1]

By the time West Indian migration to New York peaked in the early 1920s neither of the major parties had a particularly enthusiastic following in New York's black community. The major black political movements of the era were outside the mainstream parties as disillusioned blacks, both African Americans and West Indians, were drawn into the Socialist and Communist parties or into black nationalist groups. Of all of these radical alternatives, Marcus Garvey's United Negro Improvement Association was by far the most influential as well as the most Caribbean in nature. Critics within the black community often accused the Garvey movement of being West Indian-controlled and Garvey's racial politics (with his attacks on "mulatto" leaders such as W. E. B. Dubois) of being out of place in the U.S. context. In fact, Garvey's appeal cut across African-American and Afro-Caribbean lines and much of the UNIA's national leadership was African-American. Most of the New York leaders, however, were West Indian, as were most of Garvey's inner circle.

Garvey came to the United States in 1916 with the dream of founding something like Booker T. Washington's Tuskeegee movement for his native Jamaica. By the end of the decade, however, his pan-Africanist rhetoric had become increasingly strident and his appeal spread quickly throughout black America. By the early 1920s he had assembled the first genuine black mass movement in the United States. At its height the UNIA had more than one thousand chapters, thanks largely to Garvey's ability to reach the black poor and to his popularity among the clergy. Though the movement collapsed in the United States after Garvey's deportation in 1927 (remaining strong, however, in parts of the Caribbean), its veterans went on to play central roles in a variety of contexts. A number of Caribbean ex-Garveyites and nationalists from Harlem's African Blood Brotherhood went on to prominent positions in the American Communist party and in anticolonialist groups in the Caribbean (Turner and Turner 1988; Hill 1983; Marable 1985; Burkett 1978; Clarke 1974; McKay 1940).

1. The leading black political figure in New York City during the first decade of the twentieth century was Charles Anderson, a Republican and a disciple of Booker T. Washington. Like his mentor, Anderson used his influence as a distributor of federal rather than city patronage to reward friends and punish enemies in New York's black community.

It is less well known that a number of Caribbean-born Garveyites went on to distinguished careers in mainstream Democratic party politics. Indeed many of the militants who drew inspiration from the pan-Africanism of the Garvey movement in later years would have been shocked to learn that J. Raymond Jones, the Virgin Islander who in 1964 became the first black to lead Tammany Hall, had been a member of Garvey's inner circle (Walter 1989). Likewise, Wesley MacDonald "Mac" Holder, the Guyanese dean of Brooklyn's black politics and eventual Ed Koch supporter, first came to public prominence as a UNIA official (Henry 1977b).[2]

Black nationalism splintered after the Garvey movement. Though various groups rose and fell, none achieved anything approaching the UNIA's popularity among either African Americans or West Indians. The Depression and the New Deal, moreover, limited the appeal of nationalist politics and virtually killed black Republicanism. Race temporarily took a back seat to economics, and black voters poured into the Democratic party during the 1930s (Weiss 1983). In New York the primary beneficiaries of this shift were West Indians.

The Democrats had made limited overtures to the black community as early as the 1880s. While most blacks remained firm in their commitment to the Republicans, Tammany, true to form, dragooned a Tenderloin saloon keeper into being the Democratic party's first black associate. "What was I to do?" the reluctant "leader" of his race would later wonder. "I had been a Republican. But there were too many ways these fellows could make it hard for you, like licenses, taxes, etc." (quoted in Bunche n.d.:1335). For cracking the solid Republican majorities among his customers, and for scrupulously avoiding the race issue, this man would be rewarded with the control of four low-wage patronage jobs. Katznelson notes that this would be a model of black-Tammany relations for years to come.

Eventually Tammany would set up its own black subsidiary, an organization known as United Colored Democracy (UCD), which functioned from 1898 (when the annexation of Brooklyn temporarily put Tammany on the defensive and forced it to fight for every vote,

2. Despite its militant rhetoric and the hostility it inspired in whites, the black nationalism of the early 1920s was in some ways more compatible with the values of the political machine than with those of the left. Jones later insisted that "The U.N.I.A. was in no way radical. It was thoroughly American, more so than Eugene V. Debs and the Socialist Party. . . . If anything the Department of Justice should have been pleased with Garveyism . . . if one considers the trading and political connections the U.N.I.A. had established with the Caribbean and Africa" (quoted in Walter 1989:42).

even black votes) until its leadership followed the patronage jobs that were the organization's *raison d'etre* and defected en masse to the Republican-Fusion La Guardia administration after the 1933 election. The UCD was not a Tammany "club." It had no geographic base, for to create a geographically based organization would have meant disenfranchising a white clubhouse. Thus it had neither its own county committee representatives nor a voice in choosing party leadership. It was instead a segregated "broker" institution whose goals were to deliver black votes to Democrats and patronage jobs to blacks (Gosnell 1933; Snowden 1935).

Historians disagree on the efficacy of the organization. For Osofsky, the UCD represented a "taste of honey," providing a substantive foothold in local politics which in turn "proved a wedge for economic achievement" (1963:177). Katznelson, in contrast, argues that blacks achieved neither real political power nor any economic achievement to speak of during this period and that the power of both the UCD and its more respectable Republican counterparts was largely illusory. He writes:

> The political honey that Osofsky asserted was tasted by New York blacks and spooned to a few, but to very few. The political linkages fashioned . . . [during the 1920s] were the product of a white elite strategy . . . of social control that structurally linked blacks to the polity in a manner strikingly different from the decentralized machine links of other ethnic groups. White Democratic and Republican political leaders wanted, and sometimes very badly needed, black votes, but on terms that did not disturb the racial status quo. . . . Neither the U.C.D. nor the black Republican leadership was representative beyond the symbolic level. (1973:84).

West Indian immigrants joined both major parties. Yet despite ample representation among GOP workers, West Indians were largely absent from New York's black Republican leadership. In part this was due to the traditional role the party played among the black social elite. During the early twentieth century the black Republican inner circle was dominated by members of the city's leading black families and was thus extremely difficult for an immigrant to penetrate.[3] The less respectable Democrats proved more hospitable to

3. As Calvin Holder points out, the exceptions tend to prove the rule: those West Indians who became Republicans also tended to members of the black social elite. When

newcomers; in the 1920's West Indian John Shaw, who was among the UCD's leading strategists, was rewarded with the potentially lucrative patronage position of deputy tax assessor for the Borough of Queens (Holder 1980).[4]

Lacking the deep antipathy of many African Americans toward the Democratic party, West Indians were perhaps better able to assess its role in New York. If the goal of electoral politics was not social reform but patronage, it was logical to go where the patronage was centered, and that meant to Tammany. Years later, J. Raymond Jones would recall: "By 1930 any astute observer could see that Blacks were getting fed up with the Republicans. Certainly with the State Legislature, the Governor and the City Board of Alderman predominantly Democratic, the already minimal advantage of being a Republican had been further reduced. . . . We, the new Democrats, made up in great part of West Indian immigrants, had no such allegiance" (quoted in Walter 1989:51).

After the UCD collapsed, West Indians took advantage of the opportunity to join the regular Democratic clubs. The concentration of established black leaders in the Republican party and Tammany's need to make inroads into the growing black population created opportunities that West Indian politicians quickly took advantage of. Historian Calvin Holder notes:

> West Indians . . . were more aware of the political shifts taking place in the black community. They recognized that the Republican Party's traditional hegemony in the black community was being eroded. . . . Thus, joining the Democratic Party put them in a position to capitalize on these changes. . . . West Indians also had no traditional loyalty and attachments to the Republican Party, as many Afro-Americans did, particularly those of middle class backgrounds. Nor were they the victims of lynchings and other barbarities at the hands of the Democrats. To the West Indian, the Democratic Party controlled New York City . . . and this was a political reality which had to be confronted (1980:50).

During the 1930s the growing importance of the black vote within the Democratic party gave Caribbean political activists considerably more clout in making demands, albeit within the narrow parameters

the party did nominate a West Indian for the state assembly in 1926, it chose H. A. Howell, a well-known civic leader and one of the richest black men in New York (Holder 1980).

4. Many other leading UCD members were recent arrivals from the South.

of patronage politics. The Democrats were also under some pressure to counter defections to the Communist party and the American Labor party (ALP), both of which supported the New Deal at the national level but were opposed to Tammany in New York.[5] Thus, while the La Guardia years were lean for Tammany, the party's problems opened opportunities for blacks. Both the city's demographics and its ethnic political alignments were changing, and many black activists, West Indians prominent among them, used this period to plant seeds that would germinate after the Democrats came back into power in New York after 1945.

The 1930s were a growth period for the left in general and Harlem's Communist party in particular. A number of talented immigrants, veterans of the Garvey movement, the African Blood Brotherhood and the Socialist party, had become Communists during the 1920s. Indeed, Mark Naison reports that four of the five founding members of the Harlem branch of the Communist party were West Indians (1983:5). These included two of the most important of the party's early black spokesmen, Cyril Briggs, a native of Nevis, and Barbados-born Richard Moore. They would shortly be joined by the Jamaican writer and poet Claude McKay, who attended the Fourth Congress of the Communist International in 1922 at the urging of his friend Max Eastman (Cooper 1987). But soon West Indian representation in the Communist leadership began to decline.

Why this group lost its leadership role in the Communist movement is a matter of some disagreement. McKay, so deeply disillusioned by the Soviet Union that he eventually became a strident anti-Communist, would later claim that the party had purged the Caribbean leaders on direct orders from the Comintern to "Americanize itself" (McKay 1940:252). Naison, a more sympathetic chronicler of Harlem Communism, attributes the split to differences over the role of black nationalism in the movement and to the reluctance of the Caribbean militants to accept party discipline. Whatever the reasons, in 1933 the Central Committee of the American Communist

5. The American Labor party provided an opportunity for left-wing voters who had never supported a major party candidate to support the New Deal, and it provided the La Guardia administration with a ballot line that would be both pro-Roosevelt and anti-Tammany. In the 1937 election La Guardia received more than one third of his votes on the ALP line; twice as many Jewish voters voted for La Guardia on the ALP line as on the Republican (see Bayor 1978).

party placed James Ford, an African American from Chicago, in charge of the Harlem group. Briggs and Moore were accused of "petite bourgeois nationalism" and pushed out of positions of authority (Moore remained a key Communist spokesman on the Scottsboro Boys case). They were both expelled from the party in 1942 (Turner and Turner 1988; Naison 1983).[6]

Thus the combination of expanding opportunities and ideological strife on the far left pulled many black immigrants to the Democrats. The election of Herbert Bruce, a native of Barbados, as a Tammany district leader in 1935 marks the beginning of a period of West Indian ascendancy in New York black Democratic politics. Bruce was the first black man to serve on the Tammany executive committee. His election and subsequent attempts to place allies in positions in the organization sparked fears within black political circles of a West Indian takeover. Reid quotes a 1937 handbill that captured the mood of the period:

> IS THIS FAIR? BRUCE ousts Mrs. Elizabeth Ross Haynes so he can have a West Indian Woman for Co-Leader!
> IS THIS FAIR?
> Leader Bruce is a West Indian!
> The State Committeeman Thomas B. Dyett is a West Indian!
> The majority of his Negro Job Holders are West Indians!
> NOW—Mrs. Haynes must be thrown out to make room for a Co-Leader WHO IS A WEST INDIAN! (1939:169)

In the face of such charges, the usual response was to play down ethnic identity. West Indian officeholders quietly asserted that they worked in the interest of all black people and made efforts to balance the distribution of patronage jobs (Lewinson 1974). In Bruce's case such assurances were facilitated by his reputation for personal honesty, a trait so unusual among Tammany leaders of his era as to seem almost deliberately perverse. Honesty, along with independence from Harlem's powerful left, served a purpose for Bruce. It allowed him to be the first New York black politician to break the mold of white sponsorship. As Kenneth Clark would later write, "he took no

---

6. Briggs was eventually reinstated. Moore, who had long been at odds with the party leadership over his close ties to non-Communist black groups, broke with the party permanently and never looked back. He eventually became a leading advocate of Caribbean self-government (Turner and Turner, 1988).

money from Tammany to run his district and therefore, when he went 'downtown' he could demand and did not need to beg" (1965:157).

Over the next two decades, while the proportion of West Indians in New York's black community declined, the number holding positions in the Democratic party steadily increased. This would become extremely important after 1945 when the Democrats, back in power, had substantial patronage to disburse. Jones was one of the managers of William O'Dwyer's 1945 mayoral campaign and emerged from it as one of the most powerful Democrats in the city. Bertram Baker, a native of Nevis who joined a Brooklyn Democratic club shortly after becoming a U.S. citizen in 1925, became the first black state assemblyman from that borough in 1948. By 1952 four of the five Democratic district leaders in Harlem were West Indians, as was the only black district leader in Brooklyn (Lewinson 1974; Holder 1980).

One of the most notable of these men, both for his spectacular rise and his ignominious fall, was Hulan Jack. Jack, who was born in British Guiana and raised on St. Lucia, came to New York as a teenager and found work as a printer's assistant. When he joined East Harlem's notoriously corrupt Owasco Democratic Club in 1930, blacks were not yet permitted above the club's ground floor. Yet as with Jones and Baker, these early ties to Tammany would prove invaluable in later years. Unswervingly loyal to the machine, Jack profited from both growing black demographic strength and the shift of black voters to the Democrats. In 1940 he was elected to the New York State Assembly with Tammany support and in 1953 he was elected borough president of Manhattan. He thus became one of the highest ranking black officeholders in the nation and the only one not representing an overwhelmingly black constituency (Jack 1982; Lewinson 1974).[7]

7. Though Jack served his party with single-minded loyalty, he was hardly an "Uncle Tom." While in Albany he wrote numerous civil rights and antidiscrimination bills, most of which were ignored at the time only to become law decades later. As borough president he used his position to draw attention to racism, taking public stands on such issues as the murder of Emmet Till. His Tammany colleagues seem to have viewed this activity as Jack's ethnic prerogative, much as they would expect an Irish politician to make speeches about the British occupation of Northern Ireland or a Jewish one to support a Zionist homeland in Palestine. It was only on local issues that party loyalty was paramount, and there Jack could be counted on, such as when he supported Carmine Disapio's efforts to oust Congressman Adam Clayton Powell in 1958.

Jack held the borough presidency until 1960, when he was convicted of obstructing justice and of three city charter violations in connection with his use of city funds to redecorate his apartment (Jack 1982). While few of Jack's supporters ever protested his innocence, they argued that by Tammany standards his crimes were trivial, and that the party was employing a double standard because of his race. Jack held the East Harlem district leadership until 1967, and was returned to his old seat in the state assembly from 1968 until 1972. Yet his real power within the party was gone. Shortly after losing his assembly seat in 1972 he was convicted of conflict of interest, conspiracy, and several misdemeanors under the Taft-Hartley Act and served three months in federal prison. He died in December 1986, an embittered follower of Lyndon Larouche.

It should be noted that the West Indian domination of the Democratic party in the black community during the 1940s and 1950s does not reflect a monopoly on other leadership positions. Black politics has often drawn its most popular leaders, both inside and outside of electoral politics, from nontraditional political backgrounds. These alternative power bases (which reflect the lack of legitimacy accorded to the standard political structures) were (and are) common in the black community, and so many leading black public officials of this era were quite independent of the party. Some, like William Hastie (the first black appointed to the federal circuit court), Ralph Bunche, and Thurgood Marshall, had made their mark in law, civil rights organizations, and academia before being appointed to governmental positions. Others derived their leadership positions from their roles in black civil society, and particularly from the church.

Many elected officials as well had nontraditional power bases. During the 1940s several of New York's leading black political figures had independent constituencies on the left, including Communist city councilman Ben Davis, and others had support networks derived from the church. Adam Clayton Powell, Jr., Harlem's congressman after 1945, had both.[8] In fact, the rise of several leading West Indian Democrats during the 1950s reflects, at least in part, a response to

8. In *Dark Ghetto*, Kenneth Clark points out that Powell, who accepted Communist support early in his career and renounced it later, was probably the only American elected official to be openly associated with the Communist party and not to suffer for it politically, "the only one able to use the Communists and then discard them when they no longer proved useful" (1965:165).

the vacuum created by the electoral collapse of Harlem's Communist party and its American Labor party allies, just as their advancement during the 1930s was in part due to the collapse of Harlem's Republican party.

At the risk of overgeneralizing, one can say that from the return of the Democrats to power in 1946 until the election of Liberal-Republican John Lindsay in 1965, New York's black politicians were divided between those whose position was based on ties within the Democratic Party, mostly West Indians, and those who were largely independent of it, with a few notable exceptions, African Americans.

The reason for this division may well lie in the immigrants' lack of ties to the institutions of black civil society. There was no West Indian politician with an inherited position in the black church like that of Adam Clayton Powell, for example. During this period, with the number of West Indians in New York in sharp decline, Caribbean-centered institutions offered little political promise, and African-American ones, while not exactly closed to immigrants, were not really "theirs." The political club, on the other hand, was as open to them as it was to any other blacks, and the Anglo-Saxon political traditions of the islands left them at least as prepared for the operation of the New York Democratic party as were disenfranchised blacks from the South. In describing the difference between New York's two most powerful blacks of the late 1950s, Jones and Powell, Edwin Lewinson may have hit on the key difference between African-American and Caribbean political styles:

> Powell made himself a symbol of black aspirations, while Jones's career resembles that of a political leader of a white ethnic group whose members have not yet reached the middle class. For Jones, as for generations of poor white immigrant boys with ability and ambition but without formal education, political leadership has been the road to money, power and social mobility. . . . The *New York Post* accurately characterized his role when it titled a feature on him "Political Productions Need Directors as Well as Stars." Beginning in politics in the 1920's he first ran for public office in 1963. He has wielded power because of a combination of his astuteness and the growing importance of the black vote. (1974:144).

Before the mid-1960s African-American politicians often cultivated oppositional stances that were anything but typical for American politicians. Powerless to radically alter the racial division of opportunity, they could at least use public office as a stage to act out their constituents' discontents. They could be ideologues or saints or, like Powell, Robin Hoods. Whatever the role, such men were players in a drama. Thus it mattered little when the Washington press core voted Powell the least effective man in Congress (Clark 1965). His purpose was not to be effective in the traditional sense, but rather to win vicarious revenge for his powerless constituents (if annoying the white establishment is a measure of his success in this, he was very effective indeed). Yet this sort of stance was only possible because such leaders were not beholden to the party; indeed, Powell bolted the national Democratic party on several occasions and was frequently at odds with the local party leaders. But such a stance also requires that the expectations of one's constituents be for drama, not for service delivery. The types of political alliances and quid pro quo's required for normal effectiveness in the diffuse American political system are essentially foreclosed by a confrontational style like Powell's.

J. Raymond Jones functioned quite differently. Once described by Theodore White as a "master political technician" (1960:4), Jones played a simple game: he bargained votes for power and jobs. As the black vote grew, so did his power. Like other West Indian Democratic politicians of his day, Jones rejected both the constant confrontation of a Powell or a Ben Davis and the complete subservience of the old UCD. Instead he relied on what Jim Sleeper has termed "a canny mixing of confrontation and accommodation with white political machines" (1988:8) which earned him the nickname "the fox." Jones never saw politics as a redemptive force in people's lives, and he had little patience with the liberal dream of a color-blind society. When in 1960 the American Civil Liberties Union attempted to make the census drop racial categories, he called the idea "The silliest damn thing I ever heard of. How am I supposed to bargain for the Negroes if I can't prove how many there are? I'm losing too many as it is, with all of this crossing the color line" (quoted in Lewinson 1974:160).

Differences between African-American and West Indian politicians were matters of style, not of substance. No West Indian politician could be effective in New York as a "West Indian politician," nor is there any evidence that any thought of themselves in that way. All worked closely with African Americans in mixed clubhouses. None differed substantially on major issues with African Americans, and there were no identifiable "West Indian" positions. Prior to 1977 there was no unified West Indian faction within black politics, despite the importance of West Indians in the Democratic party structure.

Indeed, prominent Caribbean-American politicians ran against each other as often as not, and intraparty factional disputes often had West Indians on both sides. Jones ran against Herbert Bruce for the Harlem district leadership in 1942, and in later years he sometimes sided with Powell against fellow islander Jack. "Mac" Holder, who served for over fifty years as black Brooklyn's premier political tactician, several times ran unsuccessfully in the 1950s against Bertram Baker, then the borough's one black state assemblyman and the choice of the Democratic party. In 1962 Holder turned around and ran on the "machine" ticket for the Democratic party county committee against Barbadian Thomas R. Jones. In Brooklyn during the late 1950s and early 1960s, both black "regulars" and black "reformers" tended to be persons of Caribbean background. And when court-ordered redistricting finally created a black congressional district in Brooklyn in 1968, both of the two candidates for it in the Democratic party primary, Shirley Chisholm and William Thompson, were Brooklyn-born children of Barbadian parents.

By the 1960s, however, the passing of the first generation of pre-1930 immigrants had substantially blurred the line between African Americans and West Indians. One political veteran says: "Hey, we are Americans. I have served in the army; I marched in civil rights demonstrations. We have the same interests. If there is a difference it is one of attitudes. As expatriates we have to be more vigorous, more ambitious just to survive. That's all."

In a similar vein Chisholm has written:

> [It's] an inescapable fact, but one I have never liked to discuss because of the bad feeling it can cause, that a surprising number of successful black politicians are of West Indian descent. . . . In Brooklyn I have heard people grumbling for years, "They're taking over everything." . . . There is a strong undercurrent of resentment.
>
> It is wrong, because the accident that my ancestors were brought as slaves to the islands while black mainland natives' ancestors were brought as slaves to the States is not really important compared to the

common heritage of black brotherhood and unity in the face of oppression. . . . But the feeling is there. . . . I think that blacks from the islands tend to have less fear of whites, and therefore less hatred of them. They can meet whites as equals; this is harder for American blacks who tend to overreact by jumping from feeling that whites are superior to looking down on them as inferior. (1970:76–77)

The 1960s produced great changes in black politics in New York and the nation. The first factor in these changes was the civil rights movement and the leadership that emerged from it, which directly challenged American racism. Both Powell's redemptive drama and Jones's patronage pragmatism paled in comparison. The movement politicized a new generation and heightened interest in political involvement. The riots that followed in the movement's wake in the second half of the decade also made it unmistakably clear that the traditional political arrangements in the ghettos had become inadequate to maintain blacks' quiescence.

A second instrument of change was the Supreme Court's 1963 "one man one vote" decision. By ruling that electoral districts must be of equal size and "compact and contiguous," the Court struck down the most blatant forms of gerrymandering. This opened the way for major redistricting in New York, particularly in Brooklyn and Queens, that vastly enlarged the size of the political arena for blacks. A third major shift was the "war on poverty," the massive increase in federal participation in black neighborhoods which bypassed much of the traditional power structure and opened opportunities for groups outside the party machinery. Finally, the New York situation was transformed by the election of the Republican-Liberal "fusion" administration of John Lindsay in 1965.

As a result, with the original immigrant generation fading from the scene, a new group of African-American politicians who had come of age in the ferment of the late 1960s came to the fore. Many of these individuals made their initial mark in "great society" agencies. They also made alliances with the Lindsay administration, an inherently unstable coalition of "silk-stocking" Republicans, Liberals, old-style "good government" reformers, racial minorities, and the left. By the late 1960s a new black politics was being created by people with no experience in the traditional Democratic party clubhouses. Most of these individuals were African Americans.

The movement for decentralization of city services produced a system of parallel institutions where many of these activists received their start. The fight over school decentralization and the subsequent 1968 teachers' strike produced a sharp split between many black teachers and community activists and the traditionally liberal, predominantly Jewish teachers' union. Many of the black teachers who crossed the picket lines in 1968 subsequently left teaching, but not politics, and the community school boards remained hotbeds of minority activism.

After the Lindsay administration most of these activists found their way into the Democratic party. By the late 1970s some had become Democratic representatives in Albany and Washington. Yet they retained their independent power bases and built ties to others, particularly the black church. In Brooklyn (rapidly replacing Harlem as the center of black life in New York) a coalition of these activists founded a sort of party within a party, the "Coalition for Community Empowerment," led by Assemblyman Vann, whose most prominent members included Congressman Owens, Assemblyman Roger Green, and State Senator Velmanette Montgomery. While a number of West Indians have worked with this group and several occupy key staff positions, all of its elected officials have been African Americans (many of them first-generation emigrants from the South). Their lack of dependence on the party was illustrated both by their almost constant opposition to Democratic Mayor Ed Koch, and by the fact that on several occasions members have lost the Democratic nomination in the courts (usually by having their nominating petitions invalidated) and yet won the general elections on independent lines.[9]

At the same time, African Americans were gaining positions within the Democratic party structure as well. With the passing of the earlier immigrant cohorts, many clubs that had been dominated by West Indians gradually came to be controlled by African-American

9. In New York, where in many districts the Democratic nomination virtually guarantees election, challenging primary nominating petitions has become something of a tradition. Originally a tactic of the machine (who could rely on sympathetic judges) to cripple insurgents, it is now practiced by almost everybody including the Empowerment group, which has also often been the victim of this tactic. The practice is facilitated by New York's arcane and at times bizarre regulations governing nominating petitions that force a candidate to collect three, four, or perhaps even five times the required number of signatures in order to assure that his petitions survive challenge. In 1986 over two hundred candidates statewide, including Vann and Green, were eliminated from the primary ballot in this manner.

politicians. As the black vote grew during the 1970s Brooklyn's Democratic machine came to perceive a need for moderate alternatives to Vann and his associates, and found them in a generation of traditional clubhouse politicians who were, for the most part, African Americans. Several of these figures proved overly committed to New York Democratic party traditions: by 1984 two of the most prominent, former state senator Vander Beatty and former city councilman Sam Wright, were in prison, having been convicted of voter fraud and extortion, respectively (Sleeper 1990). Still, both inside the party and among the insurgents the number of West Indians continued to decline at the same time the immigrant population was expanding. When Shirley Chisholm retired from politics in 1982—the last figure of stature who might have served to mediate between the new immigrants—the clubhouse politicians and the Empowerment group had passed from the scene, leaving an atmosphere ripe for confrontation.

The New West Indian Politics

Waldaba Stewart, New York state senator from 1969 to 1973, identifies a crucial moment in West Indian politics: "The Caribbean community had the potential for political power from, I'd say, 1950. However, we had to reach a point when enough of those people . . . felt strong enough, comfortable enough to say 'I am a Caribbean, and I think my local politician should voice Caribbean concerns.' That period of time arrived around 1980 and became manifest, politically, in the election of 1982."

When Lamuel Stanislaus formed a support group for the mayoral candidacy of Manhattan borough president Percy Sutton in 1977, it attracted little attention. In that year's hotly contested seven-way primary, it was but one of dozens of groups of politically active New Yorkers who were raising funds or attempting to drum up support for various candidates. Nor did Stanislaus's group of mostly middle-aged, middle-class West Indians have much impact on the election's outcome, as Sutton finished near the bottom of the pack.

In light of subsequent developments, however, this group is important for two reasons. It was the first time such a group had publicly declared itself to be "Caribbeans for" anything. The new strategy asserted, if perhaps not completely intentionally, that a

[223]

Caribbean constituency existed and was able to use the political process to support West Indian interests. That this occurred at a time when New York politics was becoming increasingly racially polarized in the wake of the fiscal crisis further adds to its significance.

The group was also important in that it brought together, in a self-consciously Caribbean forum, a group of individuals who would go on to form the core of other groups over the next several years. "Caribbeans for Percy Sutton" built on ties formed among traditional immigrant associations and the WIADCA. Through it, these ties would become manifestly political. Many of its members would be central figures in a far more controversial group, "Caribbeans for Koch," in 1985.

These individuals had become uncomfortable with the direction of New York's black leadership. During the 1970s death, retirement, and elevation to the bench had depleted the ranks of the old Caribbean-American leadership, particularly in Brooklyn.[10] Thus the buffer between the new immigrant community and the black political leadership was eroding.

The political tone of "Caribbeans for Sutton" was decidedly mild, and its leadership largely comprised respectable, professional old-guard types. At the same time, however, other West Indians, including younger and more recent immigrants, were beginning to take an active role in U.S. politics. In 1980 Colin Moore, former state senator Waldaba Stewart and Trinidad-born Los Angeles congressman Mervyn Dymally organized some of this concern by founding the Caribbean Action Lobby (CAL). While this organization's membership overlapped that of "Caribbeans for Percy Sutton," it was generally younger and somewhat further to the left politically. Some members, like Moore, had backgrounds of student activism in the Caribbean, and others were educated in the United States. But like "Caribbeans for Percy Sutton," CAL attempted to mobilize ethnic ties into a political interest group. Its membership was and is pan-Caribbean and, like organizations founded by other immigrant groups, it is somewhere between a lobbying body with international concerns and a local political organization.

On a national level CAL functions as a lobbying group concerned

10. This situation was somewhat less pronounced in Manhattan, where the Harlem gerontocracy held on a good deal longer.

with Caribbean and immigration issues. Its nominal chairman, Congressman Dymally, has long been the leading proponent of aid to the Anglophone Caribbean on Capitol Hill, and has used the group to mobilize support. In New York, however, where most of CAL's membership is located, the organization quickly turned to local concerns, and both of its local chairmen—Moore and later Stewart—have attempted to use the organization to support the local agenda. Moore notes: "CAL is basically Caribbean-focused. It was founded to lobby on specific pieces of legislation, but since that time it has stretched out. It is becoming more political. It will remain Caribbean-focused, because there is a reality that Caribbean people have specific concerns, in the Caribbean, and here as well."

As an organization, CAL was not able to fully make the transition to local concerns. While it has tried to endorse local candidates, disagreements arise so often between members committed to various politicians that, as one officer put it, "we tend to agree to disagree." As its membership is based on ethnic identity, not political ideology, and as it has tried to incorporate a wide variety of opinions, it has been more of a forum for discussion than the consensus-building organization its founders envisioned. Nevertheless, the attempt to form a pan-Caribbean organization with New York political interests represents something quite new. CAL managed to bring together a cross section of the community's new intelligentsia, and for awhile it functioned something like a steering committee.

Waldaba Stewart, who succeeded Moore as the dominant figure in CAL, steered a course that put him (although not necessarily the organization) in direct conflict with the African-American leadership and particularly the Empowerment group. A Panamanian whom many see as the bridge between the older and newer Caribbean leadership, Stewart served in the state senate in the late 1960s and early 1970s, where he was known for his militant black nationalism. By the late 1970s, however, Stewart, who was involved in a wide variety of political and social service activities in Brooklyn, found himself increasingly identified with Caribbean concerns.

In 1982 the boundaries of many electoral districts were redrawn to reflect the changing demographics of the city as reported in the 1980 census. The result was the creation of a number of predominantly black districts in the outer boroughs, several of which were substantially Caribbean. Stewart and a number of other CAL members approached the Empowerment leadership concerning the possibility of selecting a Caribbean candidate to run in the Democratic primary for the newly reconstituted Twenty-first State Senatorial District. This district ran across Crown Heights and East Flatbush, and while it included Jewish and predominantly African-American enclaves, it certainly was more West Indian than anything else.

The Twenty-first's white incumbent, Martin Markowitz, found himself representing a district with a large black majority and fighting for his political life. Since the Democratic nominee is virtually assured of election in the district, primary endorsement is of signal importance. Stewart denies that he was ever interested in returning to Albany himself, only in securing the position for a West Indian, but others in the Empowerment camp believe that he was planning to run and wanted their endorsement. In any event the discussions left bad feelings on both sides. As one Empowerment team member later noted, "We were new ourselves and probably too defensive." The group selected an unknown young African American to run on a slate headed by Major Owens, their candidate for the newly redrawn Twelfth Congressional District. Markowitz obtained the endorsement of the other African-American congressional candidate, Vander Beatty.

Livid at the perceived snub, Stewart decided to embark on what he now describes as a protest candidacy. "You could not have a real candidacy without a congressional candidate on the ticket," he recalls. "If I had been serious I would have run with a congressional candidate, or I would have run for Congress. I was interested in facilitating a sense of outrage." Though he finished only third in the primary voting, Stewart's candidacy probably prevented the election of the Empowerment candidate despite Owens's strong showing at the top of the ticket. Stewart received 22 percent of the vote, enough to ensure Markowitz's victory. Even more surprising was that Markowitz apparently received significant black support in addition to the expected heavy support among Jewish voters.

Stewart's protest candidacy was not the only Caribbean electoral surprise of the year. In the neighboring Seventeenth Senatorial District, which included parts of East Flatbush and Canarsie, the black vote was split between African-American and West Indian candidates, and the white incumbent (who probably would have won in any event) came in first by a huge margin. In the Sixth Congressional

District of Queens, which included the fastest growing Caribbean neighborhoods of Laurelton, Queens Village, and Cambria Heights, the veteran white incumbent Joseph Addabbo easily beat a challenger associated with the Empowerment group, former Lindsay administration official Simeon Golar. In that case the causes were less clear: Addabbo received significant African-American support (and Golar took nearly 20 percent of the white vote), but West Indian support seemed to help the incumbent, or so CAL leaders would afterwards claim.

The bitterest of the West Indian primary fights of 1982 was probably the battle in East Flatbush's Forty-second Assembly District. Here Anthony Agard, a young lawyer who had emigrated from Trinidad in 1968, faced a Jewish incumbent in a district that, like the Twenty-first Senatorial District, was now largely black. Agard started his door-to-door campaign on a shoestring, using relatives as a staff, but with the hope that the Empowerment team would eventually endorse him, or at least stay neutral. He was shocked when most of the Empowerment leaders including Owens endorsed the incumbent, Rhoda Jacobs. He later told reporters: "[They were] trading the endorsement for Jewish support in other districts. In doing so they supported a white candidate in a district that had been specifically created to provide more minority representation" (quoted in Tennant 1984:12).

This sort of quid pro quo is, of course, fairly typical of New York politics, but it left West Indian activists bitter. At the very moment that Stewart was being berated for "tribalism" and other aspersions were being cast on West Indians for supporting white incumbents, African-American leaders had proved unwilling to support a West Indian. Agard received 42 percent of the primary vote, a quite respectable showing for a political neophyte running without a slate. Still, as in the other races, the primary beneficiaries of the African-American–West Indian split were white politicians representing primarily black districts.[11]

Despite this outcome, many West Indian politicians see the 1982 primary as a hopeful turning point. Stewart insists that "1982 de-

11. For a different interpretation of these events, which sees the power of incumbency rather than ethnic conflict as the key factor in the Jacobs and Addabbo victories, see Green and Wilson (1989). The authors agree, however, that intra-black ethnic conflict was a central factor in the Twenty-first Senatorial District.

stroyed the mythology that black leaders could automatically take for granted all of the component parts of the black community."

But it was also a year of hard lessons. Despite the growing West Indian population in many districts, mobilizing voters proved a complex task. Though the number of naturalized black immigrants was steadily increasing, most of the community was still not eligible to vote. As of 1980, surveys indicate that only 38 percent of New York's foreign-born blacks were U.S. citizens, and in heavily Caribbean neighborhoods like Crown Heights and East Flatbush the percentage was probably lower due to the concentration of recent immigrants. In addition, black New Yorkers including Caribbeans tend to be younger than their white neighbors. Over one third of blacks were too young to vote in 1980, whereas less than 20 percent of white Catholics and only about 10 percent of Jews were under eighteen (Mollenkopf 1989:12–14). Thus in some neighborhoods where West Indians constituted a large majority of the population, they were still only a minority of the potential voters. This fact was not lost on rival politicians, black or white.

The Democratic primary of 1984 proved to be largely a rematch of the confrontations of 1982. The year opened with great promise for the Empowerment group. Vann chaired the Jesse Jackson presidential bid in the city, which many saw as a dry run for a possible black mayoral candidacy, and he achieved spectacular results. Boosting voter registration and mobilizing scores of street-level campaign workers, Vann raked up huge majorities for Jackson in all of the city's predominantly black districts in the April primary, including many represented by white incumbents. Jackson's support was as strong in West Indian neighborhoods as in African-American ones, and Stewart was an early supporter. Building on these results, the Empowerment group then targeted a number of seats for the local primary in September, with Addabbo and Markowitz both high on their list.

What happened surprised almost everybody, except perhaps Markowitz. While his opponents emphasized the politics of race in the increasingly black district, Markowitz, who was assured of virtually all of the district's white votes, reached out to the black community as service consumers, home owners, ethnic group members, and every other nonracial identity he could think of. Seeing their support as increasingly crucial, Markowitz vigorously courted West Indians. He sponsored calypso contests and pop concerts, and solicited the support of the WIADCA, on whose behalf he interceded when sanitary regulations endangered its Carnival parade permit. Few Caribbean groups could hold a gathering, large or small, where he did not put in an appearance. He used his senate seat to arrange awards and proclamations in recognition of various Caribbean groups (and African-American social organizations as well). He dispensed Christmas gifts to nursing home residents, supported community business groups, and gave away tickets to baseball games. A Haitian teacher who had just received one of Markowitz's many awards in recognition of her work in bilingual education quipped: "You see Marty's converted. He's done being Jewish. Too few votes. He going to be Haitian from now on."

He was also the first politician to attempt to draw the network of Caribbean voluntary associations into New York politics. As it turned out, Markowitz's political style and high-spirited personality were more compatible with the voluntary associations than those of most local politicians. He stands in particular contrast to the dignified, almost somber Vann. One West Indian supporter commented: "It's just the way Marty is. Marty's got no wife, Marty's got no girlfriend. Marty don't want to do nothing on a Saturday night but go to seven different parties. It's his life."

Still, if the sight of the jovial, corpulent Markowitz dashing from Caribbean fete to Caribbean fete or introducing the latest calypso sensation at his free concert series inspired a good deal of humor, it also inspired respect and paid electoral dividends. If the senator seemed a bit incongruous giving out awards at association dinners to Caribbean notables or sharing the stage with Caribbean musicians, the fact was noted that he took the time to find out who the notables and appropriate musicians were. Voluntary association leaders, not used to being courted by U.S. politicians, were particularly taken with the attention Markowitz paid them. The legislator's efforts were a source of resentment for some West Indian leaders who found the act patronizing, but there can be little denying that this sort of out-reach, plus Markowitz's reputation for service delivery, was effec-tive. No politician, black or white, had previously courted West In-dians as such, and while his attempts to win new friends did often border on the comic, the fact that he made the effort was appreci-ated.

In 1984 the Empowerment team nominated the same candidate as two years previous. CAL and other Caribbean groups stayed officially neutral, but many of their members openly supported Markowitz, who formed a slate with a Crown Heights Hasidic district leader and a popular Jamaican accountant who challenged an Empowerment team member for the state assembly (leaving no base uncovered, they also slated an African-American woman for coleader). Markowitz seemed to relish the incongruities of his role, and attempts to make race an issue played into his hands. At one debate his opponent quipped, "One candidate is white, I'm the candidate that's right." Markowitz responded by striding to the podium and announcing to the mostly black audience, "Ladies and gentlemen, *I* am the white candidate." Then after a deep bow, he said, "If I don't deliver, throw me the hell out!" He won by an almost two-to-one margin, without the help of a spoiler.

In Queens, Addabbo again faced Golar for Congress, and this time the latter sought to play on Jackson's large majority in the district by emphasizing race in his campaign. The strategy backfired. Golar lost virtually all of the white vote he had taken in 1982, without making significant gains among the blacks. He received less than 33 percent of the total votes cast. In addition Jacobs easily beat an Empowerment group member in Flatbush. In Crown Heights the Empowerment group managed to hold on to an assembly seat when two West Indians entered the race, one the accountant aligned with Markowitz, and the other a schoolteacher named Maurice Gumbs, to whom we shall return.[12]

1985: The Question of Alliances

If 1984 was a disappointment for the Empowerment group, 1985 was a disaster. It was also a year in which West Indian political activ-

---

12. The Bronx proved to be an important exception to the trend of African-American–Afro-Caribbean political conflict in 1984. The election of Larry Seabrook, an African American, in the Eighty-second Assembly District over a long-time Italian-American incumbent was accomplished with considerable Caribbean support. Like the Brooklyn districts discussed in this chapter, the eighty-second covers a working-class area of the northeast Bronx that had recently seen an influx of both African Americans and Afro-Caribbeans. Unlike Brooklyn and Queens, however, the Bronx had a relatively weak black political establishment—nothing equivalent to the Empowerment group. This absence of factions may have facilitated black unity in the area. For an analysis of this election see Green and Wilson 1989.

ism reached a new height and New York's ethnic politics became substantially more complicated.

The defeat of Ed Koch had been the ultimate goal of most of New York's black political leadership for several years, and following Jackson's strong showing in the city and the election of black mayors in Philadelphia and Chicago, many felt that the time was ripe. The original consensus on a candidate who could unite blacks, Hispanics, and white liberals centered on former state senator Basil Paterson. A veteran of Harlem politics, the popular Paterson was born in New York of Grenadian parents and had long ties with white reform organizations (he received an early endorsement from Massachusetts senator Edward Kennedy) while never alienating Harlem's "regulars." His candidacy had already raised almost one million dollars when, quite unexpectedly, he announced his intention not to run.

The announcement left the forces opposed to Koch in disarray. City Council president Carol Bellamy, a white liberal, announced her plans to run, as did the Puerto Rican former congressman Herman Badillo. An organization of fifty leading blacks, the "Coalition for a Just New York," which had formed to promote the candidacy of Thomas Minter for schools' chancellor the previous year, set itself up as a nominating board in order to throw united black support behind one candidate. The Coalition included both Vann and his allies and a number of older, more traditional politicians from Harlem as well as a number of nonaligned activists. Only one of its members, Moore, was born in the Caribbean. Vann was the moving force behind the organization, and he had made it clear that he favored Badillo's candidacy. Thus it was seen as a personal defeat for Vann when Washington Heights assemblyman Herman "Denny" Farrell, a last minute entrant into the mayoral race, received the group's nomination. Vann gave Farrell a lukewarm endorsement in an effort to preserve the appearance of unity, but he made no secret of his displeasure. Badillo left the race embittered and several Empowerment members endorsed Bellamy.

Farrell, the Manhattan County chair of the Democratic party and one of the most moderate of New York black politicians, was now put forward as the unlikely candidate of black nationalism. Vann, widely perceived as a nationalist and radical, was rebuffed in his call for a progressive coalition. An additional irony stems from the fact that Farrell's parents were born in the Caribbean. He had never made

[231]

this a public issue, however, or attempted to create ties to the growing Brooklyn and Queens communities. His own district was home to few West Indians, and he had had little reason to emphasize his background over the years. His candidacy thus received little support in West Indian political circles. In any event, his underfunded campaign, believed by many to be a Koch-inspired attempt to draw votes from Bellamy, never caught fire.

CAL had originally planned to interview candidates for mayor and issue an endorsement of its own. The organization soon realized, however, that it could not reach a consensus, and in any event the point quickly became moot, for in May 1985 a large group of Caribbean notables led by Stanislaus and consisting of many former members of "Caribbeans for Percy Sutton" (as well as several CAL members) endorsed Koch for reelection. Stanislaus explained that "This group has decided we can no longer continue on a confrontational course with Koch."

The significance of "Caribbeans for Koch" went far beyond the $5,000 the group reportedly raised for Koch at its Crown Heights fund-raiser. The group brought together 150 politically active West Indians to take a stand clearly in opposition to that of the city's black leadership. Paying twenty-five dollars apiece to have their picture taken with the mayor at a "rubber chicken" gala, the group's members were not so much endorsing Koch as a politician as they were paying tribute to power. The group's leaders made few arguments in favor of Koch, and virtually none against Bellamy or Farrell. They simply argued that it was important for the community to be on the side of the winner. Stanislaus said: "I've always believed that it doesn't matter who is running. Blacks shouldn't have all of their eggs in one basket. So I advise some blacks to go with Denny Farrell and Carol Bellamy, and I'd advise other blacks to go with the Mayor" (quoted in McKenzie 1985:26). Furthermore, since Koch was likely to win, and since he desperately wanted some black support, why should West Indians not take advantage of the access to power that this opportunity seemed to promise? Stanislaus asked: "Why do black Americans and West Indians have to see eye to eye on everything? All black Americans are not going to support Farrell, I see no reason why West Indians should not support Koch" (ibid.:26).

The mayor had been courting Caribbean support for some time. During the preceding months he had invited Caribbean leaders to

City Hall, met with local West Indian groups in the Bronx and attended Caribbean cultural fetes. He had committed himself to helping Caribbean groups obtain a building for a Brooklyn cultural center
and a radio program. The reason for this interest is a matter for speculation, but it is safe to say that it had little to do with the few
thousand dollars the group could raise.[13] Nor did Koch, who was
safely ahead in the polls, really need West Indian votes. It is more
likely that the mayor was interested in demonstrating that his critics
did not speak for all blacks. Koch's Caribbean strategy was only part
of his direct pitch for black support, which was topped off by naming
"Mac" Holder, then eighty-eight years old, as his northern Brooklyn
campaign director.

As with Markowitz, it was Koch's willingness to court them, more
than any particular stands that he took, that seemed to impress Caribbean leaders most. While some spokesmen explained the endorsement with elaborate political logic, a prominent Haitian priest was
probably closer to the truth when he explained his reason for supporting Koch: "He asked us." No other politician had sought him out.
Others thought of him as merely a prominent immigrant, but the
mayor saw him as a political leader. In so doing he brought the priest
and dozens like him into electoral politics *in their ethnic capacities*.
This sort of courting changes the game. One might argue that the
Caribbean vote should go this way or that, but saying it did not exist
was now dangerous.

Reaction in the African-American media was quick and harsh. In
newspapers and on radio call-in shows, the group's members were
called traitors. Old animosities quickly came to the surface and
charges were met with countercharges. In the West Indian community itself reaction was more varied. For several weeks the strategy
was debated in political clubs and in the pages of the *Carib News*,
where a series of guest editorials argued all sides of the question.

Some activists agreed with the endorsement. As Hastick wrote:
"For too long West Indians have been taken for granted. . . . We
have to make sure that we have friends in high places." Others,
while defending the rights of the group to voice its opinion, ques-

13. Koch spent $5.1 million in the 1985 primary, or slightly over twelve dollars per
vote. In strictly financial terms, "Caribbeans for Koch" was not worth the car fare to
Brooklyn. Farrell, by contrast, spent approximately $88,000.

tioned its representativeness. Journalist Stephen Alexander noted: "I think we are confusing visibility with substance. . . . [T]he Ambassador and his friends never claimed to speak for the Caribbean community." Colin Moore condemned the Koch endorsement as an act of blatant "collaboration" with those who are "hostile to the interests of black people." At the same time he took the opportunity to chide his own African-American allies: "Caribbean American leaders suffer from a pervasive sense of frustration at their lack of political influence. . . . It is a restive and troubled community that has seen the traditional African American leadership as less than responsive to Caribbean concerns." Maurice Gumbs, on the other hand, found cause for celebration in the fact that the debate was taking place at all: "There is an excitement in the fact that Caribbeans are beginning to take an interest . . . to feel strongly about the politics of the city. A new day is dawning!"[14] While little consensus was achieved, one thing clearly emerged from the debate over Mayor Koch: the hegemony of an ethnic perspective. The creation of "Caribbeans for Koch" called for the creation of "Caribbeans for Farrell" and "Caribbeans for Bellamy." African-American politicians who had never before acknowledged the existence of a Caribbean constituency now had their own West Indian support groups and West Indian fundraising events. West Indians who had worked closely with African-American politicians including some of Koch's strongest critics suddenly became their "Caribbean liaisons" or "Caribbean community advisors." Older second-generation American West Indians found a new interest in their roots and started to participate in the new organizations. In short, the ethnic community now existed in part because people said it existed and acted as though it did.

In the end Koch seems to have done reasonably well in the West Indian community. He carried 37 percent of the black vote citywide (Farrell received only 41 percent of the black vote in the three-way race), and he carried every electoral district in Brooklyn including Vann's home district. Vann, despite the endorsement of several prominent West Indians, had become the focus of Caribbean discontent and came in a poor third in a four-way race for the borough presidency of Brooklyn, receiving barely half of the black vote.

14. The preceding quotes are from *The New York Carib News*, 11, 18, and 25 June, 1985.

Still, much of the Caribbean community was not enthusiastic about supporting the mayor, and there is little doubt that a stronger black candidate would have had their support. The lasting lesson of 1985 was not that an irrevocable split now existed in New York black politics, but rather that black politicians, like white politicians, must now pay attention to ethnic as well as racial divisions. Some black politicians and community activists had long understood this and had sought to cultivate relations with the Caribbean community. Even Vann, who had long resisted any attempt to fragment the black community, made some efforts during the 1985 race to attend specifically West Indian events and to hold specifically West Indian fund-raisers, albeit with little success.[15] Other members of his Coalition for Community Empowerment have done a better job of playing ethnic constituency politics. One of the few female ethnic leaders in the West Indian community, who is closely associated with an African-American congressman, notes: "Sometimes, something comes up where the congressman will tell me, 'now I want you to put on your Jamaican dress and your Jamaican voice and go talk to those people.'"

Ironically, though West Indians are often perceived as more conservative than African Americans, some of the most direct appeals to the Caribbean community have come from some of the most militant of New York's black activists. Since black nationalists are themselves involved in attempting to redefine black identity in cultural (pan-African) terms, it is understandable that they should make accommodations with the culturally based assertions of blacks of different backgrounds.[16]

Yet during the mid-1980s this responsiveness was not the rule. Whereas white politicians have often gone out of their way to encourage West Indian ethnic activity, black politicians, particularly Brooklyn's dominant coalition of African-American incumbents—Vann's Empowerment group—were more likely to view Caribbean

15. See *The New York Carib News*, 10 September, 1985.
16. For example, long-time black nationalist Jitu Weusi made specific appeals for West Indian support during his unsuccessful 1985 city council campaign. Stressing his own pan-Africanism, he wrote in a statement for the *Carib News*, "We have welcomed people of African descent from Haiti, Trinidad, Jamaica, Panama and other smaller nations of the Caribbean and Central America who seek a new life and greater economic opportunities in the United States. . . . Over the past years I have stood for progressive Pan-Africanism, that symbolizes the resurrection of opportunity for people of African descent wherever they reside over the world." 6 August, 1985, p. 10).

[235]

ethnicity as a nonissue or to condemn it as a result of white manipulation and West Indian "tribalism," which is a characterization many West Indians deeply resent.

> "Tribalism" has become the current club with which to bludgeon Caribbean people who dare assert any special need, an identity or even an existence within the local melting pot. . . . Tribalism is the new, subtle euphemistic replacement for other, more colorful "tropical terms of endearment" to which we have become accustomed. No more "Coconut Heads!" No more "Monkey Chasers!" No more "Banana, Boats!" Today's words are tribalism and tribalists. (Gumbs 1985b)[17]

Why were black politicians generally less receptive to Caribbean ethnic activism than white ones? During the mid-1980s whites, roughly half of the city's population, dominated New York politics to a degree far out of proportion to their numbers. In Brooklyn in particular the local government, the Democratic party machine, and the valuable network of politically active corporations and public utilities were all white-dominated, despite a rapidly growing black population. This political establishment, facing a city that was increasingly nonwhite but also increasingly ethnically diverse, seemed most comfortable with the image of the populace as a large number of small constituencies: not whites and nonwhites but rather a myriad of ethnic, class, and neighborhood interest groups vying for power and patronage, making shifting alliances, and willing to deal with those who were politically dominant. The promotion of the West Indian leadership group was consistent with this "ethnic" definition of reality.[18]

17. Obviously the notion of "tribal" divisions calls to mind the fratricidal rifts that constantly thwart African nationalism. On the other hand, the phrase has deep resonance for West Indians, as the notion of "political tribalism" is generally used to describe the deep and often violent clashes between the two major Jamaican political parties. Furthermore, the term is insulting because it is used in other contexts to describe the divisions among "primitives": Europeans have "national" divisions, but third world peoples have "tribal" ones. Many West Indians have also responded that the notion is simply inaccurate, that West Indians frequently support political candidates of other ethnic groups. There have been, they point out, organizations called "Caribbeans for Koch," "Caribbeans for Sutton," and "Caribbeans for Golden," but no "Caribbeans for Ernest Skinner," "Caribbeans for Tony Agard," or "Caribbeans for Maurice Gumbs."
18. When a black man finally did become mayor of New York in 1990, it was on the strength of a campaign that emphasized the image of the city as a "mosaic" of diverse ethnic groups. As will be discussed in the Conclusion, David Dinkins made considerable outreach to Caribbeans, Hispanics, Asians, and other ethnic constituencies, and played

Many black politicians argue instead for a more "racial" view, asserting that without racial unity all blacks will continue to be underrepresented in New York political and economic life. Andrew Cooper, editor of the Brooklyn-based blackoriented newspaper *The City Sun*, puts it this way: "We've learned simply that we have to solidify the black community electorally so that we can reward our friends and punish our enemies peacefully, like every other group in America. Without that people will never respect you and you won't get a penny. With it, you can talk about coalition and progressive efforts" (quoted in Sleeper 1985:9).

Relations between African-American and Afro-Caribbean political actors, particularly in Brooklyn, have often been subject to misunderstandings. While Vann's Coalition for Community Empowerment seemed during the mid-1980s to be an emerging black establishment to West Indians on the outside looking in, Coalition supporters knew all too well how recent, tenuous, and limited the group's power really was, and how little patronage they actually controlled in Ed Koch's New York. On the other hand, members of the Empowerment group now admit that during the mid-1980s they did not respond fast enough to the growing Caribbean community. "We've been too defensive," Assemblyman Roger Green notes. "We've misread their strength and mishandled our outreach" (quoted in Sleeper 1988:6).

The Local Politician as an Ethnic Leader

The 1985 election did not bring to the fore West Indian candidates on their own behalf. The strongest figure to emerge from the community that year was Ernest Skinner. A Trinidad-born banker and CAL member had who emigrated in 1971, Skinner mounted a well-financed and professional bid in Flatbush for the city council, only to be disqualified when his nominating petitions arrived at the Board of Elections twenty minutes after the filing deadline. Skinner has rejected the characterization of him as a "Caribbean" candidate (though

---

down racial cleavages as such. While this policy won him considerable support in these ethnic communities, including overwhelming support in the West Indian community, it seems to have been designed at least in part to reassure whites as well.

he notes, "With my accent I don't have to tell everybody I am from the Caribbean"). He steered clear of the "Caribbeans for Koch" group and attempted to maintain good relations with the Empowerment team (who nonetheless did not endorse him). His support, however, was largely Caribbean, and more than any other candidate he seemed to epitomize the new West Indian intelligentsia. His aborted campaign and the Flatbush political club he founded helped to cement relations with West Indians, and he drew enthusiastic support, much of which was inherited the following year by a fellow Trinidadian, Maurice Gumbs.

Like Skinner, Gumbs would not be comfortable with the idea of himself as a "West Indian" politician. Unlike the "ethnicity entrepreneur," the political aspirant cannot afford to be tagged as the representative of one group exclusively. The ethnic community may provide a support base but this must be balanced against the need to appeal to a wide cross section of voters. In addition Gumbs's background is closer to that of members of the Empowerment group than to most West Indian politicians. That his 1986 campaign was to go so far in mobilizing ethnic political resources illustrates the extent to which the language of ethnic politics had become important, even to politicians who had come to use this language reluctantly.

Like Vann and many other black activists of his era, Gumbs first became involved in public life as a young teacher during the 1968 Ocean Hill–Brownsville School Board dispute. Crossing the United Federation of Teachers' picket lines, he sided with black community activists in one of the bitterest disputes of the era. Unlike many of the other black leaders in the dispute, however, Gumbs remained a teacher and managed to mend his relations with the union, so well, in fact, that he was eventually invited to join its executive board. In 1983 his interest in education and his desire to make a more substantial mark on the school system led him to run for the local community school board in East Flatbush. At that time he had given little thought to the Caribbean community as a base of support. He recalls: "Interestingly enough, at that time I had no Caribbean backing, no Caribbean base. I was not even truly aware it existed. My campaign manager was white, a lot of Afro-Americans worked with me. I did not know any of the so-called Caribbean leaders at the time. The majority of my support was not Caribbean by any means. I never thought in terms of appealing to these votes."

Gumbs won his school board race and, feeling confident ("it's like the race track, you win one, you start to get cocky"), he started to plan a bid for the state assembly against a member of the Empowerment team. He realized, however, that his own lack of organizational ties presented a problem. His opponent, like so many African-American politicians, had roots in a large and politically active church. In a partial effort to compensate for this, and to build his own cadre of supporters, Gumbs founded a political club above a Nostrand Avenue storefront, which he christened with the eminently African-American name, "The Harriet Tubman Democratic Club."

The phrase "clubhouse politics" has become associated with a bygone era. It summons up images of corruption, cronyism, and backslapping, practiced largely by cigar-smoking Irish politicians. For some the clubhouse is a symbol of all that was wrong in the days before municipal reform, while for others it is remembered with nostalgia. What is generally forgotten is that the clubhouse was, and in places like Brooklyn still is, just that: a club, both a political institution and social organization. As Richard Sennett has noted, political machines, for all of their obvious failings, provided individuals a "connectedness to power and a forum for social as well as political exchange" that is generally missing in modern urban life (1970:78).

The disappearance of this institution has been greatly exaggerated. Disciplined hierarchical political machines are not at all what they used to be, but patronage politics is still a feature of the urban landscape, and its informal training ground, the political club, is certainly still with us (Guterbock 1980; Wolfinger 1972; Lowi 1964). In black communities especially, political clubs remain an important link between individuals and the state, as well as social forums. Gumbs's club, like many others, is a regular meeting place where friends come together regularly to talk, plan outings, drink, discuss the events of the day, and, on occasion, engage in the mechanics of electoral campaigns. It also provides a locus for new contacts. The invitation to "drop by the club sometime" can be extended to the leaders of ethnic associations and soccer leagues, and to ministers, local unionists, and even the occasional sociologist.

The Tubman Club's members are a mixture of schoolteachers (African-American, white, and West Indian), neighborhood people who are often black Americans, and a growing core of West Indians whom Gumbs has met through various Caribbean organizations. Friday nights are casual drop-in nights when anywhere from two or three to several dozen members will come together. Conversations may range from school board battles and local politics to the Guyanese presidential succession and V. S. Naipaul's status as a Caribbean novelist. There is plenty of ordinary gossip as well.

When an election is in gear the club converts itself into a campaign headquarters. Canvassers and petitioners are coordinated out of the back room, nominating petitions are assembled, and the press is entertained. In the weeks just before an election the pitch becomes feverish. Afterwards the club resumes its social functions, and its members, now united by combat, are bound together more tightly than ever.

For a number of reasons this traditional institution has survived better in the inner city and particularly in black areas than in white areas and the suburbs. First, office seekers in black communities, running comparatively low-budget campaigns, rely less on mass media and more on personal contacts than do their white, and particularly suburban, counterparts. Moreover, candidates in black urban areas have often failed in utilizing the broadcast media. Simeon Golar's attempts to unseat Congressman Addabbo in 1982 and 1984 are cases in point. Golar outspent his opponent and relied heavily on radio advertising, but Addabbo's following was primarily based on his personal contact with the club-house network, and Golar, despite impressive credentials, had little to show for himself in terms of local accomplishments.

Compounding such difficulties is the fact that most urban black communities are virtual one-party monopolies, which means that elections are generally decided in primaries, where turnouts tend to be low. Moreover, mayoral and city council elections are held in off years when primary turnouts are lower still. Thus "troop strength"— the number of reliable persons the candidate can count on to actually work the polls and get the vote out on election day—is crucial. If, like Gumbs, the politician lacks funds to pay poll workers, and lacks the strong ties of an established institution such as a church through which to recruit them, the club is a key way of developing the network of people who can be relied on at election time.

The clubhouse is also a vital place for new politicians, particularly those without movement connections or home bases in churches, to learn the arcane rules and techniques of the political process. The latest Board of Election ruling on the requirements for ballot petitions, tips on the most fruitful places to canvass, how to maintain a mailing list, and, occasionally, the techniques for mild electoral fraud are all passed on in the clubhouse. It is also an invaluable source of gossip, where even potential rivals will stop in to chat and occasionally compare notes.

Though the clubhouse does not necessarily have to field its own candidates, over time it will tend to do so. As a Caribbean politician in another club notes, "once the club is in place, it will tend to try to promote its own people. People want to work for their friends." The existence of several predominantly Caribbean clubs in Brooklyn today means that in the future there will probably be a steady stream of Caribbean candidates.

From his two-room clubhouse Gumbs launched his bid for the state assembly in 1984. He ran without a slate, having rejected (or, depending on who tells the story, having been rejected by) Markowitz and the Hasidic district leader as allies. The incumbent, the son of a prominent minister, not only mobilized his own church but made an alliance with a leading West Indian minister as well. Markowitz slated a Jamaican accountant for the same seat, leaving two West Indians and an African American in the race. "Running without a slate was crazy," Gumbs later recalled. "I am glad I did not know any better." Though the young Trinidadian had given little thought to his Caribbean roots before, Gumbs found himself increasingly drawn to Caribbean fetes and affairs, partially out of a change in self-awareness, partially out of an assessment of their potential political strength. He says: "I guess it's like Carl McCall once said, 'If your own people don't support you, who will?' I went to a lot of things knowing that there were not many votes there, but feeling it was something I should do. I still did not have the support of some of the old-time Caribbean leaders, but I started meeting a lot of people."

Many of these people were impressed with the soft-spoken educator. On the eve of the election the CAL endorsed Gumbs, and other West Indians were drawn into the campaign. On election day, however, Gumbs was swamped by the number of people his two opponents put on the street. He finished in third place in a tight race, with a vote generally deemed quite respectable for a newcomer. That he had done so without a slate established him as a rising star in the community.

Gumbs started to build for 1986 almost immediately. Over the next two years his club and his activities became increasingly Caribbean in tone. He started to write for the *Carib News* and to go to Caribbean affairs. He was elected to the board of the CAL. While his primary concern continued to be education, he took an interest in immigration policy as well. In addition to his usual duties on the highly politicized school board, he began to publish a newsletter. His clubhouse started to function as a meeting place for "ethnicity entrepreneurs" as well as political activists, and he also made contacts with the leaders of Caribbean social groups and sports clubs.

Gumbs and his club worked for Skinner and Farrell in 1985, and were clearly building contacts for 1986. He had originally planned another run for the assembly, but he was persuaded by a number of leading Caribbean politicians to attempt a run instead against Markowitz for the state senate.

The decision to challenge Markowitz was a potentially dangerous one. The senator had acquired a reputation for near invincibility. Yet the people around Gumbs sensed that Marty's "act" was wearing thin and that while Markowitz might use his Caribbean connections well against an African-American candidate, his ethnic appeals would be of little use against a "son of the soil." In addition, several leading African-American politicians were eager for a rapprochement. Gumbs had not supported Koch, and was therefore acceptable.

In retrospect, the Empowerment group had little to lose in the race. It had failed to unseat Markowitz twice. If Gumbs won, a thorn in their side was eliminated and Gumbs would still need the black and Puerto Rican caucus to be effective in Albany. Even if he was not "their man" he was at least as close to them as Markowitz was. If Gumbs lost, they could truthfully say that they had tried to slate a West Indian and so silence their critics.

The growing West Indian leadership, however, had much to lose. In a one-on-one race against a white opponent in the now overwhelmingly black district, they could blame only themselves for whatever happened. "There is a great deal at stake in this race," Stewart told reporters. "A failure would set us back immensely" (quoted in Blauner 1986:71). Sensing this, the Caribbean leadership seemed to unite around Gumbs. Stanislaus and veterans of "Caribbeans for Koch" joined with Moore and Skinner in supporting him. So did some "re-Caribbeanized" veterans of the earlier days of black politics. Gumbs was also initially backed by both borough president Golden (who had his own score to settle with Markowitz) and the Empowerment team's Owens. Vann, somewhat ominously, stayed neutral.

The campaign received unusual press attention during the early summer of 1986, as the New York press seemed to have suddenly discovered the West Indian community. Gumbs, played the ethnic connection for all it was worth. He raised money in calypso dance halls and put patois slogans ("Massa day done!") on his flyers. He brought members of several large Caribbean social clubs into politics for the first time, and some became tireless campaign workers.

This campaign represented a major break from the past. Previously only Markowitz had really been successful in mobilizing the voluntary associations. In 1984 a Brooklyn activist had commented:

> Caribbean leaders have never attempted to convert (the fraternal groups) into political power. No one has ever really pushed voter registration with these people. There is a group called "Four Aces and a Queen" who turns out bus trips during the summer, where you will see 75 buses going on a trip . . . all down Eastern Parkway. And I am sure most of these people have never heard of [a well known West Indian leader]. No one thinks of these groups as political. It's partly because the people resist, they are into fun and they resist the seriousness of politics.

In 1986, however, Markowitz's patronage of Caribbean organizations was suddenly an issue within the community. What was once welcome recognition came to be seen by some as empty symbolism and condescension. Skinner made this point explicitly in a series of scathing editorials in the *Carib News*:

> I was (recently) at a holiday affair given by the Hawks [a giant Trinidadian fraternal organization] and was aghast to learn that Markowitz had been given "honorary membership" status by this organization. True to form, Marty, the clown, made some ingratiating remarks when he was introduced and the presiding officer gleefully followed this by exclaiming "Dis man like bacchanal fu so!" . . . Well I am sick and tired of this bull and I am putting Marty Markowitz on notice that this charade must stop. I take my Caribbean heritage seriously and I will no longer allow an outsider who has never visited my homeland to try passing for one of us. I treat my Caribbeanage [*sic*] just as seriously as Jews take their ethnicity—it is not something to joke about. (1986a:15)

Markowitz plays Caribbeans for chumps. This clown, dressed variously in bunny suits and white tuxedos, flitters from one Caribbean organization to another, dropping a few dollars here, buying a table of tickets at another affair, providing Port-O-Sans at the parade, spending five minutes in our churches while busily handing out chocolates and invitations to the concert series at Boys and Girls High School grounds, then fleeing to his lily white confines. (1986b:15)

While politicizing the social groups proved difficult, Gumbs discovered that these organizations provided the perfect opportunity for meeting and recruiting individuals not normally involved in the political process. In early 1986 the president of the Trinidad Alliance became involved in the Gumbs campaign. This proved to be the key to unlocking the "ethnic infrastructure" of the voluntary groups, which over the years had compiled huge mailing lists and networks of contacts among Trinidadians and other West Indians who could be contacted for fund-raising and other activities. The Alliance president also turned his considerable experience at running social events to planning fund-raisers at the large Caribbean halls in Brooklyn. By the spring of 1986 Gumbs was seeing the benefits: "We worked very hard on the West Indian community and now it is paying big dividends. . . . Last night I addressed a Trinidadian club at 2 A.M.! Can you believe it, they actually turned off the music—Trinidadians! And they not only did not boo, they applauded. It's really exciting because we are reaching people who have not been reached before."

The politics of the social clubs could prove treacherous, however. To Gumbs's surprise the "Hawks" continued their open support of Markowitz. This led to charges and countercharges of "sellout" and "opportunist," with such accusations becoming increasingly bitter and personal as the summer wore on.

Outside the Caribbean community the campaign stalled. A bizarre series of ballot eligibility rulings knocked several of New York's leading black politicians off the Democratic ballot, and though Gumbs's petitions survived review, much of his financial support dried up as his new allies found themselves preoccupied with their own problems. Vann continued to refuse to back Gumbs, and other Empowerment team members seemed to cool toward him as well. Amid rumors of a rapprochement with Markowitz, the support expected from Golden never materialized. Gumbs had to lay off the one paid member of his staff.

Unable to challenge Gumbs's nominating petitions, Markowitz took him to court over the issue of residency. In August a judge ruled that Gumbs had not lived in the Twenty-first Senatorial District for the required year prior to the election and ruled him off the ballot. Gumbs, who had a lease in the area dated fourteen months prior to the election but whose utility bills had stayed in his landlord's name until only six months prior, appealed the ruling and continued to campaign, but found that his time and money were now mostly spent in court. After losing in the state appeals court he took his case to federal court, where it stayed until the day before the election. In the end his elimination stood. The courts had once more postponed the test of West Indian voting strength.

Research Note: September 1986

Early on the morning of Tuesday, September 2, 1986, the day after Carnival, a small crowd gathered in front of the federal courthouse in Brooklyn to stand with Maurice Gumbs as he waited for a decision in the final appeal regarding his candidacy. The group of two dozen or so friends and supporters included American-born whites and blacks, but most were West Indians—many, like Gumbs, from Trinidad. Together they had mounted an unusually visible electoral campaign with a great deal of enthusiasm but virtually no money. In so doing they had been bound together by moments of elation and by severe disappointments. Now, however, Gumbs's candidacy was in the hands of a judge, and there was nothing much to do but wait.

Most of the supporters were wearing campaign T-shirts and buttons, but the gathering was too low-key to be described as a demonstration. It was too early in the morning for that. They had last seen each other on Eastern Parkway less than twelve hours ago, where they had manned a table full of campaign literature in the midst of the loud Carnival crowd. Standing among the hundreds of thousands of West Indians on that street they found it hard not to believe that they were witnessing the beginnings of a major shift in New York's ethnic division of power. "You can feel it on the street," a veteran "mas man" from Tobago said. "Even if they knock Maurice off (the ballot), we will have them the next time. Look at all these people! They want a piece of the action, and there is no holding them back."

In the midst of the laughing, roaring Parkway throng, it was hard not to be convinced. But standing in front of the courthouse with the subdued assembly the next morning, one was not so sure. How would the election turn out if it was held? I was asked my opinion, and, being too tired to give an analysis at that moment, I made a joke. "Maurice will win, easy," I said, "who else could get you guys out of bed this morning?" That must have struck a chord, because the joke went around the crowd and people repeated it to new arrivals as they showed up, bleary-eyed, carrying containers of coffee. "You right," the gentleman from Tobago said, "this here is Ash Wednesday." He proceeded to tell a story about going to take the ashes with a blinding hangover after a particularly raucous Carnival of his youth. He pantomimed a wobbly-legged struggle to thrust his forehead forward, his eyes tightly shut.

In some sense it was indeed Ash Wednesday. Carnival was over and everyday life was returning. With it came the political realities. It is one thing to turn out a Carnival crowd on the Parkway, but quite another to mobilize large numbers of registered voters. Even if this could be accomplished, a few politically connected lawyers can find a legal loophole and, given the right judge, six months of work can be canceled in five minutes. Ultimately there was not much the people in front of the courthouse could do about it. You can scream about injustice, but you cannot really expect the populace to rise in outrage over a race for the state senate, and everyone knows it. In the cool of that Tuesday morning all of these facts were becoming clear. As the day wore on it also became clear that there would be no West Indian candidate in the Twenty-first State Senatorial District in 1986.

Black Rapprochement? New York Politics, 1987–1989

Following the election of 1986, ethnic conflict within the black community played a diminished role in New York electoral politics. The various reasons for this all have to do with the changing political context in which these conflicts had been played out. One key

change was the rise in crack addiction and the accompanying violence in West Indian neighborhoods, which pushed law and order
issues to the fore among voters' concerns. Another was that appeals
to Caribbean solidarity paradoxically lost salience with the decline in
strength of Brooklyn's Coalition for Community Empowerment after
the debacle of 1985. With the Empowerment group clearly less unified and on the defensive, New York's black politics appeared much
less monolithic as the decade came to a close.[19] With no clearly dominant faction, Caribbean activists had less reason to feel excluded but
no clear target on which to vent frustration.

The primary reason for increased black electoral unity at the end
of the 1980s was almost certainly the city's worsening racial climate.
On December 20, 1986, a twenty-year-old Trinidadian immigrant
named Michael Griffith was chased onto a highway by a mob of white
youths in the Howard Beach section of Queens. He was struck by a
car and killed. His death, closely followed by the killing of a Jamaican-born street vendor by New York City police officers, changed
almost overnight the attitudes of many West Indians on the subject
of race. "My son's death opened the eyes of the public," Michael
Griffith's mother told the *Trinidad Express*. "Racism was something
we read about in the Deep South. Maybe it was there all along in
New York, but I never really experienced it" (*New York Carib News*
1987:4). One of my informants, a Trinidadian woman about Michael
Griffith's age, expressed a similar sentiment: "We from the Caribbean don't think about racial matters as much. I think we have been
very naive."

Rising racial tension and worsening relations between young
blacks and the police produced a sharp sense of frustration in the
growing working-class and middle-class Caribbean neighborhoods of
Brooklyn and Queens. On the one hand residents sought protection
from drug-related violence, but on the other many felt the police
were increasingly hostile and violent toward young blacks. The attention given to the Jamaican posses and their role in the drug trade

19. After 1986 Vann and his allies were suddenly being outflanked by their more traditional, mostly Harlem-based rivals on the one hand, and a more radical faction of activist
attorneys and clergy led by Alton Maddox, C. Vernon Mason, and the Reverend Al Sharpton on the other. While the degree of the latter group's support is open to question, after
the Howard Beach killing, it was generally able to attract far more media attention than
other black groups.

during 1988 and 1989 deepened the feeling of community isolation. Many West Indians felt they were being singled out for blame for a drug scourge of which they were, in fact, the primary victims. "As far as [Manhattan district attorney] Morgenthau is concerned," complained the president of the Jamaica Progressive League, "we are all posse!" (Roberts 1989:3). For many this frustration led to increased anger at perceived white racism and stronger identification with African-Americans.

This black unity was most evident during the 1988 presidential race. West Indian voters responded to Jesse Jackson's bid even more enthusiastically than they had in 1984. Jackson had used the intervening four years to mend fences with the Caribbean community and his 1988 campaign in New York was led not by Vann, but by figures more acceptable to the Caribbean community. The deference he went out of his way to show the community paid off: not only did he take more than 90 percent of the vote in central Brooklyn and southeastern Queens, the voter turnouts in the Crown Heights and St. Albans-Cambria Heights assembly districts were among the city's highest (Mollenkopf 1989).

Local politics proved more complex. In Queens the Reverend Floyd Flake, a popular African-American minister and Addabbo supporter who had replaced the congressman after his death in 1986, was reelected with broad African-American, West Indian, and white support. In Brooklyn, Gumbs again challenged Markowitz. This time, however, Gumbs lacked the West Indian institutional support of his earlier campaign. Making overtures to African-American activists who had come to the fore in the wake of Howard Beach, Gumbs hoped to tap the enthusiasm of the Jackson campaign, with which he strongly identified himself. This strategy fell apart, however, when Markowitz endorsed Jackson a few days before the primary. Jackson, then smarting from Ed Koch's remark that "Jews would have to be crazy to vote for Jackson," welcomed the support with a well-publicized photo opportunity which looked to all the world like an endorsement of Markowitz. Thus the Jewish politician got more from the Jackson campaign for a few days of nominal support than many black politicians had for months of canvassing. After the presidential primary the underfunded Gumbs campaign struggled on, with less enthusiasm than two years before. Gumbs lost in a September primary in which, almost without exception, incumbents trounced challengers.

The mayoral race of 1989 once again pitted black insurgents against Ed Koch, but this time the black community was unified. David Dinkins, a one-time Ray Jones protégé and veteran Harlem politician, was unofficially chosen as the black candidate early in the race when the members of Brooklyn's Empowerment group made it clear that he was the one member of the "Harlem gerontocracy" that they would support. Dinkins also made early overtures to the West Indian community. He courted the West Indian press and won the enthusiastic support of the *Carib News*. He welcomed the formation of a specifically Caribbean support group, which raised funds with Caribbean fetes. On the eve of the primary he told the press: "I recognize that the Caribbean community is a very important and significant part of the total African-American community in this city, and I see them as my base, a group to which I go" (Best 1989b:16).

Dinkins' dignified political style appealed to the West Indian community, as did his rhetoric, which emphasized the idea of New York as a multicultural mosaic. He reached out to the community on its own terms, and a few days before the primary he walked the streets in East Flatbush with none other than Marty Markowitz at his side. The general sense of black rapprochement was capped off when Jones, then eighty-nine, returned to New York after years of retirement in the Virgin Islands to give the campaign his fatherly blessing. In the end Dinkins carried the Crown Heights assembly district by a margin of eight to one, and took the St. Albans-Cambria Heights district in southeastern Queens by nearly fourteen to one. He racked up similar margins in the general election against Republican Rudolph Giuliani.

At least some Caribbean observers warned, however, that the Dinkins victory did not mean a return to the old days of Caribbean invisibility. One *Carib News* columnist took the occasion of the Dinkins victory to note: "In Brooklyn . . . the modus operandi of some Black elected officials during the decade of the 1980's was one of excluding Caribbean-born politicians. . . . These office holders speak of empowerment but in turn practice exclusion. . . . That Mr. Dinkins was able to get the backing of many Caribbean voters speaks more to his appeal and character than to anything the Black leadership in Brooklyn was able to do" (Best 1989b:16).

And what of the "Caribbeans for Koch?" Koch once again had hoped that the Caribbean community would provide him considerable support and fragment the black opposition. This time, however, when he reached out to his West Indian friends, few answered the call. Some of the former "Caribbeans for Koch" supported Dinkins, and most maintained public neutrality. Only a few Caribbean supporters remained with Koch at the end, including, most notably, Wesley MacDonald Holder, who was singled out for thanks in Koch's concession speech. After praising "the dean of Brooklyn politics," the tearful mayor looked around and saw that the nonagenarian was absent from the platform. "It must be past his bed time," the mayor quietly observed.

What will New York West Indian politics be like under a Dinkins administration? As of this writing it is too early to say. The mounting number of naturalized black immigrants and the community's own political proclivities almost guarantee that West Indians will play a more visible role in the city's politics during the 1990s.[20] Yet it remains to be seen whether this role will be played as part of an increasingly powerful African-American community or in opposition to it. In any event the genie of black immigrant ethnic politics is now out of the bottle. The relative salience of race and ethnicity in people's daily lives is, and will continue to be, shaped by events, but given the force with which it has now arrived, West Indian ethnic consciousness in one form or another will no doubt influence the political life of New York City for some time to come.

---

20. This will be particularly true after 1992, when the reapportionment of legislative districts in light of the 1990 census will once again shake up established political arrangements.

Conclusion: West Indian Ethnicity and New York's Political Culture

As noted in the Introduction, theories about the nature of ethnic groups have historically tended to fall into two broad categories, the "primordial" and "mobilizationist" approaches. By now it is probably obvious that my own study was originally conceived within the latter perspective. There is little in this work that supports a strictly primordial point of view. We have examined in detail how and why individuals use ethnicity to achieve certain goals. Yet it also appears that the mobilizationist view, while not exactly wrong, is far too simple. Though the instrumental use of ethnicity is central to the public life of Afro-Caribbean New Yorkers it is shaped by at least two additional factors: the conditions of daily life within the community and the prevailing ideology of race within the broader society.

Ethnic ideas are indeed subject to considerable manipulation, but they do not spring up out of thin air. Subjective expressions of ethnicity are grounded in objective realities, such as neighborhoods, economic niches, and institutions. These realities may not determine the way that public actors express ethnic claims, but they do limit the sort of claims that will be taken seriously by audiences both within and outside the community. Group identity is created in the interplay between "ethnicity from the ground up" and "ethnicity from the top down." It is not solely a reflection of historical circumstances, but neither can it come about independent of them.

The relevant question well expressed by James McKay: "What are the historical, cultural and structural variables which account for the institutionalization and de-institutionalization of ethnic boundaries and ethnic identities" (1982:413)? In the case of West Indians in New

York, the most important of these variables has been the role of race in the larger society.

For the first major wave of West Indian immigrants to the city, an "ethnic" rather than a "racial" politics would have been impossible. Certainly cultural factors shaped their political proclivities and influenced their distinct political style, but the substance of their political activity was determined by the society in which they functioned. As far as that society was concerned, race was the paramount issue. During the 1980s a more self-consciously ethnic politics arose. This was made possible by changes within the black community. It was also greatly furthered by a white political establishment that approached the West Indian community on ethnic terms. Nevertheless, while ethnicity and race coexisted in the political life of Caribbean New Yorkers during the 1980s, there was never any real danger of the former replacing the latter. If Caribbean political actors now have more latitude in defining the community, the impact of race on the daily lives of community members continues to revitalize the political agenda. The group "Caribbeans for Koch" developed an ethnic style of politics unimaginable in earlier times, yet the Howard Beach killing and similar events quickly pushed the politics of race back to the forefront. Thus today both race and ethnicity have a role to play in shaping black immigrant politics; indeed the same individuals utilize both in different contexts.[1]

It should also be remembered that the adoption of ethnic-style politics represents a conscious adaptation to what is perceived to be the dominant political structure. Ethnicity is a resource in part because it is seen as legitimate by the wider society. Events will undoubtedly determine how useful a resource it is. Nevertheless, the idea of a distinct Caribbean subgroup within New York's black community has entered the city's political discourse. Once such an idea exists it is unlikely to disappear. The fact that the ethnic card is available to political actors changes the game, even if they do not always elect to use it.

1. What may develop in the future is a pluralist ethnic political structure *within* an overall black constituency, roughly paralleling a pluralist structure within a larger "white ethnic" constituency. Under such circumstances ethnic contests over resources and offices deemed to be within a black sphere of influence could coexist with general unity of all people of African descent in those circumstances where "black" and "white" interests are seen as being in conflict.

What does playing the ethnic card mean for West Indian New Yorkers? One thing it clearly does not mean is isolation. Richard Sennett has written that the assertion of Jewish ethnicity during the Forest Hills housing crisis of the early 1970s represented a "withdrawal from political wheeling and dealing" in the interest of preserving communal solidarity. For people in Forest Hills, modern urban ethnicity meant creating walls around an increasingly hollow identity, building a ghetto in which the sense of "who we are" becomes dependent on the rejection of others (1976:308). For New York's West Indians, by contrast, ethnic identity is largely about "wheeling and dealing." The goal of those who in the early 1980s started to make a "Caribbean" political identity was to break out of their perceived isolation. Borrowing forms of activity from the local political culture, they created rather than severed ties with those in power.

Thus, unlike the defenders of Forest Hills, today's West Indian activists seem in little danger of starting to believe their own rhetoric. "Caribbeans for Koch" made no real effort to convince anyone that Koch was the best possible mayor for Caribbeans. Their calculation was purely strategic; they argued that it was good to build ties to City Hall, and that this was the way to do it. Ethnicity was a way to create access. Is the ethnic card successful? Does it provide access to anything of value? It is too early to say definitively. It clearly provides visible appointments for certain individuals, as well as a large number of awards dinners and the occasional audience at City Hall. At a certain point in a group's political development such things may have significance, but I suspect that they have already begun to be outgrown. Sooner or later political positions based on the idea of Caribbean distinctiveness inevitably come up against the hard reality of race in America. Yet a recognition of the continued salience of race in New York City's public life in no way precludes the increasing salience of ethnic mobilization *within* the black community—to say nothing of the internal rifts within that ill-defined agglomeration referred to as "minorities."

As in many large American cities, these minorities now constitute the majority in New York's population. Early in the next century they will be a majority of the registered voters as well. Ultimately, most of these people share common interests. They share the disadvantages of a service sector economy and they have shared the costs of reduced governmental services in the wake of fiscal crises. They share a history of political exclusion and they continue to be united by racism. In short, blacks and Hispanics, regardless of ethnic background, still have far more in common with each other than with the primary beneficiaries of the Koch administration. The electoral strength these groups displayed in uniting around David Dinkins in 1989 demonstrates widespread consciousness of this fact.

Yet New York's minorities are also an extraordinarily diverse lot. They hardly speak with one voice, and political strategies that refuse to recognize this risk irrelevance. Hence, while there was certainly a great deal of justice in the demands for black empowerment during the 1980s, to the extent that empowerment came to be narrowly articulated as the election or appointment of black people to high office, it tended to flounder. Though made in the language of racial unity, such demands were essentially ethnic politics similar to that of white ethnic groups. Unfortunately, in a climate where ethnic identities are in flux, the validity of such demands is vulnerable to those who offer rival versions of ethnicity, and who would redefine ethnic boundaries in their own interests. This is particularly true when other powerful forces, such as white politicians, are actively encouraging this redefinition.

On the other hand, when empowerment is defined in terms of issues, coalitions of mutual interest become possible. This is what the Dinkins mayoral campaign understood. And while the media generally saw Dinkins's rhetorical vision of New York as a "gorgeous mosaic" as an attempt to reassure whites, this vision undoubtedly appealed to Caribbean blacks and Hispanics as well. It promised New York's various minority constituencies recognition and respect. Once this was assured, it did not take long for Caribbean political actors to see their interests as being allied with those of the rest of the African-American community.

Whether the Dinkins administration will be able to hold such a coalition together, given New York's tumultuous racial politics and current fiscal woes, is anybody's guess. What does seem certain, however, is that with Caribbean and now African immigration on the rise, New York's black community will become ever more diverse, a mosaic within a mosaic. It is probably not a coincidence that this new diversity has been accompanied by a renewed interest in Africa on the part of African Americans. African cultural symbolism may well help in the eventual creation of an ethnic political identity shared by all black New Yorkers, regardless of national origin.[2] In any event, the fecund intertwining of race and ethnicity will no doubt continue to enrich the city culturally, and at times it will probably complicate things politically. It is a future that New York's African-American political leadership seems to be increasingly comfortable with.

And what of the city as a whole? At its best, New York has always held out to its newcomers the promise of a public life in which diversity is welcomed and even rewarded. Reality has often fallen short of that promise, particularly where people of color are concerned. Perhaps in a time when many of the newcomers have dark skin, that promise will be dashed upon the shoals of racism. Still, the idea of a civic culture based on difference is what has made New York unique among American cities. That idea, and the newcomers who embody it, continue to be the last best hope for New York's survival as a cosmopolitan metropolis.

One thing is certain. Whatever New York becomes in the next century, these newcomers—the overworked nurse, the cab driver, the young black woman pushing a white baby through the park, and the political actors who seek to give all these a public voice—will play a central role in shaping it. When they come together to create the pulsating, scary, beautiful chaos that breaks out each September, the city will be once more alive with possibilities.

2. It is noteworthy in this regard that the earlier wave of Caribbean migrants was also accompanied by a rise in interest in Africa during the 1920s, and that New York, always home to the most ethnically diverse black community in the United States, has usually been the center of pan-Africanism as well.

Bibliography

Aho, William R. 1987. "Steelband Music in Trinidad and Tobago: The Creation of a People's Music." *Latin American Music Review* 8(1):26–58.

Allen, Walter, and Reynolds Farley. 1987. *The Color Line and the Quality of Life: The Problem of the Twentieth Century*. New York: Russell Sage Foundation.

Anderson, Jervis. 1981. *This Was Harlem*. New York: Vintage.

Anderson, Patricia Y. 1985. "Migration and Development in Jamaica." In Robert Pastor, ed., *Migration and Development in the Caribbean: The Unexplored Connection*, 117–39. Boulder, Colo.: Westview.

Arnold, Faye W. 1984. "West Indians and London's Hierarchy of Discrimination." *Ethnic Groups* 6:47–64.

Bakhtin, Mikhail. 1968. *Rabelais and His World*. Cambridge: MIT Press.

Banton, Michael. 1983. *Racial and Ethnic Competition*. Cambridge: Cambridge University Press.

Basch, Linda. 1987. "The Vincentians and Grenadians: The Role of Voluntary Associations in Immigrant Adaptation to New York City." In Nancy Foner, ed., *New Immigrants in New York*, 159–94. New York: Columbia University Press.

Basch, Linda G., and Joyce Toney. 1988. "Eastern Caribbean Labor Force Participation in New York: Implications For Race and Ethnicity." Paper presented at Seminar Series in Migration and Population Studies, The College of Staten Island, 6 May.

Bayor, Ronald. 1978. *Neighbors in Conflict: The Irish, Germans, Jews and Italians of New York City: 1929–1945*. Baltimore: Johns Hopkins.

Becker, Howard S. 1963. *The Outsiders: Studies in the Sociology of Deviance*. New York: Free Press.

Bell, Daniel. 1962. "Crime as an American Way of Life." In his *The End of Ideology*, 127–50. New York: Collier.

––––––. 1975. Ethnicity and Social Change. In Nathan Glazer and Daniel P. Moynihan, eds., *Ethnicity: Theory and Experience*, 141–74. Cambridge: Harvard University Press.

Bender, Thomas. 1983. "The End of the City?" *Democracy* 13:8–20.

Bendix, Reinhard. 1974. "Inequality and Social Structure: A Comparison of Marx and Weber." *American Sociological Review* 39:148–61.

Bibliography

Bernstein, Nina. 1987. "Still Nurturing Dreams." *New York Newsday*, 12 June.

Best, Tony. 1989a. "Jamaicans—Victims of an Injustice." *New York Carib News*, 28 March, 3.

——. 1989b. "That Crucial Caribbean Vote." *New York Carib News*, 19 September, 16.

Blauner, Peter. 1986. "Islands in the Sun." *New York Magazine*, 21 April, 68–73.

Blu, Karen. 1980. *The Lumbee Problem: The Making of an American Indian People.* New York: Cambridge University Press.

Bohlen, Celestine. 1989. "Residents Mobilize to Nurture Laurelton." *The New York Times*, 15 July.

Bolles, A. Lynn. 1981. "'Goin' Abroad': Working Class Jamaican Women and Migration." In D. M. Mortimer and R. S. Bryce-Laporte, eds., *Female Immigrants to the United States*, 56–84. Washington, D.C.: Smithsonian Institute.

Bonnett, Aubrey, W. 1980. "An Examination of Rotating Credit Associations among Black West Indian Immigrants in Brooklyn." In R. S. Bryce-Laporte, ed., *Sourcebook on the New Immigration: Implications for the United States and International Community*, 271–84. New Brunswick, N.J.: Transaction Press.

——. 1981. "Structured Adaptation of Black Migrants from the Caribbean: An Examination of an Indigenous Banking System in Brooklyn." *Phylon* 42(4):346–55.

——. 1982. *Institutional Adaptations of West Indian Immigrants to America: An Analysis of Rotating Credit Associations.* Washington D.C.: University Press of America.

Bourgois, Philippe. 1989. "West Indian Immigration and the Origins of the Banana Industry." *Cimarron* 2(1–2):58–86.

Briggs, Vernon. 1985. "Employment Trends and Recent Immigration Policy. In Nathan Glazer, ed., *Clamor at the Gates*, 135–60. San Francisco: Institute for Contemporary Studies.

Brown, Ernest. 1990. "Carnival, Calypso and Steelband." *Black Perspectives in Music* 18:81–100.

Browning, Rufus P., Dale R. Marshall, and David H. Tabb. 1984. *Protest Is Not Enough: The Struggle of Blacks and Hispanics for Equality in Urban Politics.* Berkeley: University of California Press.

Bryce-Laporte, R. S. 1972. "Black Immigrants: The Experience of Invisibility and Inequality." *Journal of Black Studies* 3:29–56.

——. 1979. "New York City and the New Caribbean Immigrant." *International Migration Review* 13:214–34.

Buder, Leonard. 1989a. "Accused Chief of Crack Ring Goes on Trial." *The New York Times*, 20 June.

——. 1989b. "Jury Convicts Man as Chief of Drug Ring." *The New York Times*, 26 July.

——. 1989c. "Seven Terms of Life for Drug Dealer from Brooklyn." *The New York Times*, 2 December.

Buffenmeyer, Jay Ralph. 1970. "The Emigration of High Level Manpower and High National Development: The Case of Jamaica." Ph.D. dissertation, University of Pittsburgh.

Bunche, Ralph. (n.d.). "The Political Status of the Negro." Unpublished research memorandum for *An American Dilemma*. MS., The Schomberg Collection. The New York Public Library.

Burkett, Randall K. 1978. *Black Redemption: Churchmen Speak for the Garvey Movement.* Philadelphia: Temple University Press.

Chevigny, Belle Gale. 1986. "Killer Cops." *The Nation,* 13 September.

Chisholm, Shirley. 1970. *Unbought and Unbossed.* New York: Houghton Mifflin.

Clark, Kenneth. 1965. *Dark Ghetto: Dilemmas of Social Power.* New York: Harper and Row.

———. 1980. "The Role of Race." *The New York Times Magazine,* 5 October.

Clarke, John Henrik, ed., 1974. *Marcus Garvey and the Vision of Africa.* New York: Random House.

Cliff, Michelle. 1987. *No Telephone to Heaven.* New York: Vintage.

Cloward, Richard, and Frances Fox Piven. 1975. *The Politics of Turmoil: Poverty, Race and The Urban Crisis.* New York: New York.

Coard, F.M. 1970. *Bitter Sweet and Spice.* Ifracombe, U.K.: Arthur Stockwell Ltd.

Cohen, Abner. 1974. "Introduction: The Lessons of Ethnicity." In Abner Cohen, ed., *Urban Ethnicity,* ix–xxiv. London: Tavistock.

———. 1980a. "Drama and Politics in the Development of a London Carnival." *Man* 15:65–86.

———. 1980b. *The Politics of Elite Culture: Explorations in the Dramaturgy of Power.* Berkeley: University of California Press.

———. 1982. "A Polyethnic London Carnival as a Contested Cultural Performance." *Ethnic and Racial Studies* 5:22–41.

Cohen, David Steven. 1974. *The Ramapo Mountain People.* New Brunswick, N.J.: Rutgers University Press.

Colen, Shellee. 1986. "With Respect and Feelings." In Johnnetta Cole, ed., *All American Women: Lines That Divide, Ties That Bind,* 46–70. New York: Free Press.

———. 1987. "Like a Mother to Them: Meanings of Child Care and Motherhood for West Indian Child Care Workers in New York." Paper presented at the annual meeting of the American Anthropological Association, Chicago, 22 November.

———. 1989. "Just a Little Respect: West Indian Domestic Workers in New York City." In E. Chaney and M. G. Castro, eds., *Muchachas No More: Household Workers in Latin America and the Caribbean,* 171–96. Philadephia: Temple University Press.

———. 1990. "'Housekeeping' for the Green Card: West Indian Household Workers, the State and Stratified Reproduction in New York." In Roger Sanjek and Shellee Colen, eds., *At Work in Homes: Domestic Workers in World Perspective,* 89–118. Washington, D.C.: American Anthropological Society.

Conway, Dennis. 1989. "Caribbean International Mobility Traditions." *Boletin de Estudios Latinoamericanos y del Caribe* 46:17–47.

Conway, Dennis, and Ualthan Bigby. 1987. "Residential Differentiation among an Overlooked Black Minority: New Immigrant West Indians in New York." In Constance' Sutton and Elsa Chaney, eds., *Caribbean Life in New York City,* 74–83. New York: Center for Migration Studies.

Cooper, Wayne F. 1987. *Claude McKay: Rebel Sojourner in the Harlem Renaissance.* Baton Rouge: Louisiana State University Press.

[259]

Bibliography

Cruse, Harold. 1967. *The Crises of the Negro Intellectual.* Boston: Little, Brown.

Da Matta, Roberto. 1979. *Carnavais, Malandros E Herois.* Rio de Janeiro: Zahar Editores.

Darnton, Robert. 1984. *The Great Cat Massacre.* New York: Vintage Books.

Davison, R. 1963. *West Indian Migrants.* London: Oxford University Press.

Degler, Carl N. 1986. *Neither Black Nor White.* Madison: University of Wisconsin Press.

Domingo, Wilfredo A. 1925. "The Tropics in New York." *Survey Graphic* 6(6):648–51.

——. 1926. "The West Indies." *Opportunity* 4 (October):339–42.

Dominguez, Virginia. 1975. *From Neighbor to Stranger: The Dilemma of Caribbean Peoples in the United States.* New Haven: Yale University Press.

——. 1986. *White by Definition: Social Classification in Creole Louisiana.* New Brunswick, N.J.: Rutgers University Press.

Drake, St. Clair, and Horace Clayton. 1945. *Black Metropolis.* New York: Harcourt, Brace and Co.

Du Bois, W. E. B. 1920. "The Rise of the West Indian." *Crisis* 20:214–15.

Dunbar, Barrington. 1935. "Factors in the Cultural Background of the Southern and the British West Indian Negroes That Condition Their Adjustment in Harlem." M.A. thesis, Columbia University.

Elder, J. D. 1964. "Color, Music and Conflict: A Study of Aggression in Trinidad with Reference to the Role of Traditional Music." *Ethnomusicology* 8:129–36.

Engstrom, Richard L., and Michael D. McDonald. 1981. "The Election of Blacks to City Councils: Clarifying the Impact of Electoral Arrangements on the Seat/Population Relationship." *American Political Science Review* 75:344–54.

Erie, Steven. 1985. "Rainbow's End: Old and New Urban Ethnic Politics." In Lionel Maldonado and Joan Moore, eds., *Urban Ethnicity in the United States: New Immigrants and Old Minorities,* 249–76. Beverly Hills: Sage.

——. 1988. *Rainbow's End: Irish Americans and the Dilemmas of Urban Machine Politics, 1840–1985.* Berkeley: University of California Press.

Estades, Rosa. 1980. "Symbolic Unity: The Puerto Rican Parade." In Clara Rodriquez, Virginia Sanchez-Korrol, and José Alers, eds., *The Puerto Rican Struggle: Essays on Survival in the U.S,* 82–88. New York: Waterfront Press.

Farley, Reynolds. 1986. "The Myth of West Indian Success." National Academy of Sciences Report No. 6. Washington D.C.: The National Resarch Council, Commission on Behavioral and Social Sciences and Education.

Firey, Walter. 1947. *Land Use in Central Boston.* Cambridge: Harvard University Press.

Fischer, Claude S. 1976. *The Urban Experience.* New York: Harcourt Brace Jovanovich.

Flagler, J. M. 1954. "Well Caught Mr. Holder!" *The New Yorker,* 25 September.

Foner, Nancy. 1978. *Jamaica Farewell: Jamaican Migrants in London.* Berkeley: University of California Press.

——. 1979. "West Indians in New York and London: A Comparative Analysis." *International Migration Review* 13:284–97.

——. 1983. "Jamaican Migrants: A Comparative Analysis of the New York and London Experience." Occasional Paper No. 36, New York University Program in Inter-American Affairs, New York University.

——. 1985. "Race and Color: Jamaican Migrants in London and New York." *International Migration Review* 19:708–22.

——. 1987. (ed.) *New Immigrants in New York.* New York: Columbia University Press.

Forde, F. Donnie. 1985. "Who Speaks for the Caribbean Community?" *The New York Amsterdam News*, 8 June.

Frampton, H. M. 1957. "Carnival Time in Dominica." *Canadian–West Indian Magazine* 47:9–11.

Freedman, Marcia. 1983. "The Labor Market for Immigrants in New York City." *New York Affairs* 7(4):94–111.

Gans, Herbert. 1979. "Symbolic Ethnicity." *Ethnic and Racial Studies* 2:1–17.

Garcia, John A. 1986. "Caribbean Migration to the Mainland: A Review of Adaptive Experiences." *Annals of the American Academy of Political and Social Sciences* 487:114–25.

Genovese, Eugene. 1969. *In Red and Black.* New York: Pantheon.

——. 1979. *Roll Jordan Roll.* New York: Pantheon.

Georges, Eugenia. 1984. "New Immigrants and the Political Process." Occasional Paper No. 45, New York University Program in Inter-American Affairs, New York University.

Giddens, Anthony. 1973. *The Class Structures of Advanced Societies.* London: Hutchinson.

——. 1984. *The Constitution of Society: Outline of the Theory of Structuration.* Berkeley: University of California Press.

Glantz, Oscar. 1978. "Native Sons and Immigrants: Some Beliefs and Values of American Born and West Indian Blacks at Brooklyn College." *Ethnicity* 5:189–202.

Glazer, Nathan. 1983. *Ethnic Dilemmas: 1964–1982.* Cambridge: Harvard University Press.

——. 1985. (ed.) *Clamor at the Gates: The New American Migration.* San Francisco: Institute for Contemporary Studies.

Glazer, Nathan, and Daniel P. Moynihan. 1963. *Beyond the Melting Pot.* Cambridge: MIT Press.

——. 1975. (eds.) *Ethnicity: Theory and Experience.* Cambridge: Harvard University Press.

Glick-Schiller, Nina, Josh Dewind, Marie Lucie Brutus, et al. 1987. "All in the Same Boat? Unity and Disunity in Haitian Organizations in New York." In Constance Sutton and Elsa Chaney, eds., *Caribbean Life in New York City,* 182–201. New York: Center for Migration Studies.

Goldwasser, Maria. 1975. *O Palacio do Samba.* Rio de Janeiro: Zahar Editores.

Gordon, Edmundo. 1989. "Creoles, Ideology and the Sandinista Revolution." *Cimarron* 2(1–2):119–39.

Gordon, Monica. 1979. "Caribbean Migration: A Perspective on Women." In Delores Mortimer and Roy S. Bryce-Laporte, eds., *Female Immigrants to the United States,* 14–55. Washington, D.C.: Smithsonian Institution.

——. 1980. "Identification and Adaptation: A Study of Two Groups of Jamaican

Bibliography

Immigrants in New York City." Ph.D. dissertation, City University of New York.

Gosnell, Harold. 1933. *Negro Politicians: The Rise of Negro Politics in Chicago.* Chicago: University of Chicago Press.

Greeley, Andrew M. 1971. *Why Can't They Be Like Us?* New York: E.P. Dutton.

Green, Charles, and Basil Wilson. 1987. "The Afro-American, Caribbean Dialectic: White Incumbents and Black Constituents in the 1984 Election in New York City." *Afro-Americans in New York Life and History* 11: 49–65.

——. 1989. *The Struggle for Black Empowerment in New York City.* New York: Praeger.

Gumbs, Maurice. 1985a. "Caribbean Groups: Tribal, Cannibal, Individual or What?" *New York Carib News*, 9 July:17.

——. 1985b. "A Bone Is a Terrible Thing to Fight Over." *New York Carib News*, 25 July.

——. 1985c. "Who Speaks for the Caribbean Community?" *New York Carib News*, 27 August:12.

Gunst, Laurie. 1989. "Johnny-Too-Bad and the Sufferers." *The Nation*, 13 November, 566–69.

——. 1990. "A Jamaican Posse Grows in Brooklyn." *The Portable Lower East Side* 7(1):89–100.

Guterbock, Thomas. 1980. *Machine Politics in Transition: Party and Community in Chicago.* Chicago: University of Chicago Press.

Gutman, Herbert G. 1977. *The Black Family in Slavery and Freedom: 1750–1925.* New York: Vintage Books.

Hall, Herman. 1982. "Inside Brooklyn's Carnival." *Everybody's Magazine*, November.

Hamilton, Charles V. 1984. "Political Access, Minority Participation and the New Normalcy." In L. Dunbar, ed., *Minority Report*, 3–25. New York: Pantheon.

Hannerz, Ulf. 1974. "Ethnicity and Opportunity in Urban America." In Abner Cohen, ed., *Urban Ethnicity*, 37–76. London: Tavistock.

Hanretta, John C. 1979. "Race Differences in Middle Class Life Style: The Role of Home Ownership." *Social Science Research* 8:63–78.

Harris, Marvin. 1964. *Patterns of Race in the Americas.* New York: Norton.

Hellwig, David J. 1981. "Black Leaders and United States Immigration Policy, 1917–1929." *Journal of Negro History* 56:110–39.

Hennessy, Alistair. 1984. "The Bifurcated Diaspora: An Overview on the West Indian Migration to the United States and Britain in the Twentieth Century." Paper presented at Conference on the Caribbean, Research Center for the Study of Man, New York, September.

Henry, Keith S. 1977a. "Caribbean Political Dilemmas in North America and the United Kingdom. *Journal of Black Studies* 7:373–85.

——. 1977b. "The Black Political Tradition in New York: A Conjunction of Political Cultures." *Journal of Black Studies* 7:455–84.

Herbstein, Judith F. 1978. "Rituals and Politics of the Puerto Rican Community in New York City." Ph.D. dissertation, City University of New York.

——. 1983. "The Politicization of Puerto Rican Ethnicity in New York, 1955–1975." *Ethnic Groups* 5:31–55.

Hicks, G. L., and D. I. Kertzer. 1972. "Making a Middle Way: Problems of Mohegan Identity." *Southwestern Journal of Anthropology* 28:1–24.

Higham, John. 1982. "Leadership." In Stephan Thernstrom, ed., *The Politics of Ethnicity*, 69–72. Cambridge: Harvard University Press.

Hill, Donald. 1981. "New York's Caribbean Festival." *Everybody's Magazine* 5 (August/September):33–37.

Hill, Donald, and Robert Abrahamson. 1980. "West Indian Carnival in Brooklyn." *Natural History* 88:72–84.

Hill, Errol. 1972. *The Trinidad Carnival*. Austin: University of Texas Press.

Hill, Robert A. 1983. *Marcus Garvey and the Universal Negro Improvement Association Papers*. Berkeley: University of California Press.

Holder, Calvin. 1980. "The Rise of the West Indian Politician in New York City." *Afro-Americans in New York Life and History* 4:45–59.

——. 1987. "The Causes and Composition of West Indian Immigration to New York City." *Afro-Americans in New York Life and History* 10:7–27.

Hunt, Lynn. 1984. *Politics, Culture and Class in the French Revolution*. Berkeley: University of California Press.

Hunter, Albert. 1975. "The Loss of Community: An Empirical Test Through Replication." *American Sociological Review* 40:537–52.

Isaacs, Harold. 1975. *Idols of the Tribe: Group Identity and Political Change*. New York: Harper and Row.

Jack, Hulan. 1982. *Fifty Years a Democrat: The Autobiography of Hulan E. Jack*. New York: The Benjamin Franklin House.

Jackman, Mary R., and Robert W. Jackman. 1980. "Racial Inequality and Home Ownership." *Social Forces* 58:1221–34.

Jackson, Peter. 1988. "Street Life: The Politics of Carnival." *Environment and Planning D: Society and Space* 6:213–27.

Jamaica Weekly Gleaner. 1983. "Reggae at Brooklyn Carnival." 15 August (North American Edition).

James, C. L. R. 1953. *Mariners, Renegades, Castaways*. New York: Published by C.L.R. James.

Janowitz, Morris. 1952. *The Community Press in the Urban Setting: The Social Elements of Urbanism*. Chicago: University of Chicago Press.

Johnson, Charles S. 1938. *The Negro College Graduate*. Chapel Hill: University of North Carolina Press.

Johnson, James Weldon. 1925. "The Making of Harlem." *Social Graphic* 6(6):635–40.

——. 1930. *Black Manhattan*. New York: Knopf.

Johnson, Michael, and James Roark. 1984. *Black Masters: A Free Family of Color in the Old South*. New York: Norton.

Kain, John F., and John M. Quigley. 1972. "Housing Market Discrimination, Home Ownership and Savings Behavior." *American Economics Review* 62:263–77.

Kasinitz, Philip. 1987a. "The Minority Within: The New Black Immigrants." *New York Affairs* 10:44–58.

——. 1987b. "The City's 'New Immigrants.'" *Dissent* 34:497–506.

——. 1988. "From Ghetto Elite to Service Sector: A Comparison of Two Waves of West Indian Immigrants in New York City." *Ethnic Groups* 7:173–204.

Bibliography

Kasinitz, Philip, and Judith Fridenberg-Herbstein. 1987. "Caribbean Celebrations in New York City: The Puerto Rican Parade and the West Indian Carnival." In Constance Sutton and Elsa Chaney, eds., *Caribbean Life in New York City: Social and Cultural Dimensions*, 327–49. New York: CMS.

Katznelson, Ira. 1973. *Black Men, White Cities: Race, Politics and Migration in the United States and Britain*. Chicago: University of Chicago Press.

———. 1981. *City Trenches: Urban Politics and the Patterning of Class in the United States*. Chicago: University of Chicago Press.

Kilson, Martin. 1975. "Blacks and Neo-Ethnicity in American Political Life." In Nathan Glazer and Daniel P. Moynihan, eds., *Ethnicity: Theory and Experience*, 236–67. Cambridge: Harvard University Press.

———. 1984. "What Is Africa to Me." *Dissent* 31:433–40.

Kim, Ilsoo. 1981. *The New Urban Immigrants: The Korean Community in New York*. Princeton: Princeton University Press.

Klein, Herbert S. 1986. *African Slavery in Latin America and the Caribbean*. New York: Oxford University Press.

Knight, Franklin W. 1978. *The Caribbean: The Genesis of a Fragmented Nationalism*. Baltimore: Johns Hopkins University Press.

Kornblum, William. 1983. "Racial and Cultural Groups on the Beach." *Ethnic Groups* 5(1–2):109–23.

Krasner, Michael A. 1980. "Two Districts: Another Look at School Decentralization." *New York Affairs* 6:58–69..

Kristol, Irving. 1972 [1966]. "The Negro Today Is Like the Immigrant of Yesterday," In Peter I. Rose, ed., *Nation of Nations: The Ethnic Experience and the Racial Crisis*, 197–210. New York: Random House.

Krivo, Lauren. 1986. "Homeownership Differences Between Anglos and Hispanics in the United States." *Social Problems* 33:319–33.

Ladurie, E. Le Roy. 1979. *Carnival in Romans*. New York: George Braziller.

Laguerre, Michel S. 1984. *American Odyssey: Haitians in New York City*. Ithaca, N.Y.: Cornell University Press.

Lewinson, Edwin R. 1974. *Black Politics in New York City*. New York: Twayne.

Lewis, David. 1984. *Reform and Revolution in Grenada: 1951–1980*. Havana: Ediciones Casa de Las Americas.

Lewis, Gordon. 1968. *The Growth of the Modern West Indies*. New York: Modern Reader.

Lieberson, Stanley. 1980. *A Piece of the Pie*. Berkeley: University of California Press.

Lieberson, Stanley, and Mary C. Waters. 1986. "Ethnic Groups in Flux: The Changing Ethnic Responses of American Whites." *Annals of the American Academy of Political and Social Science* 487:79–91.

Light, Ivan. 1972. *Ethnic Enterprise in America*. Berkeley: University of California Press.

Logan, John, and Harvey Molotch. 1987. *Urban Fortunes: The Political Economy of Place*. Berkeley: University of California Press.

Lovelace, Earl. 1979. *The Dragon Can't Dance*. Essex, U.K.: Longman.

Lowenthal, David. 1967. "Race and Color in the West Indies." In John Hope Franklin, ed., *Color and Race*, 302–48. Boston: Beacon Press.

——. 1972. *West Indian Societies.* New York: Oxford University Press.

——. 1978. "West Indian Emigrants Overseas." In Colin Clarke, ed., *Caribbean Social Relations,* 82–95. Monograph No. 8, Centre for Latin American Studies, The University of Liverpool.

Lowi, Theodore. 1964. *At the Pleasure of the Mayor.* New York: Free Press.

Lyman, Stanford. 1974. *Chinese Americans.* New York: Random House.

Machado, Deirdre Meintel. 1981. "Cape Verdean Americans." In Joan Rollins, ed., *Hidden Minorities,* 227–50. New York: University Press of America.

Maingot, Anthony P. 1985. "Political Implications of Migration in a Socio-Cultural Area." In Robert Pastor, ed., *Migration and Development in the Caribbean: The Unexplored Connection,* 63–90. Boulder, Colo.: Westview.

Mann, Evelyn S., and Joseph Salvo. 1984. "Characteristics of New Hispanic Immigrants to New York City." New York City Department of City Planning.

Manning, Frank. 1978. "Carnival in Antigua: An Indigenous Festival in a Tourist Economy." *Anthropos* 73:191–204.

——. 1983a. (ed.) *The Celebration of Society: Perspectives on Contemporary Cultural Performance.* Bowling Green, Ohio: Bowling Green University Popular Press.

——. 1983b. "Get Some Honey for Your Money: Gambling on the Wages of Sin. In Frank Manning, ed., *The Celebration of Society: Perspectives on Cultural Performance,* 80–99. Bowling Green, Ohio: Bowling Green University Popular Press.

——. 1984. "Symbolic Expression of Politics: Cricket and Carnival." Paper presented at the Conference on New Perspectives on Caribbean Studies, Hunter College, 30 August.

Marable, Manning. 1985. *Black American Politics: From the Washington Marches to Jesse Jackson.* London: Verso.

Marger, Martin. 1986. "Ecological Factors in the Formation of Ethnic Community." Paper presented at the American Sociological Association meeting, New York, 30 August.

Marshall, Dawn. 1980. "Emigration as an Aspect of the Barbadian Social Environment." *Migration Today* 8(4):6–14.

——. 1985. "Migration and Development in the Eastern Caribbean." In Robert Pastor, ed., *Migration and Development in the Caribbean: The Unexplored Connection,* 91–116. Boulder, Colo.: Westview.

Marshall, Paule. 1981 [1959]. *Brown Girl, Brownstones.* Old Westbury, N.Y.: The Feminist Press.

——. 1985a. "Gone to Heaven at the Apollo." *The New York Times Magazine,* pt. 2: "The Worlds of New York," 28 April.

——. 1985b. "The Rising Islanders of Bed-Stuy." *The New York Times Magazine,* pt. 2: "The Worlds of New York," 3 November.

Marx, Karl. 1974 [1857]. *Grundrisse.* Trans. Martin Nicolaus. London: Penguin and New Left Books.

Massey, Douglas, and Nancy Denton. 1988. "Suburbanization and Segregation in U.S. Metropolitan Areas." *American Journal of Sociology* 94:592–626.

Massing, Michael 1989. "Crack's Destructive Sprint across America." *The New York Times Magazine,* 1 October, 38–62.

Bibliography

McKay, Claude. 1940. *Harlem: Negro Metropolis.* New York: E. P. Dutton.

McKay, James. 1982. "An Exploratory Synthesis of Primordial and Mobilization Approaches to Ethnic Phenomena." *Ethnic and Racial Studies* 5:395–415.

McKenzie, Alecia. 1985. "Lamuel Stanislaus: Man of the Year." *Everybody's Magazine* 9:25–27.

McLaughlin, Megan E. 1981. "West Indian Immigrants: Their Social Networks and Ethnic Identification." Ph.D. dissertation, Columbia University.

McLemore, Leslie Burl. 1972. "Toward a Theory of Black Politics—the Black and Ethnic Models Revisited." *Journal of Black Studies* 2 (March):323–30.

Miles, R. and A. Phizacklea. 1979. "Class, Race, Ethnicity and Political Action." *Political Studies* 25:491–507.

Miliband, Ralph. 1977. *Marxism and Politics.* Oxford: Oxford University Press.

Miller, Luther G. 1985. "Linking Tourism and Agriculture." In Robert Pastor, ed., *Migration and Development in the Caribbean: The Unexplored Connection,* 289–300. Boulder, Colo.: Westview.

Mintz, Sidney W. 1974. *Caribbean Transformations.* Baltimore: Johns Hopkins University Press.

Mollenkopf, John H. 1983. *The Contested City.* Princeton: Princeton University Press.

———. 1989. *The Wagner Atlas: New York City Politics 1989.* New York: Robert F. Wagner Institute of Urban Public Policy.

Moore, Colin. 1985. "Some Reflections on the Labor Day Carnival." *New York Carib News,* 24 September.

Morgan, Thomas. 1988. "Caribbean Verve Gives New York a Lift." *The New York Times,* 3 June.

Naison, Mark. 1983. *Communists in Harlem During the Depression.* New York: Grove Press.

New York Carib News. 1985a. "Carib Shootout in New Jersey," 13 August.

———. 1985b. "Caribbean American Awareness Day," 9 April.

———. 1986. "Brooklyn Mourns Day Care Deaths" (editorial), 9 December.

———. 1987. "Mrs. Griffith Speaks Out," 10 March.

———. 1989a. "Jamaicans on DA's Drug List," 21 March.

———. 1989b. "Trinidadians Now Linked to Posses," 28 March.

———. 1989c. "Interview with Michael Manley," 4 April.

New York Times. 1987. "Spirit of Trade Winds and Palm Trees in Brooklyn," 20 September.

———. 1988. "Jamaican Emigres Bring Thrift Clubs to New York," 19 June.

Office of Immigrant Affairs. 1985. "Caribbean Immigrants in New York City: A Demographic Summary." New York: Department of City Planning.

Oser, Alan. 1988. "Tapping the Market in Central Brooklyn." *The New York Times,* 2 October.

Osofsky, Gilbert. 1963. *Harlem: The Making of a Ghetto.* New York: Harper and Row.

Ottley, Roi. 1943. *New World A'Coming.* Boston: Riverside.

Ottley, Roi, and William Weatherby. 1967. *The Negro in New York.* New York: Oceana.

Papadenetriou, Demetrios G. 1983. *New Immigrants to Brooklyn and Queens.* New York: Center for Migration Studies.

Parcel, Toby. 1982. "Wealth Accumulation of Black and White Men: The Case of Housing Equity." *Social Problems* 30:199–211.

Pastor, Robert A. 1985. "Introduction: The Policy Challenge." In Robert Pastor, ed., *Migration and Development in the Caribbean: The Unexplored Connection* 1–40. Boulder, Colo.: Westview.

Patterson, Orlando. 1975. "Context and Choice in Ethnic Allegiance: A Theoretical Framework and Caribbean Case Study." In Nathan Glazer and Daniel P. Moynihan, eds., *Ethnicity: Theory and Experience*, 305–47. Cambridge: Harvard University Press.

——. 1977. *Ethnic Chauvinism*. New York: Stein and Day.

——. 1987. "The Emerging West Atlantic System: Migration, Culture and Underdevelopment in the United States and the Circum-Caribbean." In William Alonso, ed., *Population in an Interacting World*, 227–62. Cambridge: Harvard University Press.

Pearse, Andrew. 1956. "Carnival in Nineteenth Century Trinidad." *Caribbean Quarterly* 4:250–62.

Pearson, David G. 1981. *Race, Class and Political Activism*. Westmead, U.K.: Gower Press.

Petras, Elizabeth McLean. 1987. *Jamaican Labor Migration: White Capital and Black Labor 1850–1930*. Boulder, Colo.: Westview.

Pettigrew, Thomas M. 1981. "Race and Class in the 1980's: An Interactive View." *Daedalus* 110:223–55.

Philpott, Stuart B. 1973. *West Indian Migration: The Montserrat Case*. New York: Humanities Press Inc.

Pinderhaus, Diane Marie. 1977. "Interpretations of Racial and Ethnic Participation in American Politics: The Case of Black, Italian and Polish Communities in Chicago, 1910–1940." Ph.D. dissertation. University of Chicago.

Piore, Michael. 1979. *Birds of Passage*. New York: Cambridge University Press.

Powell, Adam Clayton, Jr. 1945. *Marching Blacks*. New York: Dale.

Powrie, B. E. 1956. "The Changing Attitudes of the Colored Middle Class towards Carnival." *Caribbean Quarterly* 4:224–32.

President's Conference on Homebuilding and Home Ownership. 1931. *Report of the Committee on Negro Housing*. Washington, D.C.

Priestley, George. 1985. "Diggers: The Men Who Dug the Panama Canal." *Everybody's Magazine* 9(1):12–16.

——. 1989. "Panama: Ethnicity, Class and the National Question." *Cimarron* 2:28–42.

Rae, Douglas W. 1967. *The Political Consequences of Election Laws*. New Haven: Yale University Press.

Raphael, Lennox. 1964. "West Indians and Afro-Americans." *Freedomways* 4:438–45.

Reid, Hazel E. 1983. "Caribbean Children in New York." *Everybody's Magazine* 7(6):32–34.

Reid, Ira De A. 1939. *The Negro Immigrant: His Background, Characteristics and Social Adjustment, 1899–1937*. New York: AMS Press.

Reimers, David M. 1985. *Still the Golden Door: The Third World Comes to America*. New York: Columbia University Press.

Bibliography

Rex, John. 1968. "The Sociology of a Zone of Transition." In Raymond Pahl, ed., *Readings in Urban Sociology*, 211–31. London: Pergamon.

——. 1982. "West Indian and Asian Youth." In Ernest Cashmore and Barry Troyna, eds., *Black Youth In Crisis*, 53–71. London: Allen and Unwin.

——. 1983. *Race Relations in Sociological Theory*. London: Routledge and Kegan Paul.

Rex, John, and Sally Tomlinson. 1979. *Colonial Immigrants in a British City: A Class Analysis*. London: Routledge and Kegan Paul.

Reyes, Angelita. 1983. "Carnival: Ritual Dance of Past and Present in Earl Lovelace's 'The Dragon Can't Dance'." *World Literature in English* 24:107–20.

Richardson, Bonham C. 1983. *Caribbean Migrants: Environment and Human Survival in St. Kitts and Nevis*. Knoxville, Tenn.: University of Tennessee Press.

Ricketts, Erol. 1987. "U.S. Investment and Immigration from the Caribbean." *Social Problems* 34:374–87.

Rieder, Jonathan. 1985. *Canarsie: The Jews and Italians of Brooklyn against Liberalism*. Cambridge: Harvard University Press.

Ringer, Benjamin. 1983. *'We the People' and Others: Duality and America's Treatment of its Racial Minorities*. New York: Tavistock.

Roberts, Michael D. 1989. "Jamaicans Protest D.A.'s Action: We Will Not Be Crucified." *New York Carib News*, 4 April.

——. 1990. "Grenadian: Nobody Will Run Me Out." *New York Carib News*, 20 February.

Rodney, Walter. 1981. *A History of the Guyanese Working People: 1881–1905*. Baltimore: Johns Hopkins University Press.

Roehler, Gordon. 1984. "Calypso and Social Confrontation in Trinidad: 1970 to Present." Paper presented at the Conference on New Perspectives on Caribbean Studies, Hunter College, 30 August.

Rosenwaike, Ira. 1972. *The Population of New York City*. Syracuse, N.Y.: Syracuse University Press.

Salins, Peter. 1983. "New York in the Year 2000 Revisited." *New York Affairs* 7:4–19.

Sanjek, Roger. 1984. "Review of Michael Banton's. *Racial and Ethnic Competition*." *American Ethnologist* 11:629–31.

——. 1990. "Conceptualizing Caribbean Asians: Race, Acculturation and Creolization." In his *Caribbean Asians: Chinese, Indian and Japanese Experiences*. Asian American Center Working Papers, Queens College, Flushing, New York.

Sassen-Koob, Saskia. 1980. "The Internationalization of the Labor Force." *Studies in Comparative Economic Development* 15:3–25.

——. 1981. "Exporting Capital and Importing Labor: The Role of Caribbean Migration to New York City." Occasional Paper No. 28, New York University Program in Inter-American Affairs, New York University.

——. 1984. "The New Labor Demand in Global Cities." In Michael Smith, ed., *Cities in Transformation* 139–72. Berkeley: Sage.

See, Katherine O'Sullivan. 1986. *First World Nationalism: Class and Ethnic Politics in Northern Ireland and Quebec*. Chicago: University of Chicago Press.

Segal, Aron. 1983. "Background to Grenada." *Caribbean Review* 7:40–44.

Selwyn, Ryan. 1985. "Tobago's Quest for Autonomy." *Caribbean Review* 13:7–9.

Sennett, Richard. 1970. *The Uses of Disorder: Personal Identity and City Life.* New York: Vintage Books.

——. 1976. *The Fall of Public Man.* New York: Vintage Books.

Shils, Edward. 1968. "Color, the Universal Intellectual Community, and the Afro-Asian Intellectual." In John Hope Franklin, ed., *Color and Race*, 1–17. Boston: Beacon Press.

Singham, A. W. 1968. *The Hero and the Crowd in the Colonial Polity.* New Haven: Yale University Press.

——. 1985. "Coalition Building: Race and Culture Play Critical Roles." *The City Sun*, 17–23 April. New York.

Skinner, Ernest. 1986a. "Where Are Caribbeans' Loyalties in the Battle for the 21st Senatorial Seat?" *New York Carib News*, 1 April.

——. 1986b. "Marty Markowitz Betrays Caribbean Community." *New York Carib News*, 7 May.

——. 1986c. "Caribbeans in New York—A People in Limbo." *Le Critique* 1:8–11.

Sleeper, Jim. 1981. "Building a New Black Politics." *Village Voice*, 9–15 December.

——. 1985. "Black Empowerment Blues." *In These Times*, 9(16–22 January):8–9.

——. 1988. "Playing the Ethnic Card in New York City." *American Visions*, April:6–10.

——. 1990. *The Closest of Strangers: Liberalism and the Politics of Race in New York.* New York: W.W. Norton and Company.

Smith, M. G. 1965. *Stratification in Grenada.* Berkeley: University of California Press.

Smith, Neil, and Richard Schaffer. 1987. "Harlem Gentrification: A Catch 22?" *New York Affairs* 10:59–78.

Snowden, George. 1935. "The Growth of Negro Office Holders and Employees in the Government of New York City Since 1898." M.A. thesis, New York University.

Soto, Isa Maria. 1987. "West Indian Child Fostering: Its Role in Migrant Exchanges." In Constance Sutton and Elsa Chaney, eds., *Caribbean Life in New York City: Social and Cultural Dimensions*, 131–49. New York: Center for Migration Studies.

Sowell, Thomas. 1975. *Race and Economics.* New York: David McKay.

——. 1978. "Three Black Histories." In Thomas Sowell, ed., *Essays and Data on American Ethnic Groups*, 7–64. Washington, D.C.: The Urban Institute.

——. 1981. *Ethnic America.* New York: Basic Books.

——. 1983. *The Economics and Politics of Race: An International Perspective.* New York: Morrow.

Spurling, John Jasper. 1962. "Social Relationships between American Negroes and West Indian Negroes in a Long Island Community." Ph.D. dissertation, New York University.

Steinberg, Stephen. 1981. *The Ethnic Myth.* Boston: Beacon Press.

Stone, Carl. 1976. "Class and the Institutionalization of Two Party Politics in Jamaica." *Journal of Commonwealth and Comparative Politics* 14:177–96.

Bibliography

——. 1980. *Democracy in Clientelism in Jamaica*. London: Transaction.

Suttles, Gerald. 1968. *The Social Order of the Slum: Ethnicity and Territory in the Inner City*. Chicago: University of Chicago Press.

——. 1972. *The Social Construction of Communities*. Chicago: University of Chicago Press.

Sutton, Constance R. 1987. "Introduction." In Constance Sutton and Elsa Chaney, eds., *Caribbean Life in New York City: Social and Cultural Dimensions*, 1–3. New York: Center for Migration Studies.

Sutton, Constance R., and Susan R. Makiesky. 1975. "Migration and West Indian Racial and Ethnic Consciousness." In H. I. Safa and B. M. Dutoit, eds., *Migration and Development: Implications for Ethnic Identity and Political Conflict*, 113–44. The Hague: Mouton.

Tabb, William. 1982. *The Long Default: New York City and the Urban Fiscal Crisis*. New York: Monthly Review Press.

Tannenbaum, Frank. 1947. *Slave and Citizen: The Negro in the Americas*. New York: Knopf.

Tauber, Karl. 1983. "Residential Segregation in 28 Cities: 1970–1980." Working Paper 83–12, Department of Sociology, University of Wisconsin.

Taylor, Edward. 1976. "The Social Adjustment of Returned Migrants to Jamaica." In Frances Henry, ed., *Ethnicity in the Americas*, 217–20. The Hague: Mouton.

Tennant, Jennifer. 1984. "Anthony Agard." *Everybody's Magazine* 8(7):12–14.

Thomas-Hope, Elizabeth. 1978. "The Establishment of a Migration Tradition: British West Indian Movements in the Hispanic Caribbean after Emancipation." In Colin Clarke, ed., *Caribbean Social Relations*, 66–81. Monograph Series No. 8, Centre for Latin American Studies, The University of Liverpool.

——. 1985. "Return Migration: Its Implications for Caribbean Development." In Robert Pastor, ed., *Migration and Development*, 157–77. Boulder, Colo.: Westview.

Truab, James. 1981. "You Can Get It If You Really Want." *Harpers* 264:27–31.

Turner, Victor. 1983. "The Spirit of Celebration." In Frank Manning, ed., *The Celebration of Society: Perspectives on Contemporary Cultural Performance*, 103–24. Bowling Green, Ohio: Bowling Green University Popular Press.

Turner, W. Burghardt, and Joyce Moore Turner. 1988. *Richard B. Moore, Caribbean Militant in Harlem*. Bloomington: Indiana University Press.

University of the West Indies. 1969. "The Development Problem in St. Vincent: A Report by the U.W.I. Development Mission." Institute for Social and Economic Research, Kingston, Jamaica. Mimeo.

van Capelleveen, Remco. 1985. "Schwarze Erfahrung und Marginalitat." *Peripherie* 20:36–58.

——. 1987 [1984]. "Caribbean Immigrants in New York City and the Transformation of the Metropolitan Economy." In *The Caribbean and Latin America*, 260–72. Free University of Berlin and the John F. Kennedy Institute for American Studies. Berlin: Verlag Klaus Dieter Vervuert.

van den Berghe, Pierre. 1978. "Race and Ethnicity: A Sociobiological Perspective." *Ethnic and Racial Studies* 1:401–11.

Vickerman, Milton. 1991. "Distancing Behavior in Jamaican Men." Ph.D. dissertation, New York University.

Volsky, George. 1987. "Jamaican Drug Gangs Thriving in U.S. Cities." *The New York Times*, 19 July.

Waldinger, Roger. 1987a. "Beyond Nostalgia: The Old Neighborhood Revisited." *New York Affairs* 10:1–12.

———. 1987b. "Changing Ladders and Musical Chairs: Ethnicity and Opportunity in Post-Industrial New York." *Politics and Society* 15:369–402.

Walter, John C. 1989. *The Harlem Fox: J. Raymond Jones and Tammany, 1920–1970*. Albany: State University of New York Press.

Walzer, Michael. 1982. "Pluralism in Political Perspective." In Stephan Thernstrom, ed., *The Politics of Ethnicity*. Cambridge: Harvard University Press.

———. 1986. "Public Space: The Pleasures and Costs of Urbanity." *Dissent* 33:470–75.

Ware, Caroline F. 1965 [1935]. *Greenwich Village: 1920–1930*. New York: Harper and Row.

Waters, Anita M. 1985. *Race, Class and Political Symbols: Rastafari and Reggae in Jamaican Politics*. New Brunswick, N.J.: Transaction.

Watsby, Stephen L. 1982. *Vote Dilution, Minority Voting Rights and the Courts*. Washington, D.C.: Joint Center for Political Studies.

Watson, Hilbourne. 1985. "The Caribbean Basin Initiative and Caribbean Development: A Critical Analysis." *Contemporary Marxism* 10:1–37.

Weber, Max. 1968. *Economy and Society*. Berkeley: University of California Press.

Weiss, Nancy J. 1983. *Farewell to the Party of Lincoln*. Princeton: Princeton University Press.

Wellman, Barry. 1979. "The Community Question: The Intimate Networks of East Yorkers." *American Journal of Sociology* 84:1201–31.

White, Theodore H. 1960. "Perspective 1960." *Saturday Review* 43 (March 14):4–5.

White, Timothy. 1983. *Catch a Fire: The Life of Bob Marley*. New York: Holt, Rinehart and Winston.

Wiley, Norbert F. 1967. "The Ethnic Mobility Trap and Stratification Theory." *Social Problems* 15:147–51.

Wilkinson, Alec. 1989. *Big Sugar: Seasons in the Cane Fields of Florida*. New York: Knopf.

Williamson, Joel. 1980. *New People: Miscegenation and Mulattoes in the United States*. New York: Free Press.

Willie, Charles V. 1978. "The Inclining Significance of Race." *Society* 15(5):10–15.

Wilson, Basil, and Charles Green. 1988. "The Black Church in the Struggle for Community Empowerment in New York City." *Afro-Americans in New York Life and History* 11:51–79.

Wilson, Peter. 1973. *Crab Antics*. New Haven: Yale University Press.

Wilson, William Julius. 1978. *The Declining Significance of Race: Blacks and Changing American Institutions*. Chicago: University of Chicago Press.

———. 1987. *The Truly Disadvantaged: The Inner City, the Underclass and Public Policy*. Chicago: University of Chicago Press.

Wirth, Louis. 1956 [1926]. *The Ghetto*. Chicago: University of Chicago Press.

Bibliography

Wolfinger, Raymond E. 1972. "Why Political Machines Have Not Withered Away and Other Revisionist Thoughts." *Journal of Politics* 34 (May):365–98.
Woodward, C. Vann. 1955. *The Strange Career of Jim Crow.* New York: Oxford University Press.
Wrong, Dennis H. 1968. "Identity: Problem and Catchword." *Dissent* 15:427–35.
———. 1972. "How Important Is Social Class?" *Dissent* 19:43–55.
———. 1979. *Power: Its Forms, Bases, and Uses.* New York: Harper and Row.
Yancey, William L., Eugene P. Eriksen, and Richard N. Juliani. 1976. "Emergent Ethnicity: A Review and Reformulation." *American Sociological Review* 41:391–403.

Index

[273]

Index

Index

Congress of Racial Equality (CORE), 185
Conway, Dennis, 21, 56–57
Cooper, Wayne F., 214
Costa Rica, 21
Credit associations (*Susu*), 87–88
Crime: drug trade, 66–67, 79–85, 247–48; numbers racket, 94–95
"Crop Over" celebration, 134
Crosswaith, Frank, 43
Crown Heights, 55, 59, 61, 64, 142–43, 181, 226, 230
Cuba, 21

Darnton, Robert, 135
Davis, Ben, 217
Degler, Carl N., 33
Democratic party: 1982 primary, 225–28; 1984 primary, 228–30; 1985 mayoral election, 230–35; and political clubs, 209, 211, 239–42; United Color Democracy (UCD), 211–13; West Indian politicians and, 213–20, 222–23
Denton, Nancy, 57
Dinkins, David, 249–50, 254
Dominica, 29
Domingo, Wilfredo A., 8, 43, 47, 50, 94, 114–15
Dominican Republic, 21–22
Dominicans, 101–2, 104, 183n
Drug trade, in West Indian neighborhoods, 66–67, 79–85, 247–48
DuBois, W. E. B., 94, 210
Duke, St. Clair, 43n
Dymally, Mervyn, 174, 224–25

Eastern Parkway, 142
East Flatbush, 64–65, 226–27
East Indians, 14–15
Eastman, Max, 214
Education: decentralization dispute in, 222; higher, 78, 95, 98; Ocean Hill–Brownsville dispute, 40, 238; private institutions, 73–76; public, 77–78; in West Indies, 75–76, 94
Edwards, Delroy "Uzi," 83–85
Employment: affirmative action, 98; discrimination, 98–99; during economic decline, 96–97, 99; expansion of opportunities, 97; female, 92, 104–5; professional, 95–96, 120–21; rate of, 101–2; in service sector, 103–6, 109; voluntary associations and, 120–21
Empowerment group, 191, 192, 222, 226–30, 235–37, 242, 244, 247, 249, 254
Erie, Stephen, 198n
Eriksen, Eugene P., 187

Ethnic entrepreneurs, 163–64, 177n; as leaders, 176–202
Ethnicity: defined, 4–5; mobilizationist view of, 251; and neighborhood, 39–41; pluralism and, 196–97; and politics, 40–41, 161, 252; and race, 5–7, 35–37, 50–54, 252; symbolism of, 39. *See also* West Indian ethnicity
European Carnival tradition, 135–36
European immigrants, 6
Everybody's magazine, 71–72, 119–20, 168
Exposito, Meade, 192

Farley, Reynolds, 91–92, 96, 101–2, 107
Farrell, Herman "Denny," 76n, 231–32, 234, 242
Female-headed households, 107–8
Fischer, Claude, 68, 118–19
Flagler, J. M., 112
Flake, Floyd, 248
Flatbush, 55, 57, 65–66, 230; East Flatbush, 64–65, 226–27; "Flatbush USA," 65–66
Florestan, Joe, 72–73
Foner, Nancy, 59, 174, 204
Ford, James, 215
Forde, F. Donnie, 188–95
Forest Hills housing crisis, 253
Freedman, Marcia, 97

Gairy, Eric, 22–23, 172–73, 175n
Ganja trade, 85
Gans, Herbert, 11
Garvey, Marcus, 22, 37, 43, 113–14, 121, 155, 210–11
Genovese, Eugene, 20
Georges, Eugenia, 112, 183n
Giuliani, Rudolph, 249
Glantz, Oscar, 91
Glazer, Nathan, 27, 91, 111, 190, 197
Glick-Schiller, Nina, 23
Golar, Simeon, 227, 230, 240
Golden, Howard, 10, 186–87, 196, 243–44; and black vote, 191–92; and "Caribbean-American Awareness Day," 192–93
Goldwasser, Maria, 137
Gordon, Monica, 21
Gorin, Rufus, 141, 147
Gosnell, Harold, 209, 212
Green, Charles, 98, 230n
Green, Roger, 194, 222, 237
Grenada, 22–23, 29, 166, 167n; national identity in, 175; politics in, 172–73, 183–84; Stanislaus appointment, 173–74, 176; U.S. invasion of, 173, 202

Index

Index

Labor Day Carnival, 1–2, 133, 134; background of, 140–42; bands and costumed in retinues, 144–45, 147; ethnic identity and, 134, 141, 148–53; lack of central organization, 143–44, 146–48; politicians and, 153–59; procession of, 146–47; scheduling and site of, 142–43
Labor force. *See* Employment
Ladurie, E. Le Roy, 135
Laurelton, 57, 67, 227
Leadership: ambivalent attitude toward, 161–63; of ethnicity entrepreneurs, 163–64; militant, 202–6, 224–25; of old guard, 163–76, 224
Leeward Islands, 21
Left-wing intellectuals, 203–4
Lewinson, Edwin R., 51–52, 215–16, 218–19
Lewis, Arthur, 168
Lewis, Gordon, 115–138
Lezama, Carlos, 141–42, 147, 149, 152, 154–55, 158
Lieberson, Stanley, 98
Light, Ivan, 91
Limon, Costa Rica, 21
Lindsay, John, 218, 221
Literature, West Indian, 78–79
Logan, John, 85
London Carnival, 134, 140
Long Island University, 78
Lowenthal, David, 19–20
Lowi, Theodore, 239
Lubavitcher sect, 61
Lyman, Stanford, 111

McCall, Carl, 241
McCarran-Walter Act, 26
Machado, Deirdre M., 33n
McKay, Claude, 5, 43, 44, 47, 95, 210, 214
McKay, James, 251
McKenzie, Alecia, 232
McLaughlin, Megan, 87
Maddox, Alton, 247n
Maingot, Anthony P., 22
Makiesky, Susan R., 142, 174n
Manley, Michael, 80n, 82, 117n
Manley, Norman, 22, 117n
Manning, Frank, 133–34, 139
Marable, Manning, 210
Marger, Martin, 39
Markowitz, Marty, 192, 196, 241, 249; courting of West Indian vote by, 228–29, 243–44; Gumbs challenge to, 242–45, 248; and Labor Day Carnival, 143,

153–55; in 1982 primary, 226; in 1984 primary, 230
Marshall, Dawn, 20–22
Marshall, Paule, 38–39, 53, 59, 115–16
Marshall, Thurgood, 217
Marx, Karl, 21
Mason, C. Vernon, 247
Massey, Douglas, 57
Massing, Michael, 81, 84
Medgar Evers College, 78, 194–95
Mexican Americans, 5n
Middle class neighborhoods, 66–67
Miles, R., 112
Miller, Luther G., 21
Minter, Thomas, 231
Mintz, Sidney W., 20
Mollenkopf, John H., 176–77, 228, 248
Molotch, Harvey, 85
Montgomery, Velmanette, 222
Montserrat, 167n
Moore, Colin, 158, 204–6, 224–25, 234, 242
Moore, Richard, 43, 214–15
Motley, Constance Baker, 208
Moynihan, Daniel Patrick, 91, 111, 190–91, 197
Music, calypso/reggae split, 150–52

Naipaul, V. S., 240
Naison, Mark, 214–15
Naturalization: promotion of, 189–90; rate of, 31, 174
Neighborhoods: community control of, 40; decline of ghetto institutions, 97–98; and ethnicity, 39–41. *See also* Harlem; West Indian neighborhoods
Netherlands Antilles, 3n
New Jewel Party, 172–73
New National Party (NNP), 173–74, 184
New York Carib News, 72, 78, 82, 86, 193, 201, 204, 233, 242–44, 249
New York University, 78
Nicaragua, 21
Numbers racket, 94–95
Nyerere, Julius, 173

Ocean Hill–Brownsville dispute, 40, 238
O'Dwyer, William, 216
Olmstead, Frederick Law, 142
Oset, Alan, 66
Osofsky, Gilbert, 42–43, 47, 212
O'Sullivan, Katherine, 4
Ottley, Roi, 45–47, 112–13
Owasco Democratic Club, 216
Owens, Major, 72, 174, 201–2, 222, 226–27, 243

[277]

Index

Trump, Fred, 64
Tubman (Harriet) Democratic Club, 239–42
Turner, Joyce Moore, 210, 215
Turner, Victor, 135, 137
Turner, W. Burghardt, 210, 215
Twenty-year myth of immigrant adaptation, 199–201

Unemployment, 28–29, 102, 107
United Colored Democracy (UCD), 211–13
United Negro Improvement Association (UNIA), 113, 210–11
Unity Democratic Club, 169

Van Capelleveen, Remco, 87
Van den Berghe, Pierre, 5
Vann, Albert, 154, 191–94, 196, 222, 223, 228, 231, 234–35, 237, 243–44
Vann, Robert L., 46
Venezuela, 21
Vickerman, Milton, 204
Vincentians, voluntary associations of, 112n, 115, 117
Virgin Islands, U.S., 21
Volsky, George, 81
Voluntary associations. See Community organizations

Waldinger, Roger, 96, 99, 108
Walrond, Eric, 43
Walter, John C., 211
Walzer, Michael, 68
Waters, Anita M., 80n
Watson, Hilbourne, 28n
Wattle, Jesse, 140
Weatherby, William, 45, 47, 112–13
Weber, Max, 207
Weiss, Nancy J., 211
Wellman, Barry, 85
West Indian American Day Carnival Association (WIADCA), 142–43, 146–49, 152–57, 169, 229
West Indian ethnicity: as adaptive strategy, 11; community organization promotion of, 112, 122; cultural divisions and, 150–52; defining, 3–5; encouraged by white politicians, 10–11; and expectation of return, 35; Forde on, 190–91; Labor Day Carnival impact on, 134, 141, 148–53; and migrant tradition, 22–23; Pan-West Indian, 134, 149–50; pre-1965 vs. post-1965, 8–9; race and, 154, 252–54; second generation, 53–54; transportation in, 23

West Indian immigrants: in black neighborhoods, 43–47, 52; British connection of, 47–48; businesses owned by, 93–95, 99, 101, 118, 185–86; economic success of, 90–93, 107–10; educational and occupational status, 94; illegal, 30–31; relations with African Americans, 44–47, 154, 156–57, 204; support networks of, 87–88
West Indian immigration, 19–37; in Britain, 26; economic motives for, 28–29; first wave of, 8–9, 23–25, 93–95; intra-Caribbean, 20–21, 20–23, 175; racial categorization in, 32–33; second wave of, 25–27; short-term, 23n; from small territories, 166–67; as survival strategy, 19–20; third wave of, 7–32, 35–37, 55, 96–110; transnationalism of, 31–32; twenty-year myth of adaptation, 199–201
West Indian neighborhoods: commercial enterprises in, 68–70, 103; Crown Heights, 55, 59, 61, 64, 142–43, 181, 226, 230; drug trade in, 66–67, 79–85, 247–48; East Flatbush, 64–65, 226–27; English/Spanish speaking enclaves, 56–57; Flatbush, 65–66, 230; formation of, 58; geographic distribution of, 55, 57–58, 66; home-buying in, 58–59; middle-class enclaves, 66–67; self-sufficiency of, 85–89. See also Community organizations; Community press; Education
West Indian population: defined, 24n; in 1930s, 24–25, 42; post-1965, 54–55
West Indians in politics: accusation of tribalism, 236–37; African-American vs. Caribbean political styles, 218–21; and black electoral unity, 246–50, 253–55; black power advocates, 204–6, 224–25; "Caribbeans for Koch," 170, 173, 188, 198, 204, 224, 232–34, 249–50, 252–53; "Caribbeans for Percy Sutton," 169–70, 223–34; community organizations and, 111, 121–23, 168–69, 181, 243–44; community press coverage of, 72; in Democratic party, 212–20; and ethnicity entrepreneurs, 163–64, 176–202; Gumbs/Markowitz campaign, 242–46; in Harlem, 95; identification with broader black community, 207–8; independence movements and, 113–15; involvement in Caribbean politics, 122, 174; left-wing intellectuals and, 203–4; in 1982 primary, 225–28; in 1984 primary, 228–30; in 1985 mayoral election, 230–35; old

Anthropology of Contemporary Issues

A SERIES EDITED BY

ROGER SANJEK

Library of Congress Cataloging-in-Publication Data

Kasinitz, Philip, 1957–
    Caribbean New York : black immigrants and the politics of race /
Philip Kasinitz.
      p.   cm. — (Anthropology of contemporary issues)
    Includes bibliographical references and index.
    ISBN 0-8014-2651-0 (cloth : alk. paper). — ISBN 0-8014-9951-8
(paper : alk. paper)
    1. West Indian Americans—New York (N.Y.) 2. Ethnicity—New York
(N.Y.) 3. New York (N.Y.)—Politics and government—1951– 4. New
York (N.Y.)—Social conditions. I. Title. II. Series.
F128.9.W54K37 1992
305.896′972907471—dc20   .   91-55539